Ottoman Rule of Law and the Modern Political Trial

Modern Intellectual and Political History of the Middle East
Fred H. Lawson, *Series Editor*

SELECT TITLES IN MODERN INTELLECTUAL
AND POLITICAL HISTORY OF THE MIDDLE EAST

Becoming Turkish: Nationalist Reforms and Cultural Negotiations in Early Republican Turkey, 1923–1945
Hale Yılmaz

Emirate, Egyptian, Ethiopian: Colonial Experiences in Late Nineteenth-Century Harar
Avishai Ben-Dror

The Iranian Constitutional Revolution and the Clerical Leadership of Khurasani
Mateo Mohammad Farzaneh

Jurji Zaidan and the Foundations of Arab Nationalism
Thomas Philipp

Mirror for the Muslim Prince: Islam and the Theory of Statecraft
Mehrzad Boroujerdi, ed.

Mohammad Mosaddeq and the 1953 Coup in Iran
Mark J. Gasiorowski and Malcolm Byrne, eds.

National Elections in Turkey: People, Politics, and the Party System
F. Michael Wuthrich

Syria from Reform to Revolt, Volume 2: *Culture, Society, and Religion*
Christa Salamandra and Leif Stenberg, eds.

Ottoman Rule of Law and the Modern Political Trial

THE YILDIZ CASE

Avi Rubin

SYRACUSE UNIVERSITY PRESS

First Edition 2018

18 19 20 21 22 23 6 5 4 3 2 1

∞ The paper used in this publication meets the minimum requirements of the American National Standard for Information Sciences—Permanence of Paper for Printed Library Materials, ANSI Z39.48-1992.

For a listing of books published and distributed by Syracuse University Press, visit www.SyracuseUniversityPress.syr.edu.

ISBN: 978-0-8156-3597-0 (hardcover)
978-0-8156-3601-4 (paperback)
978-0-8156-5455-1 (e-book)

Library of Congress Cataloging-in-Publication Data

Names: Rubin, Avi, 1971– author.
Title: Ottoman rule of law and the modern political trial : the Yıldız case / Avi Rubin.
Description: First edition. | Syracuse, New York : Syracuse University Press, 2018. |
Series: Modern intellectual and political history of the Middle East |
Includes bibliographical references and index.
Identifiers: LCCN 2018031028 (print) | LCCN 2018039614 (ebook) |
ISBN 9780815654551 (E-book) | ISBN 9780815635970 | ISBN 9780815635970 (hardback : alk. paper) |
ISBN 9780815636014 (paperback : alk. paper) | ISBN 9780815654551 (e-book)
Subjects: LCSH: Trials (Political crimes and offenses)—Turkey—Historiography. |
Midhat Paşa, 1822–1884—Trials, litigation, etc. | Abdülaziz, Sultan of the Turks, 1830–1876—
Death and burial. | Justice, Administration of—Turkey—History—19th century. |
Rule of law—Turkey—History—19th century. | Abdülhamid II, Sultan of the Turks, 1842–1918. |
Turkey—History—Ottoman Empire, 1288–1918.
Classification: LCC KKX41.Y55 (ebook) | LCC KKX41.Y55 R83 2018 (print) |
DDC 345.5601/31—dc23
LC record available at https://lccn.loc.gov/2018031028

Manufactured in the United States of America

In memory of my father, Dov Rubin, 1936–1996

And the memory of my nephew, Noah Dov Rubin, 1998–2017

Contents

Illustrations

Acknowledgments

I OWE A GREAT DEBT OF GRATITUDE to a number of individuals. I want to particularly thank Yener Bayar for his invaluable assistance and advice. I cherish the friendship and scholarship of Iris Agmon, Haggai Ram, Omri Paz, Boğaç Ergene, Yoram Meital, Hakan Karateke, Dror Ze'evi, Ehud Toledano, Safa Saraçoğlu, Judith Weil, and Aliza Uzan-Swisa, all of whom were involved in this project in this way or another. I am grateful to Peter Gran and the anonymous readers of the manuscript for their valuable suggestions, as well as the support and kindness of Alison Maura Shay and Kelly Balenske from Syracuse University Press. Thanks are also due to Fred Lawson, the editor of the series Modern Intellectual and Political History of the Middle East, for his thoughtful suggestions. I am equally grateful to Annette Wenda for her excellent work. I thank my colleagues from the Department of Middle East Studies at Ben-Gurion University for their collegiality and friendship. Thanks are due to the staff of the Başbakanlık Archives in Istanbul and the National Archives in Kew Gardens, London. This research was supported by the Israeli Science Foundation (grant no. 17/14).

I owe the greatest debt of gratitude to my wife, Ronit Rubin, who had to endure the strange destiny of living with a person who spent long weeks, months, and years talking to a dead Ottoman paşa. I am equally deeply grateful to our children, Mai, Adam, and Ella, who keep me going. You are my rising stars.

Prologue

Historical Resonances

ON JULY 13, 2013, the retired chief of the general staff of Turkey, General Mehmet İlker Başbuğ, published on his Internet blog a bitter post, where he discussed the similarities between his ordeal and the situation of an unforgettable Ottoman hero who lived more than twelve decades earlier. The fact that the retired general wrote this post while in prison, waiting for his trial, was but one of many oddities that make up contemporary Turkish politics. In the aftermath of a brilliant military career of nearly a half century, General Başbuğ was about to stand trial for playing a key role in the famous Ergenekon network, which had allegedly conspired to overthrow the government ruled by the Justice and Development Party (Adalet ve Kalkınma Partisi [AKP]), purportedly resorting to terrorist means.[1] Başbuğ was one of almost three hundred military officers, journalists, and opposition lawmakers charged with membership in the Ergenekon network and convicted at the Istanbul Heavy Criminal Court. This ongoing episode, bizarre in more than one respect, has come to be a defining feature of Turkish political life in recent years, reaching the boiling point that was the coup attempt of July 15, 2016. A mishmash of conspiracy theories, possible and less than possible facts, rumors, and official propaganda about the shadowy existence of a state within a state, or "Deep State" (*Derin Devlet*) as it is known in Turkey, this ever-developing story has been a challenge for anyone trying to make sense of Turkish politics.[2] The habitual affinities between politics and law have become a Gordian knot in the era of the Justice and Development Party, making the task of distinguishing facts from speculation and fiction more and more difficult. Modern historians have been contemplating the meaning of facts in historical writing, but for Başbuğ and the other individuals who were convicted and sentenced to grave penalties, some of them to life sentences, distinguishing facts from fiction was not a philosophical matter. Rather, it was a matter of life and death.

Başbuğ's blog post on the eve of his trial makes a perfect point of departure for my discussion of the trial that took place in the Yıldız (Star) Palace during June 27–29, 1881.[3] This dramatic event, or perhaps tragicomic event, to paraphrase General Başbuğ's description of his own situation when he was led to prison in January 2012, involved two of the highest-ranking politicians of the day, both of whom had served in the most senior position of Ottoman officialdom. Both Midhat Paşa and Mütercim (Translator) Rüştü Paşa had served as grand viziers. The spotlight of Ottoman, European, and American media of the late nineteenth century turned to Midhat Paşa rather than the three ignorant defendants who stood the same trial. On the social spectrum that separated Midhat, a celebrity statesman in both Europe and the Ottoman Empire, and the three anonymous individuals who were charged with murdering an ex-sultan, there were a few political figures of lesser caliber, yet they were as influential as some of the defendants in the Ergenekon trials taking place more than a century later. Without belittling the prominence of General Başbuğ, he certainly is not in Midhat Paşa's league, as far as the history of the world is concerned. Midhat has become a legendary icon in parts of the modern Middle East and the Balkans, associated with Ottoman liberalism and constitutionalism, as well as rational modern administration. He became an idol in the histories of the Balkans and Iraq, also revered by Kemalist Turks. Owing to the liberal legacy associated with Midhat, his name was subject to both commemoration and negation in modern Turkey, depending on the political circumstances there.[4] Nevertheless, familiar clichés along the lines of "history repeats itself" are irresistible when thinking about these two episodes, namely, the trial of İlker Başbuğ and the trial of Midhat Paşa 132 years earlier, which is the subject of this book. This seemed to be General Başbuğ's state of mind when writing his blog post in July 2013.

In the first part of his blog post, Başbuğ provides some details about Midhat's career that would be familiar to most educated Turks of our days: Midhat the successful governor of Bulgaria and Baghdad; Midhat as a kingmaker, playing a key role in the deposition of two sultans and the enthronement of another; Midhat the champion of the constitution; and Midhat as the biggest threat to the despot Sultan Abdülhamit II. Başbuğ moves on to offer a sketchy description of the trial that marked the courageous Paşa's ultimate downfall. Başbuğ's narrative about the trial is somewhat haphazard, but it delivers the point already familiar to Turks since 1909, namely, Midhat fell victim to a mockery of justice masterminded by one of the most despotic sultans in Ottoman history. One of the bullet points that make up Başbuğ's historical account deserves our special attention. He correctly notes that the trial of Midhat took place in a tent erected in the yard of the Yıldız Palace and that the audience entered with tickets. "It was desired that the court hall would resemble a theatrical scene," Başbuğ observed. Later I will discuss the performative quality of this particular trial, a quality that is evident in every trial to a certain extent but assumes shocking dimensions in political trials. Başbuğ concludes this part of his post with the following question: "Are there similarities between the contemporary Specially Authorized Courts [Özel Yetkili Mahkemeler] and the trial of Midhat Paşa, who lived 132 years ago? Some similarities are easily evident." At this point, he indicates a good number of features of Midhat's trial that sustain his conclusion. Most of the points are worth citing here, as they illustrate the conventional narratives about Midhat's trial in particular and common ideas about the meaning of "political trials" in general:

- "The phase of the investigation has to be secret. Yet in this phase, condemning essays were written following leaks to the media. This task has been fulfilled with great success by the Ahmet Midhats of yesterday and today. This way, people are tried by public opinion without standing trial." (Başbuğ refers here to the condemnatory articles published by a former protégé of Midhat Paşa, who ended up a foe. See chapter 3.)
- That court operated in Yıldız Palace under the shadow of the Sultan. The [present-day] Specially Authorized Courts were established in the prison campus.

- A tent was erected for the Criminal Court of Appeal (*Istinaf Cinayet Mahkemesi*), and the audience entered with tickets. For inexplicable reasons, the palace turned this court into a theatrical tent, not only in terms of contents but also in terms of the way it was displayed. The Specially Authorized Courts, too, took place in a sports arena turned into a courthouse.
- Many people, Tuncay Güney, the falsifier of the Ergenekon case being the first among them, openly said that the Ergenekon case was a drama.[5]
- The special courts often violate the Code of Criminal Procedure.
- In the trials, the statements made by some witnesses and defendants were identical to the bills of indictment, as if someone dictated it to them. They changed their statements, and then they repeated them word-for-word.
- The court did not allow Midhat Paşa to cross-examine the witnesses that had testified against him. The same situation is often evident in the latter-day Specially Authorized Courts.
- Midhat Paşa asked the court persistently to have Abdülaziz's mother heard as a witness, but this request was not accepted. A similar situation occurs these days, when the courts avoid hearing critical witnesses.
- Another important similarity is the disregard of evidence and documents.
- Midhat's defense lasted nine hours. The court issued its decision an hour later. This is a demonstration of the fact that the court had made its decision before the trial, failing to consider the defenses.

Başbuğ concludes the list of allegations with the following gloomy words: "Was the lesson learned from political trials such as the exemplary trial of Midhat Paşa, which took place 132 years ago? . . . Absolutely not!" He then warns his readers that one should not forget Midhat's last words in the trial: "At this point, when the judges exchanged positions with the suspects, history is the judge."

The Turkish General Başbuğ, aged seventy in 2013, wrote this post from the position of a person who knew that there was a good chance that he would end his life in prison, a possibility that would make any person fretful. Some 132 years earlier, the Ottoman statesman Midhat, at the age of sixty, knew that he might end his life on the scaffold. Başbuğ was a professional soldier, but he is also an amateur historian who published bestselling books on the founder of the Turkish Republic, Mustafa Kemal.[6] His enthusiastic patriotism is not to be questioned, judging not only by his military career but also from another book he published in 2015, titled *Armenian Allegations and Facts* (*Ermeni Suçlamalari ve Gerçekler*).[7] In this book he takes upon himself the dubious challenge of equipping the Turkish reader with accessible historical "facts" that would allow him or her to cope with "Armenian allegations" about the tragedies of 1915. For Başbuğ the historian, the problem is not only one of facts gotten wrong but also one of bad publicity for the Turkish cause, as he perceives it, so he offers some advice as to how the Turkish lobby should handle the Armenian one. Başbuğ, like many other Turkish officials who have gained some experience in dealing with accusations about the darkest chapter in what is commonly considered "Turkish history" (more accurately, modern Ottoman history), is aware of the force of rhetoric. His description of the historical episode known as the Yıldız court contains its own share of fiction. For instance, Başbuğ attributes to Midhat the phrase "The only true things in this bill of indictment are the *besmele* at the beginning, and the date," adding that even these truths are not evident in today's bills of indictment.[8] Besides the fact that such a statement has no trace in the records of the trial, no Ottoman legal document, be it a bill of indictment, an interrogation protocol, or court decision, bore the phrase *besmele* (in the name of God). Also, there is no known record of the last dramatic words that Başbuğ attributes to Midhat. In fact, after the presiding judge informed Midhat that he was sentenced to death and that he could use his right to appeal the Court of Cassation within a week, Midhat simply said, "I thank you."[9]

The retired general was more fortunate than the retired Ottoman grand vizier. On August 2013, the special court that operated in the Silivri Prison found the general guilty of establishing and leading a terrorist organization and attempting to destroy the Turkish government and sentenced him to life imprisonment. The Constitutional Court quashed this heavy sentence in March 2014 on procedural grounds, a ruling that necessitated Başbuğ's immediate discharge from prison. His torment ended the following day, when an Istanbul criminal court overturned the conviction. In theory the prosecution could revise the bill of indictment and call for a retrial, but it was clear to all that such a move would not take place. It is tempting to praise the Turkish Court of Cassation for its role as the gatekeeper of the rule of law against recurring attacks by power-crazed politicians. However, passing judgments on the work of Turkish judges, in this case the court that convicted Başbuğ in the first place, would be counterproductive in terms of the present discussion. Clichés about letting history judge might be as meaningless as truisms about "historical perspective" in certain cases, if not in all cases. There is no want of documents on the Yıldız trial; actually, we probably know more about it than we know about the trial of İlker Paşa.[10] Nevertheless, every attempt at evaluating the fairness of the Ottoman judges of Midhat and the other defendants who stood trial in Yıldız Palace has left behind question marks and unsolved mysteries. Some of the details that I will present in this study will complicate rather than clarify "the truth" about the trial. If the assessment of the work of judges is a challenge resulting from different paths taken by judges and historians, such an endeavor becomes a dead end in the case of political trials.

Ottoman Rule of Law and the Modern Political Trial

Introduction

(Not) Letting History Judge

NEW ACCESS TO THE TRUTH OF THE MATTER?

Sharia court records (*sijill*) have nourished the work of social historians of the Ottoman Empire for decades. For historians, the *sijill* has been a mine of information on social practices, allowing a rich crop of historical analyses. We owe a great debt to hundreds of Ottoman *katib*s (scribes) and *kadı*s (judges) who industriously produced and archived court records across the Ottoman realms and centuries. Even though they did not have us in mind when writing down summaries of cases brought before the local *kadı*s, their work allowed a plethora of economic histories, histories from below, histories of elite groups, histories of women and non-Muslim groups, and legal history, to name but a few fields that have developed thanks to the *sijill*. Although *sijill*-based studies have been expanding impressively since the 1960s, only recently has the Sharia court become a subject matter in its own right. As argued by Iris Agmon and Ido Shahar, "Until the mid-1990s, most social historians ignored the fact that these *sijill* records were produced in courts of law, in the context of particular legal traditions and cultures, and with the purpose of attaining particular legal outcomes."[1] The few works that have taken the court of law as a subject matter offer groundbreaking insights but at the same time demonstrate the existence of a significant lacuna in our knowledge of the everyday practice of Ottoman law in its most important site. Like any other gap in historiography, the reasons are to be found in scholarly fashions, patterns of training, and above all the possibilities and limitations of the sources at hand. At any rate, the *sijill* records do not resemble Inquisition court records or modern judicial protocols. They provide dry and usually succinct *summaries* of cases, which make the task of recovering the voice of the judge quite difficult. Their style also reflects the logic of a judicial system that lacked an elaborate mechanism of judicial review; but, more important, the pre-nineteenth-century court records reflect the logics of the pre-nineteenth-century type of state.

The nature of court records changed in the course of the nineteenth century because the judicial system as a whole was changing. The court system changed profoundly, along with other state institutions, owing to the Tanzimat, an extensive reform project administered by four generations of Ottoman officials who developed new perceptions of state and society and new administrative practices, partially inspired by European models and embedded in the international circumstances of the day.[2] In chapter 1, I provide a brief account of this development in the judicial field while addressing the new meanings assumed by the concept of the rule of law. For now, it is the changing nature of the legal document that I wish to emphasize and its potential for historical analysis of judicial work. Two major trends changed the contours of the Ottoman judicial system in a gradual process that started in the early 1840s: codification and the transition to a hierarchical review system. Both developments were utter innovations, reflecting the process of administrative centralization that defined the entire project of the Tanzimat, but they also reflected a new understanding of justice, defined by legal formalism and procedural correctness. With the emergence of the Nizamiye court system in the 1860s and its experimental predecessors in the provinces during the 1840s and 1850s, good administration of justice came to be associated with detailed representations of the "truth" as it was played out in court. Proceedings became more inquisitorial in style, requiring new procedures for recording evidence and testimonies. The fact that every criminal trial was subject to judicial review by higher instances, a novelty of the nineteenth century, necessitated a new way of registering evidence, hence the new form of the "case file." As shown by Omri Paz, a case file was a collection of documents produced by the various functionaries who dealt with the case from the moment it was brought to the attention of the authorities until its conclusion at the final judicial instances.[3] Obviously, simple criminal and civil cases meant thin files, whereas serious crimes or civil disputes involving high sums of money or large estates meant thicker files. The establishment of appellate instances in the second half of the nineteenth century meant that judges had to spend a good many hours reading other judges' takes on this or that case of murder, theft, or debt, in addition to reading protocols of trials, pretrial documentations such as bills of indictment, reports of investigating magistrates, and other written evidence. This sort of judicial labor was very different from the work of their early modern predecessors, whose effort at getting to the truth of the matter centered on oral testimonies in court.[4] Potentially, the elaborate paper trail signifies a whole new pasture for historians, always hungry for "new evidence." The new types of documentation that emerged in the nineteenth century meant a much-richer registration of everyday practices as compared to the pre-nineteenth-century *sijill*, similar to the detailed files of the Inquisition, which have allowed brilliant microhistories.[5]

Take, for instance, the interrogation protocols (*istintaknames*). This genre of documentation became the core of criminal proceedings in the middle decades of the nineteenth century. They registered everything from exchanges between interrogators and suspects, statements of defendants and witnesses, affidavits, and every verbal exchange that could serve the judges in future stages of the trial. Covering both pretrial and trial proceedings, Ottoman legal professionals came to view the interrogation protocols as a major, if not the exclusive, access to past realities addressed by the courts. For the social historian, the possibilities of historical reconstruction and analysis opened up by the availability of fully recorded conversations between ordinary people are immense. Interrogation protocols from the second half of the nineteenth century appear in the form of questions and answers, confirmed by the signatures of the suspect or defendant or his fingerprint if he was illiterate. For sociolegal historians, this richness of judicial materials provides an opportunity to analyze legal change from a "law in action" perspective while highlighting nuances that historians of early modern Ottoman law and society can only fantasize about.[6] Hence, the new recording procedures that emerged in the middle of the century opened up new access to the past, for both the judges of the

1. Sultan Abdülaziz. The picture was taken in 1867, during his visit to Britain. Photographer: W&D Downey, from an album of "Royal Portraits" compiled by Queen Victoria (1819–1901). Courtesy of the Royal Collection Trust / © Her Majesty Queen Elizabeth II 2017.

past and the historians of the present, two professions that carry the burden of reconstructing and analyzing past "realities."

The Yıldız Trial (June 27–29, 1881) was different from the many scandals of the preceding Ottoman centuries, not least because it was documented in a new way. This feature of the trial, enabled by three decades of extensive judicial reforms that had set up an industry of legal documentation, signified a new way of struggling against injustice attributed to the state. Midhat's trial haunted his son, Ali Haydar Bey, who waged a public war on Abdülhamit II with the objective of clearing his father's reputation and thereby spreading the word of Abdülhamit's evil, in the meanwhile cultivating his own political career in the ranks of the exiled opposition, the Committee of Union and Progress (CUP). The question of "murder or suicide" of Sultan Abdülaziz in 1876 has occupied historians. A few days after his deposition, on the afternoon of June 4, Abdülaziz was found dead in his chambers, his arm veins cut. Did he fall victim to power-hungry politicians who conspired to kill him, or did he perhaps take his own life? This question fascinated historians of the Turkish Republic. Both the judges of Midhat and the historians who tried to pass judgment on their work enjoyed an abundance of documentation when trying to understand what had happened. Hence, a comment about the old—and perhaps even exhausted—comparison between judges and historians and its relevance to the trial of Midhat is called for.

A MULTITUDE OF VERSIONS

Thanks to the new recording proceedings that were introduced in the nineteenth century, historians enjoy a healthy number of narratives about the events that led to the premature death of the deposed Sultan Abdülaziz. There are several accounts of the trial of the men who were accused of murder and complicity in the crime, among them Midhat Paşa. These narratives are available in testimonies gathered for the consideration of the judges, in addition to bills of indictment, reports written by foreign and local journalists who witnessed the trial, and the actual rulings of the criminal court and the Court of Cassation. We are fortunate to have verbatim protocols that appeared in Ottoman and foreign newspapers as well as a verbatim report supposedly written by Midhat in his memoirs. There are also published memoirs of senior officials and the accounts and studies published by professional historians. As we will see later on, some of these accounts are contradictory, while others share some commonalities but disagree in nuances. All these versions share the claim of representing what "really happened," while many of them take issue with the credibility of competing accounts about the events in question. Does this abundance of narratives get us any closer to providing definitive answers to questions about Midhat's culpability and about the conduct of the tribunal that convicted him? Before trying to answer this question, sketching out the types of documents that made up the reservoir of versions at hand might be helpful. The following list includes the major types of documentation that contain narratives about the deposition of Abdülaziz in 1876, the enthronement and deposition of his successor Murat V the same year, the death of Abdülaziz, and eventually, the arrest, trial, and ultimate fate of the convicts.

Official Narratives

- Indictment committee reports: This type of report initiated judicial proceeding based on the public prosecutor's recommendation. The report consisted of the opinion of the public prosecutor and the opinion of the indictment committee, composed of three members appointed by the presiding judge of the relevant court. This body was in charge of defining the severity of the case in line with the standard categories defined in the Code of Criminal Procedure. This document provided the "green light" for issuing an arrest warrant.
- Interrogation documents: These documents were verbatim transcripts of exchanges between interrogators and suspects in the form of questions and answers. In line with the procedural requirements in an inquisitorial system, each page of the interrogation record bore the signatures of the interrogator and the suspect, to confirm its authenticity. The examining judge (*müstantık*) was the official in charge of this procedure. The interrogation documents present the suspects' version of the events in question as well as their responses to the interrogators' attempts to destabilize these versions. The interrogation records of Midhat Paşa and Rüştü Paşa, who was the grand vizier (*sadrazam*) at the time of Sultan Abdülaziz's death, present their versions of events.
- Police reports (*fezleke*): These reports provided a summary of the interrogation, written by the examining judge, to be submitted to

the public prosecutor (*müddei-i umumı*), together with the interrogation record.

- Bill of indictment (*ithamname*): This type of document, authored by the public prosecutor, presents the criminal offenses attributed to the defendant, specifying the major evidence. It also includes recommendations of the penalties, in accordance with the relevant clauses in the Penal Code.
- Depositions: These documents are written statements of defendants and witnesses recorded prior to the trial.
- Court decisions (*ilam*): The Yıldız court, which was defined as a *Cinayet* Penal Court, that is, a penal court authorized to address severe criminal cases, produced two verdicts. One verdict referred to Midhat, and the other referred to the other defendants. Each court decision includes the verdict and the sentence. These decisions were brought to the discretion of the Court of Cassation, which issued its own ruling.

Nonofficial Narratives

- Verbatim transcripts: These transcripts of the trial recorded the exchanges between presiding judge Sururi Efendi and his deputy Hiristo Forides Efendi and the defendants and witnesses, in addition to oral statements made by defendants, witnesses, and the prosecution. These reports include some background details, such as the order of seating and a description of the physical setting, in addition to occasional descriptions of gestures. There are two major transcripts at hand. One of them recorded by reporters of the *Annales judiciaires de l'Empire Ottoman*, a short-lived legal journal in French that was published in Pera, the cosmopolitan district on the European side of Istanbul (today's Beyoğlu district). The *Annales judiciaires* contained reports about legislation, jurisprudence, and legal cases heard in the courts. On July 9, 1881, the journal published a special issue dedicated to the full transcript of the Yıldız Trial.[7] Historian İsmail Hakkı Uzunçarşılı, who published three monographs about the trial and has been considered the ultimate authority on it in Turkey, drew on the reports of the *Annales judiciaires*, which he translated into Turkish.[8] Another version of the transcript appeared twenty-eight years after the trial, in the daily newspaper *Tanin*, the mouthpiece of the CUP, the political body that initiated the Young Turk Revolution and led the empire until its demise. The newspaper serialized the transcript, which spread over numerous issues beginning on June 12, 1909, and ending on July 29 of the same year.[9] A third version of the transcript is available in Midhat's memoirs, published by his son, Ali Haydar Midhat, in 1909. The transcript provided in the memoirs is not as complete as the other two; it is limited to the hearing of Midhat.[10] The value of this source as an authentic transcript of the trial is highly questionable, since it is not likely that Midhat was able to reconstruct a verbatim transcript from memory, all the more so while enduring the hardships of his daily life in prison. The possibility that it was his son's creation is quite plausible and will be discussed in chapter 4.

- Biographies and memoirs: A few contemporaries of Midhat published their takes on the trial and the preceding events, from the perspective of those individuals who had been in the midst of the affairs. An especially detailed account of the trial and its aftermath is provided in the memoirs of the Albanian Ismail Kemal Bey (Ismail Qemali, as he is known in Albania), who was a protégé and close friend of Midhat Paşa.[11] One of the most detailed accounts of the trial is available in the biography of Midhat, written by his son, Ali Haydar Bey, while in exile. This book was the apex of Ali Haydar's early-life project, namely, clearing his father's name, in itself a story worth telling, which will be discussed later. Ali Haydar published his book in the early 1900s in Ottoman Turkish, English, and French.[12] The book contains copies of official documents as well as reports of the *Times* correspondent to the trial. The last major source that I wish to mention at this point is the memoirs of Fahri Bey, a former chamberlain (*mebeynci*) of Sultan Abdülaziz and one of the individuals who were convicted in the trial. This document was actually a manuscript written by Fahri Bey while in prison, which came out as an edited book in 1968 thanks to the efforts of a Turkish historian, Bekir Sıtkı Baykal. The memoirs contain transliterations of the bill of indictment as well as transliterations of the statements of the convicts.[13]

- Petition for retrial: Published as a book in Ottoman Turkish in 1910, this petition is signed by Tomaidis Hirisantos, the attorney of Midhat's son, Ali Haydar Bey, and Fahri Bey, who had been released from jail following the revolution, after spending almost three decades in the Taif prison. The petition specified the legal reasons that justified a retrial, offering another version of the events.[14]

Does the relative abundance of sources get us closer to the truth of the matter? For the purpose of the present discussion, it is important to stress that the pretrial part of this repertoire has served both judges and historians. It is equally significant to frame the present discussion in terms of competing *narratives* about the past, to be distinguished from *sources*. A comparison with the *sijill*-based scholarship will be helpful once again in emphasizing the potential opportunities, unprecedented in Ottoman history. The Ottoman court records that were produced by hundreds of Sharia courts over the centuries and across the empire are quite limited in terms of the "voices" they reflect. Always written by trained court scribes and approved by the *kadı*, they sometime provide the voices of plaintiffs, defendants, and witnesses, albeit in a summarized way, mediated by the clerk.[15] Nevertheless, these records do not even come close to the level of specificity, or rather authenticity, of the voices heard in the court, provided by the new types of records introduced in the nineteenth century. What is the meaning of this potential advantage, from the perspective of historians who wish to evaluate the work of past tribunals? I will use this question as a point of departure for addressing the issue of historians as judges.

HISTORIANS AND JUDGES ON THE BENCH

In the questioning of Midhat Paşa, on the second day of the three-day trial, Judge Forides Efendi, who substituted for the presiding judge for reasons that I will discuss later, asked him how and from whom he learned about Sultan Abdülaziz's death. According to the transcript provided by the correspondent of the *Annales judiciaires*, Midhat replied: "I went to the Sublime Porte [the Bab-ı Ali, the government building] on Sunday in order to attend a meeting. When I arrived there, I could not find anybody. I was told that only the undersecretary (*müsteşar*), Said Efendi, was around. I went to his office, and he informed me of what had happened. This news saddened me, all the more so when I started to think that the world will be suspicious."[16] In this answer, Midhat delivered the message that the news of the sultan's death came to him as a surprise. It is the last sentence in Midhat's response that catches the eye. The newspaper *Tanin* provides a slightly different version of Midhat's reply, whose last sentence was "I cannot describe the extent to which I was saddened by this news, because everybody will have doubts about this death."[17] Midhat's awareness of the possibility of assassination is evident in both versions. The judge told Midhat in response that Said Efendi contradicted his words, and Midhat replied, "It is of no importance, probably he did not have a choice other than making this statement." The court came back to this matter in Midhat's second hearing, which took place on the third day of the trial. Judge Forides Efendi asked Midhat once again for his response to the undersecretary Said Efendi's statement, which contradicted Midhat's version as to how he learned about Sultan Abdülaziz's death. Midhat replied: "I already answered yesterday concerning the deposition of Said Efendi. He said in his interrogation that it is not true that on Sunday, the day of the sultan's death, I went to the Bab-ı Ali and learned from him about what had happened. However, it did happen this way. The fact that he says that I am lying is of no importance. Maybe it is good that he said so, because saying the truth may have caused him troubles."[18]

What should we make of this conflict between versions? Either Midhat Paşa or Said Efendi was lying to the court. If we are to accept the basic position shared by most of the commentators who have written on this historical episode, namely, that the Yıldız court was a mockery of justice, we must take into consideration the possibility that undersecretary Said Efendi was a false witness arranged by the prosecution with the court's knowledge. In fact, this belief is the standard judgment of the Yıldız court, shared by historians and commentators. Nevertheless, a letter preserved in the Ottoman archive raises some questions. On the first day of the trial, the presiding judge, Sururi Efendi, sent a written inquiry to Said Efendi. In this letter, he asked him to respond to Midhat's statement, in which Said is quoted as saying to Midhat, who was worried that he might be suspected, "Relax, Abdülaziz killed himself." In this letter, the judge says to Said Efendi, "For the sake of legal procedure I have to ask you the following questions (answer them): What time was it when Midhat Paşa came to your room at the Porte and what did you discuss there?" Following is the written answer that the undersecretary sent to the judge:

> One should always tell the truth. Because I follow this rule, obviously I strive for revealing all that I know. However, at that time I was employed at a low-level position in the Bab-ı Ali. Besides, I am not one of the people who possess greater prestige than his post. I was also not in the circle of Midhat Paşa and I was not his man [that is, protégé]. So because it is inappropriate that Midhat Paşa would come to my room and talk with me in this way, I do not even dream of this.[19]

Said Efendi concludes his letter with an absolute denial of the conversation reported by Midhat. This was a tall tale; Said was a senior official who used to attend the most important meetings of the cabinet. This sort of attempt at covering one's tail is known in Turkish by the phrase "playing with the three monkeys: I don't see, hear and know" (*üç maymunu oynamak: görmedim, duymadım, bilmiyorum*). Said Efendi was clearly trying to save his neck.

In any case, this exchange of letters between Judge Sururi Efendi and the witness is quite extraordinary and certainly not in line with the standard procedure. Why did the judge decide to correspond with the witness instead of simply asking him this question in the hearing? Said Efendi's oral testimony and written deposition would certainly meet the legal requirements. This exchange is all the more unusual when thinking about the trial as a staged show trial, which surely did not require such private correspondence. What was it that bothered Judge Sururi Efendi? Could this correspondence be an indication of his integrity, contrary to subsequent allegations about the partiality of this court? Or, alternatively, was it a sign of the judge's cunning mind? In his written memo to the witness, the judge asked what time was it when Midhat came to Said's room. Had Said specified the hour, the judge would have addressed the same question to Midhat during the hearing, and the latter's inaccurate answer could be regarded as a discrepancy. We have no way to know for certain.

No historian interested in the story of Midhat's demise can disregard three books that were published by one of the forefathers of Turkish historiography, İsmail Hakkı Uzunçarşılı. Born in 1888, Uzunçarşılı witnessed the collapse of the Ottoman civilization, the creation of the national order in the Middle East and elsewhere, and the successful project of Turkish nation formation. In fact, he was not merely an observer of the latter development but also a contributor to the politics and scholarship that sustained it. After graduating from Darülfünün in 1912, the institution of higher education that became Istanbul University in 1933, Uzunçarşılı embarked on an exceptionally fruitful scholarly career, which was not disturbed by years of political activity. In the years that followed his graduation, he worked as a teacher in the school system. In 1927, four years after the declaration of the republic, he became a member of Parliament (MP), a position that he maintained until 1950. During the 1930s, he taught at the History Department of Istanbul University, where he became a full professor of history. Uzunçarşılı published numerous books on a dazzling range of subjects related to Ottoman history. The historical reconstruction of the Ottoman bureaucracy was a major theme in his work, in addition to urban histories and pioneering work based on the *sijill*. A striking feature of Uzunçarşılı's work is the breadth of his research interests in terms of historical epochs. It is impossible to imagine a present-day Ottomanist, or historian of any other period for that matter, practically publishing on all periods of Ottoman history and thereby challenging the very concept of specialization. Such a span of research interests would also deny the fact that *Ottoman civilization* is an arguable term used to capture diverse societies, cultures, and even languages. Uzunçarşılı, however, published books on the very early stages of the Ottoman state as well as its very late ones. Such an extraordinary array of professional interests was made possible by his admirable linguistic skills but primarily by his *approach* to history writing. According to Buşra Ersanlı, Uzunçarşılı is a representative of Turkish traditional narrative history. Judging him as an exemplar of historical positivism, historians of later generations criticized him for the absence of analysis in his work and its lack of sophistication.[20] Uzunçarşılı upheld a strictly Rankean perception of the historian's duties, based on the conviction that the facts are there for harvest and presentation, with as minimal interpretation as possible. This approach, antiquarian as it sounds today, qualifies some of his writings as "primary sources" in their own right.[21] This approach also rendered him the obvious historian as magistrate in assessing the Yıldız court.

Uzunçarşılı's interest in the Yıldız Trial spanned more than three decades. His first book on the subject appeared in 1947 under the title *Documents Concerning the Arrests of Midhat Paşa and Rüştü Paşa* (*Midhat ve Rüştü Paşaların Tevkiflerine dair Vesikalar*).[22] Rather than a piece of scholarship, this book is really a collection of official Ottoman documents that Uzunçarşılı edited and transliterated to modern Turkish and to which he added a list of résumés of the main characters. It includes interrogation records, reports, and correspondence related to the pretrial stage. In 1950 this diligent historian (and politician) published his second book on the subject, titled *Midhat Paşa and the Convicts of Taif* (*Midhat Paşa ve Taif Mahkumları*), which is a reconstruction of the posttrial phase, namely, the years that the convicts spent in the prison of Taif.[23] A sort of development in the quality of his work is notable in Uzunçarşılı's book about the posttrial events. Whereas his first book was merely a compendium of documents, this second book offered a narrative of the events, supported by the presentation of actual documents framed in lengthy footnotes. Nevertheless, the narrative reads like a report about the facts, devoid of any interpretation or analysis. It took Uzunçarşılı sixteen years to publish his most significant contribution on the trial, which covered the trial itself, titled *Midhat Paşa and the Yıldız Court* (*Midhat Paşa ve Yıldız Mahkemesi*).[24] This thick book consists of a factual narrative as well as copies and summaries of Ottoman documents transliterated into modern Turkish, in addition to summaries and allusions to news reports. It also contains photographs of key characters and original archival documents. We may consider this book as the historian's verdict, concluding a "case file" prepared through meticulous work that lasted more than three decades. To be sure, like most other Turkish historians of his time, in 1967 Uzunçarşılı did not really succumb to the general trend of deserting Rankean conceptions of historical work, a trend that had been in motion for quite a while in Western European and American academia. His verdict was there, even if expressed in a very subtle fashion, not leaving a doubt as to the historian's commitment to an objective, scientific unfolding of the facts. An illustration of the subtlety of his verdict is available in the following passage taken from the introduction to the book, which begins with a brief summary of the events: "The bill of indictment was prepared in accordance with statements that were taken with the use of torture in order to support this allegation [against the defendants]. At the end of the trial death sentences were issued, confirmed by the Court of Cassation. Eventually, the objective was realized through conviction of Midhat Pasha, of whom Abdülhamit was most afraid."[25] This passage leaves no question marks as to the key issues that had surrounded the events since 1881. In this account, the pursuers inflicted torture in order to produce false testimonies, and the entire trial was the scheme of the despotic Sultan Abdülhamit, who was eager to get rid of his political foe, a committed constitutionalist.

In the introduction to the book, Uzunçarşılı mentions two of his own predecessors in the task of revealing the truth, historians Abdurrahman Şeref Bey and İbnülemin Mahmud Kemal İnal, who commented briefly on the question of whether Abdülaziz's death resulted from murder or suicide. Neither author, according to Uzunçarşılı, was able to reach a conclusion or a verdict.[26] Carefully unfolding his own detective work, Uzunçarşılı explains how he dealt with his own doubts. In the introduction, actually the only part of the book where he allows himself to disclose "an opinion" (to be distinguished from "the facts"), he reveals that the documents he had read initially led him to suspect that Abdülaziz was murdered. Nevertheless, there was one reservation that troubled him: the death of the deposed sultan occurred on a certain Sunday, when the palace to which he was confined, Feriye, was filled with people already awake in late morning. Uzunçarşılı wonders, how could the three murderers enter the palace and kill the stout sultan without a struggle, without being noticed or heard by the ladies of the harem, the servants, and the always-watchful sultan's mother, the valide sultan, all of whom were waiting outside the sultan's room? Uzunçarşılı tells his reader that this doubt required a deeper excavation into the reservoir of trial documents.

A more effective scrutiny of documents that he had already read before, and the examination of newly accessible archival records, brought Uzunçarşılı to the conclusion that some of the defendants were subject to two types of interrogation, formal and informal. The informal interrogation was applied to the three alleged killers and to the chamberlain Fahri Bey, who was found guilty of assisting the murderers. Then the interrogators recorded information from this interrogation as a formal document, while the defendants were forced to confirm it by fingerprints, signatures, or seals. Eventually, the interrogators officially confirmed this document.[27] Uzunçarşılı repeatedly mentions the application of torture, but he provides no clear evidence to support it. Obviously, proving torture would be difficult, if not impossible, considering that the application of torture in penal proceedings had been banned for decades. As recently argued by İbrahim Kalkan, nineteenth-century Ottoman reformers sought to eradicate torture from criminal legal practice because it became ineffective and contradictory to the new ideas about the use of political power. In addition, in a new legal culture that favored proof over confession, torture as a means of substantiating culpability in the legal process became irrelevant.[28] But even if we accept Uzunçarşılı's assumption of torture, the interrogators must have made sure to clean the records of any trace of this practice whenever they applied it. Hence, Uzunçarşılı could not take it as a "fact." In the final analysis, he admits that no decisive answer to the question of whether Abdülaziz fell victim to a murder or took his own life is possible, because the evidence, plentiful as it is, does not allow such a verdict. Yet Uzunçarşılı's inclination to the option of suicide is quite clear. In addition, he tries to show that in either scenarios, suicide or murder, Midhat was not involved. Thus, for Uzunçarşılı, Midhat's situation was totally independent from Sultan Abdülaziz's death. The reader is left, then, with the impression that the verdict is there, even if not formally sealed.

Herein lies the problem of the historian acting as a judge, a point that Ginzburg framed with much skill and that I wish to address in the following chapters. Uzunçarşılı, and any other historian for that matter, would never be able to "convict" the murderers of Abdülaziz, to the extent that the sultan was indeed murdered. On the other hand, the historian could never "acquit" Midhat and the other convicts, either. A historical indictment of the judges who tried Midhat and the other suspects is equally a mission impossible. Bearing in mind Ginzburg's observations, this entire endeavor might be futile because the function of *historical* evidence is different from the purpose of *legal* evidence in a penal proceeding. These two types of evidence refer to two different types of contexts.

While a good number of Turkish historians of later decades did challenge the historical positivism that Uzunçarşılı represented, the overall persistence of Rankean perceptions of the historical craft in Turkish historiography is quite remarkable. Interest in the Ottoman past has been growing exponentially in recent years, evident in numerous publications on Ottoman themes. One of the reasons for this scholarly flourishing is the improvement in the service provided by the Turkish national archive, the Prime Minister's Ottoman Archives (Başbakanlık Osmanlı Arşivi) in recent decades (Uzunçarşılı, by the way, died in the Topkapı Archives at the age of eighty-nine).[29] However, the growing accessibility of documents during the second half of the twentieth century came with a considerable price, all the more so in an intellectual environment still largely shaped by dichotomous conceptualizations such as East-West, religious-secular, and development-underdevelopment.[30] Document fetishism, sustained by the bottomless pit that is the Ottoman archive, seems to stifle analysis. In such an atmosphere, historiography is often the business of document hunting, while presentation of these documents in the form of mass production of soft-cover monographs reflects a general belief in the ability of documents and facts to "speak for themselves."[31] In terms of the present discussion on judgmental historiography, historians often present the exposure of more documents as a matter of bolstering a case, even if it does not lead to any decisive verdict.

In 1968, a year after the publication of Uzunçarşılı's book on the trial, Turkish historian Bekir Sıtkı Baykal published the memoirs of Fahri Bey and a collection of newly discovered documents that were supposedly written by the prisoners of Taif, namely, those individuals who had been convicted in the Yıldız Trial. As mentioned before, Fahri Bey was the young chamberlain of Sultan Abdülaziz and one of the individuals convicted by the Yıldız court for complicity in the conspiracy to kill the sultan. Baykal, who published the documents and wrote the introduction of the book, provided a dry account of what is otherwise a rather exotic story of history as detective work. According to Baykal, while serving his life sentence in the citadel of Taif together with Midhat and some other convicts, Fahri Bey managed to smuggle his account of events to Istanbul, together with a few other documents signed by his fellow prisoners. Fahri Bey's family kept the documents for many years, until it delivered them to the Turkish Historical Foundation (Türk Tarih Kurumu), the institutional gatekeeper of the historical profession in Turkey. Baykal, who confirmed the text's authenticity by comparing the handwriting to archival documents attributed to Fahri Bey, points to the importance of Uzunçarşılı's work. He mentions the existence of an original file related to the trial that had been prepared by Sultan Abdülhamit. Nevertheless, since this document was burned to ashes because of a fire (a common explanation for disappearance of documents in Turkey), it might be impossible to determine whether Abdülaziz's death was a matter of murder or suicide.[32] The file published in the book contained three statements supposedly written by the three individuals who allegedly performed the actual murder of the sultan, Mustafa "the Wrestler," Hacı Mehmet, and Mustafa "the Algerian." In these statements, the convicts argue that they were innocent and that their confessions in the trial were the outcome of torture. Each of these statements was confirmed by the signatures of Midhat Paşa and the former *şeyhülislam* (the highest position in the hierarchy of the learned class), Hayrullah Efendi, who had been jailed (without a trial) for his supposed part in the conspiracy. Does this discovery get us any closer to the task at hand, namely, revealing the truth about the culpability of the convicts or, alternatively, of whether the judges who tried them betrayed their professional integrity? It does not, because there will always be "reservations," to use Uzunçarşılı's wording, that will form an impediment for the historian as magistrate in making a verdict. In this case, a single person, Fahri Bey, put on paper the statements of the three individuals who had been accused of the murder. It might make sense, given that the three alleged murderers were simple fellows and probably illiterate, in which case Fahri Bey wrote down whatever they told him, and he then had his fellow prisoners confirm the version. Nonetheless, the possibility that Fahri Bey made it all up with the intention of smuggling the materials to Istanbul, which he did, is just as probable. So once again, the "facts," embodied in "the documents," fail to speak for themselves, and history remains impoverished.

For all the known limitations of Uzunçarşılı's Rankean approach, the merits of good old professional historiography stand out when juxtaposed with popular history, which is quite a successful genre in Turkey. While the Yıldız Trial itself has not received much attention within this genre, the question that the court addressed, namely, whether Sultan Abdülaziz committed suicide or was murdered, has never lost relevance in modern Turkey. References to this historical enigma have become a Pavlovian response to developing political crises, which are never in shortage in Turkey. In Turkish collective memory, the year 1876 encapsulates an aggregation of issues that have haunted Ottoman and then Turkish political life ever since, namely, the nature of constitutions, the ever-present likelihood of coups d'état, political murders and sudden deaths, and the elusive meaning of the rule of law in the context of a statist political culture. In addition to the usual fascination of ordinary Turks (much like Britons) with the drama of their ancestors' palace life, the murder of Abdülaziz is a convenient metaphor that allows allusions to burning issues of the hour. Most of these popular contributions, which take the form of television series, documentaries, or newspapers or magazine coverage, involve historians as interviewees or consultants. The vast majority of these productions share and reproduce the thesis that a junta of which Midhat Paşa was a member murdered Abdülaziz. Historical anachronism is ubiquitous, often serving as ammunition in the service of the conservative (so-called Islamist) or ultranationalist camps. In the television series *Filinta* (*Firearm,* 2014–16), for instance, Abdülaziz appears as a martyr killed by subversive anarchists. The dramatic moments of his slaughter are accompanied by Islamic symbolism, such as scenes of a whirling dervish in the background and the sound of Quranic verses. In his last moment in this world, the bleeding sultan whispers the şehadet, the affirmation of faith. *Filinta* was broadcasted on the channel TRT1, the official state channel that represents the AKP line.[33] Another example is a televised lecture given by Kadir Mısıroğlu (2016), an Islamist eighty-three-year-old historian, author, and jurist, who argues that Midhat was a crypto-Jew and a traitor who joined forces with other traitors in an effort to demolish the sacred Ottoman state.[34] Other documentaries convey more subtextual ideological positions, but they nonetheless share the strong conviction that Abdülaziz was a murder victim, while presenting a rather shaky empirical basis in support of this thesis.[35] Considering the instrumental readings of Abdülaziz's death in the Turkish media, one can see why Uzunçarşılı's pedantic project has submerged in the abyss of Turkish collective amnesia, present only as a footnote in professional historiography.

AN ALTERNATIVE FRAMEWORK OF ANALYSIS: A SOCIOLEGAL PERSPECTIVE

The Yıldız Trial has not received systematic scholarly attention since Uzunçarşılı's "last word" on the subject in 1967 and Baykal's "commentary" from 1968. The lack of scholarly interest in the trial is puzzling, given Ottomanists' mounting interest in the history of the "long nineteenth century." Document fetishism in Ottomanist scholarship, especially as it is practiced in the conservative centers of Ottoman studies in Turkey, might be a major reason for the fact that the trial has never received the scholarly attention that it deserved, despite the relative abundance of documentation. Historians missed the possible effect that the trial had on future conceptualizations of the law in Turkey and other successor states of the Ottoman Empire. After all, Uzunçarşılı read all the documents that needed to be read, and no new documents have been "discovered"—hence the dead end. At the same time, perhaps the fact that the trial involved high-ranking Ottomans and a good deal of elite politics has reduced it to a marginal footnote in the historiography of the period. The more analysis-driven camp in Ottoman studies has been focusing on social and cultural histories and history from below while cultivating something of an antipathy to political history.

I contend that from the perspective of sociolegal analysis, the question of whether Sultan Abdülaziz killed himself or was killed by others is actually a nonissue, and so is the question of Midhat's liability. The schemes and interactions exposed in the trial, as well as the way it appeared in the post-Hamidian era of the CUP, provide remarkable opportunities in terms of political history, which historians should explore. However, it is the sociolegal angle that I wish to emphasize in this study. The trial coincided with the ripening of a four-decade process of judicio-administrative reform that generated profound change in the Ottoman court system. This process entailed features typical of "the passage to modernity" visible in nineteenth-century bureaucracies across Eurasia, namely, administrative state centralization, professionalization, and standardization. The judges who tried Midhat, his interrogators, the lawyers who defended him and the other defendants, the clerks who recorded their statements—all these functionaries were bound by the Code of Criminal Procedure, promulgated three years earlier. This code, which was enacted in tandem with the Code of Civil Procedure and the Law of the Nizamiye Judicial Organization, formed the apex of a long process of codification, which really changed the mentality of Ottoman legal professionals, a change that was also evident in other parts of Eurasia.

Political and legal elites across Europe and Asia employed codification as a major means for advancing the ideology of legal positivism. Some of them truly believed that the law could be structured and practiced as a scientific endeavor, while others saw the potential of formalism in advancing goals that were not only opportunistic but also antithetical to the common good. Legal positivism was a legal culture in itself, which developed a fetish for procedures, a problem that remains an integral part of legal practice to this day, long after the decline of legal positivism. The fixation on procedure was embedded, and still is, in the ideology of the rule of law, which is the idea that all people, especially those individuals who exercise political power, should obey the written laws. But this definition of the rule of law is merely a crude phrasing of a seriously contested idea, which encapsulates a good deal of myth and demagogy alongside substantive legal practice. The notion of the rule of law is Dr. Jekyll and Mr. Hyde. It is a platform for liberal mechanisms aimed at restraining political power and the protection of individual rights, and at the same time it provides a perfect legal tool kit for dictators and serial abusers of individual rights. In this context, modern political trials are legal laboratories in which all these modern legal concepts and reflexes are tested, performed, used, and abused. Contrary to the image of a declining entity lagging behind its peers, Ottoman elites were usually quite effective in adapting to changing circumstances and the adoption of new practices, a quality demonstrated by the very ability of a single dynasty to rule a strong state over centuries.[36] This book will advance the argument that the Yıldız Trial was a modern political trial, which resorted to a new legal idiom that was entrenched in legal positivism and, surprising as it might sound, equally rooted in the rule of law. It was a demonstration of the immense potential of modern rational law when hitched to political goals.

To look at the Yıldız Trial from a sociolegal perspective is to analyze it as a societal and a political, rather than a purely legal, event. The historian-as-magistrate mission that dictated the way that Uzunçarşılı and others approached the subject was a far cry from both social and legal approaches, treating it as an isolated event with no heed for the societal, political, and legal processes that allowed it. Indeed, such a parochial exploration of the trial misses the opportunity it provides to learn about a large-scale process of sociolegal change. Hence, to look at the Yıldız Trial sociolegally, as I wish to do in this study, is to look at it primarily as a social construct framed and performed through legal idioms, thereby problematizing the division between law and society. Obviously, one can interpret every trial in the past and the present as a demonstration of norms and social developments that are space and time specific; *the social,* in that sense, is an umbrella term signifying economic, political, and cultural specificities.[37]

Political trials bring out the inseparability of law and society in a most concrete fashion, when the boundaries of law and politics are constantly redrawn and challenged. The performative aspects of this dynamism of pulling and pushing the boundaries of "the legal" vis-à-vis "the political" are often evident in the physical settings of political trials, which are often unique. The Turkish general İlker Başbuğ mentioned the theatrical features of the Turkish Specially Authorized Courts and the Ottoman Yıldız court, the former taking place in an arena, while the latter took place in a circus-like tent. The Turkish political court referred to by Başbuğ operated in a prison. The Ottoman special court operated in a palace. These exceptional locations, as far as the administration of justice is concerned, are not a matter of prosaic needs, even if the producers of political trials always present them as such. Rather, these sites reflect careful choices meant to generate a certain type of dialogue between presenters and audience, an aspect of the trial that I discuss in chapter 3. The two gilded chairs reserved for the Ottoman minister of justice right behind the presiding judge and the public prosecutor at the Yıldız Trial were intended to transmit a powerful message. The minister of justice, Cevdet Paşa, a great reformer in his own right, happened to be one of Midhat's political foes. This rivalry, both political and personal, is one among several layers that form the subject of the present microhistorical exploration.

1

Ottoman Legalism

THE YILDIZ COURT was a legal scandal because it consisted of numerous compromises of numerous standards. It was neither a universal corpus of standards nor some celestial principle of absolute justice that the court violated. Rather, the many infractions evident in the trial can be considered as such only when assessed against a certain legal culture that I identify here as *legalism*. This specific context was a new development in Ottoman sociolegal history, an outcome of some three decades of experimentation with new procedures and a gradual advent of a new legal culture. The following exchange between Midhat and his judges could not take place before the nineteenth century. It took place during the second day of the trial, when the judges were just about to conclude the hearing of the defense speeches of the defendants:

MIDHAT PAŞA: I demand that each of these men [the defendants] will be interrogated again in front of me. Have them make their statements here, one by one. Clause 277 in the Code of Criminal Procedure provides me with this right. Yes, I have the right to summon all the defendants and the witnesses to the court and interrogate them separately or jointly. So let us begin with interrogating the murderers.

JUDGE FORIDES EFENDI: They were interrogated many times; as late as yesterday they testified publicly and in front of the court. As for the decision regarding the necessity of a new interrogation, it is up to the court to decide, not you.

MIDHAT PAŞA: The code provides me with this right. Read clause 277 (Midhat opens the copy of the code and reads aloud): "After the witnesses present their statements, the defendant may ask the court to summon them and hear them separately or together. . . ." You see, the law is clear and unequivocal. You have no choice other than to indulge my request.

PUBLIC PROSECUTOR: The law indeed provides the defendant with the right to reinterrogate the witnesses. However, Midhat Paşa has no right to demand to reinterrogate the defendants who said nothing against him.

MIDHAT PAŞA: I said at the outset of my defense speech that if I could prove that Sultan Abdülaziz had killed himself, ipso facto I will be able to prove my innocence. In order to prove this [that is, Abdülaziz's suicide], it is necessary that I interrogate each of the defendants and witnesses. If you disagree, give me a written assurance that statements of these defendants are unrelated with me.

JUDGE FORIDES EFENDI: The witnesses that concern you were heard yesterday in your presence. As to the defendants, they also testified in public. The court does not see a need for a new interrogation.

MIDHAT PAŞA: I insist on applying the clause that I cited.

Following this tense conversation, the judge decided to comply with Midhat's request, so he summoned Mustafa the Wrestler, who was one of the defendants accused of killing the sultan on June 4, 1876. But Midhat interrupted his testimony, and the dispute continued:

MIDHAT PAŞA: This [testimony] cannot be conducted in the presence of the [other] defendants. I want to have them interrogated one by one. Else, have the defendants step aside.

FORIDES EFENDI: It has nothing to do with you.

MIDHAT PAŞA: It is absolutely my concern.

FORIDES EFENDI: Defendants cannot be heard as witnesses. It is against the law.

MIDHAT PAŞA: These defendants are testifying for me, and legally I have the right to demand that they be interrogated again.

PUBLIC PROSECUTOR: I request to deny the defendant's insistence.

The judges retired to discuss Midhat's request and returned to the bench to inform him that they accepted it under the condition that each of the defendants would be interrogated in the presence of the other defendants. To this, Midhat replied, "I will interrogate," but the judge told Midhat, "Here you are neither a judge nor an examining magistrate; you are a defendant and perhaps a convict. You will address your questions to the court, and the court will question the defendants." When permitted to speak, the defendant Mustafa the Wrestler reiterated his statement, which had been presented on the first day of the trial. But Midhat was far from satisfied. He wanted to present questions to each of the witnesses and demanded to summon the ladies of the harem and the sons of the dead sultan Abdülaziz. These members of the imperial family had not appeared on the witness list, as required by legal procedure. He also demanded to subpoena all the physicians who examined the body of the deceased sultan right after the alleged murder. The judge refused, and Midhat, in response, refused to present his defense speech. The following conversation concluded this debate between Midhat and his judges, actually putting an end to the hearing part of the trial, before the presentation of the verdict:

JUDGE FORIDES EFENDI: Will you present your defense?

MIDHAT PAŞA: Not unless you apply clause 277.

JUDGE FORIDES EFENDI: As far as the court is concerned, your repetitive insistence on this unacceptable request is a case of contempt of the court.

MIDHAT PAŞA: Condemn me for this case too and write your decision on my gravestone.[1]

Three times the judge asked Midhat to make his defense speech, but Midhat stuck to his refusal. Eventually, the court carried on to the last phase of the trial.

This specific pattern of bickering between Midhat and the people who were about to decide his fate could not have happened a few years earlier. It could not have happened in any of the preceding centuries. Every single sentence uttered in this dialogue was dictated by a new legal culture that

2. A secretary is reading a newspaper to Midhat Paşa. Photograph taken from the journal *Resimli Kitap*, July 23, 1910.

rendered procedure the focal point of the law. Midhat and his judge were arguing about the meaning of a codified clause. The idiom they used was dictated by other clauses, even when both sides did not indicate the specific numbers of these clauses. The part of the procedural code that specified the rights of defendants and witnesses determined whether Midhat was eligible for the right to interrogate the other defendants. The clauses that determined the procedure of registering and distributing the written depositions provided the rationale of Midhat's request to read the written depositions of the witnesses. The judge mentioned the fact that the court had already heard the witnesses "publicly." What he meant really was that his court implemented the clauses of the procedural code that dealt with the publicity of trials. Similarly, the intervention of the public prosecutor in the dialogue between Midhat and the judge was made possible by the procedural clauses that not only invented the Public Prosecutor as a legal function, unheard of in Ottoman classical legal system, but also equipped him with exceptional powers in the field of legal procedure.

After 1879 legal procedure became the judicial front line, allowing attorneys and their clients, along with judges and prosecutors, endless possibilities of procedural maneuvering when making their cases. I argue that any reading of the trial as a political trial must take into account the context of legalism, which determined the strategies, idioms, and performances of every individual who was involved. In some paradoxical fashion, the context of legalism allowed this particular trial to appear as a rational administration of justice and a mockery of justice at the same time. My objective in this chapter, then, is to unfold the nature of Ottoman legalism, which was apparent in two aspects of the law, codification and judicial practice. A brief explanation of the concept of legalism, the way I use it here, is called for.

THE IDEOLOGY LEGALISM

I believe that Judith Shklar's book on legalism, published for the first time more than a half century ago, remains one of the most powerful analyses of the modern imagination of the law. Many of the points made by Shklar have been developed in later years by the school of critical legal studies (CLS) and by students of sociolegal studies who focused on the gap between the liberal rule-of-law morals, founded on Montesquieu's dogmas, and the reality "on the ground."[2] I believe that Shklar was the first to problematize the concept of the rule of law by identifying its sustaining platform, legalism, as an ideology. Presenting Shklar's key arguments about legalism in a concise form might be somewhat unfair given the nature of her text, which possesses the prose of a philosophical essay rather than an empirical study. However, the clarity of her writing compensates for the risk of oversimplification.

Shklar defines legalism as "the ethical attitude that holds moral conduct to be a matter of rule following, and moral relationships to consist of duties and rights determined by rules."[3] Through this basic definition, Shklar points to the rudimentary linkage that bonds morals to rules, duties, and rights. The "-ism" part of the concept is the crux of her argument about the nature of legalism as a mode of thinking, as an ideology. Rather than upholding any rigid or sophisticated understanding of the term *ideology* or understanding it as a detailed program, Shklar refers to ideology as an open-ended category that signifies a certain preference of people who share a certain social experience.[4] Therefore, there is little point in trying to subject legalism to lexical definitions. It is the quality of legalism as a reifying ideology that is presented lucidly in the following two passages:

> The tendency to think of law as "there" as a discrete entity, discernibly different from morals and politics, has its deepest roots in the legal profession's view of its own functions, and forms the very basis of most of our judicial institutions and procedures. That lawyers have particularly pronounced intellectual habits peculiar to them has often been noticed, especially by historians and other students of society whose views differ sharply from those of the legal profession. As one English lawyer has put it, "A lawyer is *bound* by certain habits of belief . . . by which lawyers, however dissimilar otherwise, are more closely linked than they are separated. . . . A man who has had legal training is never quite the same again . . . is never able to look at institutions or administrative practices or even social or political policies, free from his legal habits or beliefs."[5]
>
> A practicing lawyer might not rest with noting the difference between himself and others; he would insist that his was simply the right and true view. That is the meaning of legalism as an ideology.[6]

Hence, for practicing lawyers, whether attorneys, judges, or prosecutors, the societal and political trajectories that had led to the corpus of rules they abide by make no difference, all the more so the conflicts and political intricacies that make up these trajectories. Legalism is primarily an ethos whose fundamentals are not open to debate among the practitioners of law, and it is in this sense that it is imagined as a primordial construction. In Shklar's words, "It relies on what appears already to have been established and accepted."[7] Legalism as an ideology that reveres orderliness is served by formalism, and, according to Shklar, the repressive nature of formalism is perfectly compatible with legalism.[8]

Later theorists of the rule of law, such as Brian Tamanaha, Michael Neumann, Joseph Raz, and others, contributed to a nuanced discussion of the meanings of the rule of law, thereby resolving much of its theoretical fuzziness. Nevertheless, Shklar was able to capture the dogmatism of legal formalism by insisting on its ideological nature.[9] Formalism, according to Shklar, allows lawyers to imagine ("treat," in her words) the law as "a conceptual pattern entirely distinct from all political, moral, and social values and institutions." This mode of reasoning is bound to a closed circuit of logical deductions from given premises. This treatment of the law as an entity isolated from politics and morals, according to Shklar, is "a refined political ideology, the expression of a preference."[10] Hence, there is nothing "natural" or obvious about it; neither is it a universal feature of legal systems. The Ottomans, who were reinventing their judicial system in the nineteenth century through a gradual process, adopted the ideology of legalism in tandem with other ruling elites throughout Eurasia.

During the second half of the nineteenth century, the Ottoman judicial system underwent a sweeping refashioning. The jurisdiction of the Sharia courts, which until then had operated as the main judicial body of the empire, was reduced to matters of personal status and pious foundations. A new court system, known as the Nizamiye courts, was responsible for addressing civil, commercial, and criminal matters. This new judicio-administrative structure was officially pronounced in 1864, but it had been preceded by judicial organs and arrangements in the provinces, where new legal notions and practices evolved, partially in response to local necessities and partially in the context of legal borrowing from the French legal system. In terms of its structure, the French court system served as an inspiration. As any other case of legal borrowing in the legal history of the world, however, adoption was selective.[11] The Ottoman reformers adopted the three-tier configuration of first, second, and cassation instances as well as functions such as the examining magistrate (*müstantık*) and the public prosecutor (*müddei-i umumı*). They adopted a considerable number of French procedures that defined daily proceedings in the courts of law, in addition to some key concepts that delineated the substantive aspects of the judicial work, such as the distinction between private and public rights. This distinction affixed the fundamental separation between civil and criminal law, in itself a doctrinal novelty, from the Ottoman point of view.[12]

Borrowing from the French legal system was a highly selective venture. The reformers left out many features of the French system, such as the institution of jury trial, the administrative courts, and the codification of family laws (which were codified as late as 1917). However, describing the reformed legal system as a matter of eclectic transplantation of foreign law would be a reductionist description of this large-scale process of legal change. The reformed judicial system was a truly innovative amalgam evident in the legal sources, which combined adaptations and adoption of French positive law together with Islamic legal principles. Fusion was also evident in the professional backgrounds of the staff, coming from both Shar'i and Nizamiye training paths.[13] The fusion of legal traditions was even apparent in the elastic division of labor between the Nizamiye and Sharia courts, which deliberately allowed a considerable diffusion of cases between both flanks of the court system. Indeed, rather than two separate legal systems, the Sharia courts and the Nizamiye courts were two overlapping and at times interrelated segments of a single judicial system.[14]

Elsewhere I provided a comprehensive description and analysis of the main institutional and doctrinal features of the Nizamiye court system, presenting it as a case of Ottoman legal modernity. I also analyzed the legal culture brought about with the development of the Nizamiye courts, and perhaps *mentality* would be a better term for what was actually a commitment of Ottoman lawyers (judges, prosecutors, attorneys) to the ideology of legalism, apparent in their extreme dedication to formalism.[15] Committed to the argument of the present study, namely, that the political trial of Midhat Paşa can make sense only when analyzed within the context of a legalistic ideology, I would like to dwell on the project of

Ottoman legal codification, which signified the emergence of Ottoman legalism. Codification in the modernizing Ottoman Empire, I will try to show, was a local display of a global trend that changed the way that legal and nonlegal elite groups imagined the law. It was concurrently a catalyst and a response to legalism.

OTTOMAN CODIFICATION: A DOCTRINAL PLATFORM OF LEGALISM

The Code of Criminal Procedure, which was the exclusive guide and reference for all things procedural in the Nizamiye criminal courts, was a relatively late development in the general process of legal codification, which started in the early 1840s. Codification was a key feature of Ottoman legal reform in the nineteenth century. The government enacted penal codes in the 1840s and early 1850s, codification in the fields of commerce and land law took place in the 1850s and early 1860s, a civil code was enacted between 1869 and 1876, and the work of the Nizamiye courts was regulated by procedural codes enacted in 1879. Codification even continued in times of severe trouble, as was the case of the Family Law of 1917, which was the last codified statute enacted by the Ottoman state. Through the following comments about Ottoman codification, I hope to add to the few studies that look at it as a legal phenomenon in its own right.[16] I advance two related arguments: first, that Ottoman codification provided the doctrinal platform of Ottoman legalism and, second, that its nature as a *modern* sociolegal artifact becomes apparent only when depicted as a local manifestation of a global trend of codification. This notion is not to be confused with the old "impact of the West" narrative of the 1950s and the 1960s, which assumed a passive and incomplete reception of "Western" institutions in a time line customarily characterized as "first in the West and then in the rest." This specific conceptualization of change was contingent on a representation of two polarized and reified cultural entities, "the East" and "the West."[17]

The eminent English jurist Jeremy Bentham coined the term *codification* in 1815 to signify a distinctive legal doctrine rather than the mere technical act of putting laws together.[18] In his comprehensive and groundbreaking study, Csaba Varga describes the earliest versions of written law as forms of codification. He does not question the decisive change brought about by eighteenth-century codification, but he situates this change in a long history of codification, going back to antiquity.[19] Other scholars emphasize the difference between *codes* and *compilations* of law, arguing that the latter aimed at organizing existing laws and customs, whereas codes were the products of state legislation intended to introduce a new framework of positive law that may or may not include older statutes; hence, they identify a substantial difference between compilation and codification.[20]

Most of the legal compilations produced before the late eighteenth century were bodies of laws arranged along a varying degree of consistency. Such was the case of the Justinian laws of the sixth century or the Ottoman *kanun*s in the fourteenth through the sixteenth centuries. The Chinese penal code from the seventh century, known as the Tang Code after the Tang dynasty, was an exception to the rule. It contained some of the features attributed to modern codes, namely, it was well classified, systematic, and comprehensive. Rooted in a casuistic tradition of thought reminiscent of modern legalism, classical Chinese legalism emphasized the equality of all people before the law as well as the subordination of the ruler to the law.[21] The Tang Code had an impact in East Asia during the centuries that followed, but it never generated a global codification movement. The Prussian Allgemeines Landrecht für die Preussischen Staaten (General State Laws for the Prussian States) of 1794 defined the key features of modern codification. This elaborate code was designed to replace the haphazard myriad of Prussian laws with a unified system of clauses aimed at regulating all aspects of daily life. In the Prussian context, the code was primarily a vehicle for attaining state centralization. Prussian codification was also a vehicle for facilitating the work of the complex bureaucratic machinery that had emerged in previous years.[22] The implications of the Allgemeines Landrecht went beyond the immediate political and social circumstances of the Prussian state. It was an expression of a new vision about the *appearance* of the law, allowing jurists to *imagine* the legal sphere as a perfect consistency based on logical classifications and as a systematic organization of a gigantic number of clauses (nineteen thousand overall). The vision of completeness corresponded with the vision of legibility to all, which the Prussian legislature stated as such.[23]

As far as the global dissemination of codes is concerned, Napoleonic codification was the tipping point that accelerated codification in other parts of the world and determined its future general contours. In places where codification was debated and eventually rejected, as were the cases of Britain and the United States, the *Code Civil* (1804) served as the ultimate point of reference for both supporters and opponents of codification. Regardless of its revolutionary context, French codification concluded an internal process of three centuries during which partial codification took the form of *ordonnances* that had been published in France from time to time. The *ordonnances* of the seventeenth and eighteenth centuries created in the minds of jurists, philosophers, and political leaders the linkages between concepts such as reason, legal and social reform, natural law, and natural rights. A slow but steady doctrinal development rendered an overall systematic codification a "natural" outcome of the French Revolution.[24] Hence, on the one hand, French codification, which encompassed the civil, commercial, criminal, and procedural aspects of the law, envisioned a completely *new* legal order founded on human reason and consistency. It exhibited revolutionary ideals such as equality and natural rights as well as the desire to do away with the ancien régime; on the other hand, the Napoleonic codes formed the apex of a long process of doctrinal development, which preserved existing laws and customs.[25]

Motivations for codification across the world were quite diverse. While the Prussian and the French codification projects made jurists around the world aware of the benefits of codification for purposes of sweeping legal reform and social engineering, decisions to codify were preceded by debates that sometimes postponed the act of codification for decades. Such was the case, for instance, with Germany, where the government enacted a civil code as late as 1896, when the Ottoman civil code had been in existence for more than twenty years and more than fifty years after the enactment of the first Ottoman Penal Code. In Britain jurists and politicians debated the need for codification in the nineteenth century, eventually rejecting it.[26] In Russia the Digest of the Laws of the Russian Empire came into force in 1835. As argued by Tatiana Borisova, this project exhibited ideas about legality, also promoting legal professionalization.[27] In the United States, debates over the need to move away from the common law system continued throughout the century, and in one case—Montana in 1895—it even resulted in actual codification.[28] In Latin America codification progressed throughout the century. As in other regions of the world, Latin American legislators drew inspiration from French law, yet Latin American codes included a wide variety of other legal sources, such as Spanish and Portuguese laws, being remnants of the colonial period.[29] The global dissemination of codification made its impact in East Asia in the later part of the "long nineteenth century"; the Meiji reformers of Japan codified civil, criminal, commercial, and procedural law during the 1890s.[30] Chinese reformers saw in Japanese codification a model for their own codification project, which gained momentum during the 1920s and the 1930s.[31] Already in the first half of the nineteenth century, Muhammad Ali and his successors, who ruled Egypt after gaining de facto (though not de jure) independence from the Ottoman Empire, experimented with a system of partial codification in the criminal field.[32] As shown recently by Kenneth Cuno, the codification of Egyptian family law (beginning in the 1920s) involved the invention of the "personal status" category.[33] These examples are only a few that demonstrate the appeal of codification across the world. They equally demonstrate the novelty of the legalistic imagination of the law, advanced through these codification projects.

What made codification a worldwide venture was much more than the legislative-technical act of producing legal collections that possessed the same basic features everywhere in terms of their appearance (but not in terms of their contents). The universal sorts of classification and method evident in the codes are merely one reason for analyzing them in a global context; more significantly, the codes set the ground for a transnational common imagination of what a modern law ought to look like. Duncan Kennedy offered one of the best-known analyses of legal globalization, explaining its contents and mechanism from 1850 to 2000.[34] Kennedy identifies three phases in the process, each phase possessing distinctive features. Phase one (1850–1914) is marked by the spread of what Kennedy calls *classical legal thought*. Phase two (1900–1968) signifies the emergence of *the social* as a major subject of legal activity along with a growing criticism of classical legal thought. Phase three (1945–2000) suggests a global tendency to view law as a guarantor of human and property rights through the notion of the rule of law. It is the first globalization that is of interest for the purposes of the present discussion of the advent of Ottoman legalism. According to Kennedy, what was globalized in the late nineteenth century was a certain mode of legal thinking, a *consciousness* that perceived law as a coherent *system* founded on the distinction between private and public law, individualism, and commitment to legal formalism. These traits were integrated in an ideology associated with the Western nation-states, which attributed to the government the role of protecting the rights of legal persons in order to help them realize their wills, "restrained only as necessary to permit others to do the same."[35] Originally molded by German legal scholars, this mode of legal thinking globalized through interactions in both Western nation-states and imperial contexts. For instance, the British, the French, and the Dutch exported their versions of this legal model to their colonies outside Europe, while the United States, Britain, and British colonies imported German legal thought to their domains. The process of dispersion was not always an outcome of an outright imposition through colonial rule, yet according to Kennedy, "opening" to Western law was a precondition set by the Great Powers for those countries who wished to board the alluring ship of Western trade, which was the case of the Ottoman Empire, China, Egypt, and Iran.[36]

The Ottoman project of codification, then, was a local interpretation of a certain mode of legal thought classified as "classical" only in hindsight. For the Ottoman reformers, like anybody else, codification was a powerful tool for control and state centralization that also meant progress, entailing a promise for effective social and administrative engineering. In the early stages of codification, it also possessed specific political objectives dictated by contingent circumstances. As convincingly argued and demonstrated by Cengiz Kırlı, the Ottoman ruling elite designed and applied the first Ottoman code, the Penal Code of 1840, with the intention of neutralizing political opponents to the Tanzimat. This was done through prosecuting senior officials on the charge of corruption, in itself a category obscurely defined, for practices of gift giving that had been deemed legitimate before the enactment of the code.[37]

The fact that local customary law found its way to the *Code Civil* and other legal codes inspired by it is not in contradiction with the fact that codification rendered local contexts extraneous from the sovereign's perspective. On the contrary, as far as the legislator was concerned, the codified law was the only legitimate space where customary law could exist, except for specific localities where the sovereign allowed special arrangements. The difference between the premodern sultanic law, the *kanun*, and the Ottoman codes of the nineteenth century is a demonstration of this point, also demonstrating the novelty of modern Ottoman codification. The *kanunnames*, which were law books distributed to the provinces beginning from the late fifteenth century, were enactments of written versions of customary and sultanic law, mostly in matters of criminal law, land tenure, and taxation. It is important to stress that these law books were not aimed at uniform application across the empire; rather, they were valid in the designated province, often reflecting pre-Ottoman legal practices and jargon.[38] In his seminal study on premodern Ottoman criminal law, Uriel Heyd refers to the *kanunnames* as "codes." While accepting the view that most of the *kanunnames* were incomplete and unsystematic private replications of official texts, a conclusion that social historian Ömer Lütfi Barkan had offered, Heyd defines the criminal *kanuns* of Bayezid II and Süleyman the Lawgiver as "official codes of law." Nevertheless, his characterization of these *kanuns* gives the impression that they were almost the antithesis of the modern code. According to Heyd, the criminal *kanunnames* share with the other *kanuns* "a great many deficiencies, such as incompleteness, repetition, contradictions between different sections, and interpolations. The sections were not numbered or even clearly separated. Like the other *kanuns*, they were not conceived as a whole but were composed of statutes, mostly summaries of firmans, which were issued in different periods and were later put together, often in piecemeal fashion. . . . Most important [the *kanun*] makes no attempt to elaborate general and basic principles of crime, punishment, evidence, etc., from which the detailed statutes could be logically derived."[39]

Similarly, James Baldwin has argued recently that in the seventeenth century, the *kanun* "was becoming a legal literature rather than a set of statutes, and its authority was no longer depended on official promulgation," thus becoming a sort of common law.[40] The modern Ottoman codes, by contrast, exhibited a different logic: the exclusive authority of the law was legislation, and each of the numbered clauses in every single code was meant to be applied across the imperial territories in the same manner, reflecting a deductive approach to legal situations.[41] As such, the code was the embodiment of the modern state, with its desire for legal and bureaucratic standardization across the board.

Ottoman codification involved a good deal of legal transplantation. None of the Ottoman codes inspired by the French quintessence was a replica of it. As Tobias Heinzelmann demonstrates convincingly with regard to the Ottoman Penal Code of 1858, amalgamation of traditional rhetoric and new legal terminology was an effective strategy for legitimizing innovations in the field of codification.[42] The enactment of the Land Code (1858) and the civil code, the Mecelle-i Ahkam-ı Adliye, however, signified a deviation from the general inclination of Ottoman reformers toward transplant of French codes as the desirable course of action. Both codes were based on the *fiqh*. As noted by Heinzelmann, the authors of the Mecelle made sure to avoid defining it a code, thereby sidestepping the legitimacy issues, a potential minefield, related to any attempt at codifying the Sharia.[43] Nevertheless, designed for accessibility and coherence through its systematic classifications and numbered clauses (amounting to 1851 clauses overall), the Mecelle possessed the features distinctive of a modern code. The structure of the Mecelle and its mode of application as a legal standard in the official courts leaves no doubt that the legislature and the courts perceived it as a full-fledged civil code.[44]

Codification is probably the most powerful expression of legalism. While Shklar's debunking of legalism draws attention to its mythical aspects, it is important to stress that in itself, legalism as an ideology is not a blessing or a curse. Rather, it is a precondition for modern legal regimes that can advance authoritarian ends or, alternatively, promote liberal politics and protect individual rights.[45] Political trials reveal this Janus-faced nature of legalism in the most intense fashion, an issue that I will address in the next chapter. For the Ottomans, as was the case for the other countries that adopted codification in the later nineteenth century or early twentieth century, the promulgation of the code was a junction that could lead to several routes, all of which were imagined in terms of legalism. In the twentieth century, these routes would lead to liberal democracies as much as to fascism and totalitarianism. The immediate aftermath of the adoption of legalism, consisting of "moments" expressed through the promulgation of major codes, could last for several decades, during which legalism could be either used for promoting liberal justice or, alternatively, abused in the service of oppressing regimes.

LEGALISM AND THE RULE OF LAW

In previous studies, I argued that the Ottoman judicial reforms of the late nineteenth century were meant to establish the rule of law, in addition to advancing state centralization. Commitment to the rule of law was evident in the Basic Law of 1876 (Kanun-ı Esası, also known as the first Ottoman Constitution) through clauses that secured principles such as the independence of the courts and separation of powers. The abolition of the Basic Law in 1878 had no impact on these commitments, which endured overall. In fact, the Ottoman government was so efficient in applying these principles that British consuls were astonished to discover in the 1880s and 1890s that their habit of interfering in trials through the help of allied governors became ineffective, as the latter officials were losing their foothold in the courts of law.[46] While I remain convinced that codification was one of the key forces that generated a new legal culture centered on formalism, as I have argued, some reflexive criticism is called for with regard to my use of the rule of law as a descriptive category. Here I would like to advance some criticism on the tendency to employ the rule of law as an objective benchmark used for normative assessments of legal performance.

In his recent book, which provoked heated debates among scholars of the Middle East, Timur Kuran argues that some inherent features of Islamic law institutions are responsible for the departure of the Middle East from the path of economic development. In addition to structural peculiarities of institutions such as Islamic laws of inheritance, partnership, and *waqfs*, Kuran blames the societies of the Muslim Middle East for their culture of corruption, also referred to as "norms of state-subject interaction involving nepotism, bribery and rule bending as a matter of course." He contrasts this centuries-old state of affairs with "campaigns to modify and strengthen the rule of law."[47] The thesis offered in the book is evocative of the old theme of Oriental structural backwardness. Although Kuran's perspective of economic history provides a fresh twist to the classic Orientalist argument while diverting the discussion from the out-of-date province of moral evaluations of Middle Easterners' decadence and backwardness, he resorts to cultural essentialism nonetheless. Kuran's argument about a "culture of corruption" is not in accord with several important studies. For one, what many European observers interpreted as corruption was actually a practice of gift giving defined by the norms of a society composed of complex social networks of patronage.[48] Second, abuse of power associated with bribery surely existed in Ottoman societies, as it does in every other society, yet there is no evidence that Ottoman administration was more or less corrupt than contemporary European societies. There is evidence, however, indicating that effective policies aimed at eradicating administrative corruption already existed prior to the nineteenth century.[49] In addition to the fact that state law was a constitutive force in Ottoman societies, serving as a major point of reference in spheres such as ruler-subject relations, property relations, and family relations, efforts at eradicating public corruption force us to rethink common usages of the rule of law when describing the passage of Ottoman societies to modernity.

The breadth of the literature dedicated to explaining the meaning of the rule of law as a descriptive category, as well as its repertoire of empirical evidence, is an indication of the opacity of this concept the way it is commonly used. Most theoretical discussions on the rule of law recognize a fundamental conceptual distinction between formalist and substantive versions of the rule of law, also known as "thin" and "thick" versions, respectively. Both paradigms differ in their treatment of what liberal theory considers as the essential contours of state and society. Theorists of the rule of law consider Joseph Raz's formulation of the rule-of-law doctrine a theoretical point of departure for formalist interpretations. Raz outlines several key elements of the concept, among them clarity of the laws, availability of general rules, independence of the judiciary, adherence to principles of natural justice, and accessibility of the courts. Raz's theory of the rule of law is consciously almost devoid of moral stipulations on questions of equality, justice, and fundamental rights. On the other side of the divide, Brian Tamanaha offers a substantive theory that attributes some importance to legal formalism yet renders liberal democracy and secured individual rights and human rights as prerequisites, hence ruling out any other version as a true rule of law regime.[50] The thin-thick divide in the realm of legal theory resonates with the three rule-of-law trajectories that emerged in the nineteenth century, namely, the English rule of law (with its North American rendering), the German *Rechtstaat*, and the French *état de droit*. Each of these venues signified a distinctive perception of such matters as individual rights versus public rights, political representation and legislation, the powers and working of the judiciary, and the boundaries over the free hand exercised by the state in general.[51]

Philosophically stimulating as it might be, this theoretical discourse on the rule of law fails to provide practical descriptive tools suitable for non-European contexts before and during the nineteenth century and prior to the emergence of nation-states. Given its treatment of Western European history of the nineteenth and twentieth centuries as the exclusive repertoire of evidence, the resulting concept, often referred to as a "model," represents a rather limited range of historical experiences. In fact, some of the canonical theories of the rule of law are committed to philosophical rather than empirical integrity.[52] When used in the context of analyzing legal experiences outside the historical contexts from which it had emerged, the rule of law becomes a reified standard against which other legal experiences are measured. Yet Eurocentrism is not the only problem here. Rather, to use the rule of law as an objective benchmark is to contribute to its mystification, thereby losing its value as a category of analysis that can capture the multifaceted relations between legal and political institutions. The rule of law often appears as an ideological dogma in the service of political action, but its failure to capture the complexity of law and politics relations, not only in the non-West but also in the West, might be a feature that is immanent to the concept. As noted by Lauren

Benton in a review of a study that compares rule of law in India and China, "One begins to wonder, then, what we gain from approaching the 'rule of law' as a powerful concept whose 'impact' we then trace over the fields of culture and politics."[53]

To argue that the rule of law (in its analytical sense) is a myth is not to rule out its employment in analysis of legal experiences. Once approached as an imagined rather than an objective measure for legal practices, it becomes a fascinating historical phenomenon demarcated in various ways by multiple historical contexts. Paul Kahn's agenda for approaching the rule of law as a cultural phenomenon provides a methodological platform to my own argument that legalism became a defining feature of Ottoman legal culture, which was experimented in the trial of Midhat. According to Kahn, the rule of law should not be understood as anything other than an experience of meaning. This methodological rule of thumb positions the rule of law in the realm of historical phenomena, thereby removing it (or, shall we say, rescuing it) from the province of abstract doctrine defined by sets of criteria, the way it was conceived by most theorists of the rule of law. As an imagined venue, the law's rule possesses contradictions and gaps between ideals and daily practice as much as life itself, namely, contradictions that people experience on a daily basis, often with no need to "solve" them. In the "real world" of political passions, norms, power relations, and institutions, there can be no singular imagination of the rule of law. In Kahn's words, "The rule of law is not the product of anyone's or any institution's effort at rational design, whether conscious or unconscious. It was not constructed according to a systematic plan and it exhibits no single, rational order."[54] Appreciating the flexibility of this conception of the rule of law, however, one should be aware of overstretching it, thereby falling into the trap of historicism. The rule of law is a constitutive feature of the modern state, part of an aggregate of concrete phenomena and concepts that are time specific.

The Ottoman endorsement of legalism in the second half of the nineteenth century was not a matter of replacing incomplete law with a rule of law then. Rather, it was another way of imagining the law's rule. Beginning from the early 1840s, three generations of Ottoman officials, judges, and other decision makers in the judicial sphere became accustomed to thinking in terms of legalism. The domination of legalism over the Ottoman judicial sphere could not happen without codification, which provided the conceptual building blocks of the formalist imagination of the rule of law, especially but not exclusively through the procedural codes. Codification made possible the system of judicial review created in the second half of the nineteenth century. The concept of evaluating lower court decisions in higher judicial instances, mainly through checking conformity of decisions with procedural standards, was much more than a technical and an institutional innovation. It was a new way of imagining the law's rule. According to Kahn, the mechanism of judicial review renders the rule of law a permanent order attached to a permanent object, a linkage that allows imagination of the rule of law as perfect and timeless.[55] In constitutional countries, the constitution serves as the permanent object. In code countries (defined as continental law, civil law countries, or whatever definition that describes countries where the judicial sphere is regulated by codes), the code establishes permanence. Elsewhere, I have demonstrated in detail the obsession of the Nizamiye judiciary with procedure and the way these courts applied the codified clause (*madde*) as a focal point of adjudication in both criminal and civil proceedings.[56] As Baldwin has demonstrated recently, procedure played a considerable role in Ottoman court practice in the eighteenth century, and it even attracted some criticism concerning its negative influence on the ability of the court to attain justice.[57] Nevertheless, there was a striking difference between the legalist mentality of the late nineteenth century and earlier understandings of justice. Legalism changed the rules of the game when compared to the preceding judicial order, which lacked a *system* of judicial review based on codes. I have already pointed to the reasons for not considering the old *kanunnames* as artifacts of codification. I wish to emphasize that the *kanun* lacked the permanence of the modern code. Even if most newly enthroned sultans merely ratified the preceding *kanuns*, the rule that rendered all *kanuns* null and void upon the death of a sultan signified its temporary nature and its attachment to the body of the sultan. The code, by contrast, was imagined as permanent, serving the basis of an imagined permanent legal order.

PROCEDURAL CORRECTNESS AND INCORRECTNESS IN THE YILDIZ TRIAL

As argued by Shklar, the adoption of the ideology of legalism, in itself, says little about fairness, impartiality, and other normative aspects of the judicial work. In fact, an imaginary alien observer from another planet who would find a way to travel between premodern and modern courtrooms might end up thinking that formalist legal regimes are imbued with injustice and violation of the rules thus less just when compared to the premodern courts. Nostalgia for good old simple justice set aside, there is some optic illusion here, caused by the intense energies invested in procedural discussions by all the parties who operate in sites of modern law: judges, lawyers, defendants, and institutions. The Ottoman system of judicial review and the procedural laws that sustained its daily working, like all other modern formalist systems, was mostly about pursuit of procedural infractions. It does not mean that substantive considerations were absent. The judges certainly took them into account, but whenever possible they framed the substantive aspects in procedural terms. In a sense, more regulation calls for more irregularities. We can make the argument that procedural irregularities were a distinctive feature of the Yıldız Trial only because its planners had made a decision to perform it as a Nizamiye trial. As such, the Code of Criminal Procedure served as its legal Polaris for the procedural aspects, and the Penal Code determined the nature of the discussions as far as the substantive aspects were concerned. As we shall see soon, to argue that the codes were the exclusive points of reference is not to argue that violations were absent or minor.

The main interrogation of Midhat took place on the ship that transferred him from Izmir to Istanbul, immediately after his arrest. The circumstances of this interrogation were exceptional, but the resulting documents adhered to the procedure of the Nizamiye courts. Adhering to the logics of the inquisitorial system, Nizamiye trials laid the emphasis on pretrial documentation. The conversation with Midhat was recorded in an interrogation protocol (*istintakname*), in the form of questions posed by the interrogator, an officer called İbrahim Hilmi, and Midhat's answers that followed. The interrogation was then summarized in a report (*fezleke*) signed by the police officer. As in any other Nizamiye interrogation, Midhat signed on each page of the protocol to confirm its authenticity.

The interrogation protocol, the report that summarized the interrogation, and the bill of indictment that was written based on the report reveal the positivist consciousness that had been indoctrinated in each member of the Nizamiye staff who was in charge of producing documents, beginning with the initial stage of gathering depositions and ending with the court decision. None of these documents reveals the personal voice of the official who wrote them, thereby creating the impression of interpretation-free representations of narratives. The report that summarized the interrogation of Midhat does not say anything about the interrogator's impression with regard to the reliability of the suspect's version, possible contradictions, and the very issue of culpability. There are no recommendations whatsoever but a straightforward representation of the suspect's narrative. For instance, the interrogator asked Midhat about the circumstances of his escape from his mansion in Izmir as soon as he heard about his upcoming arrest. He replied that when he was in bed, his own "secret agents" came to inform him that three armed squads were about to enter the harem of the house. He left hastily through the back door. Facing the threat of guns, as he put it, he did not have time to consider his options, so he got on a carriage. He entered the French consulate because it was the first open gate that he had come across in the neighborhood of the foreigners. The protocol presents this narrative as is, also phrasing it in the third-person form.[58] The entire report reveals that the police officer who had interrogated Midhat and then prepared the report understood his duty as a mere representation of the suspect's version about the event. In fact, as far as the judicial perspective is concerned, the report was a superfluous document; the suspect's version was available to the judges through the interrogation protocol and his deposition. The complete absence of pejorative rhetoric or even explicit interpretation of "the facts" was a typical feature of the Nizamiye discourse, which was apparent throughout the trial. The entire rhetoric evident in these documents was geared toward the ultimate question of conformity of actions with codified clauses.

The second day of the trial concluded with the conviction of all the defendants. The court found Mustafa the Wrestler, Hacı Mehmet, and Fahri Bey guilty of premeditated murder. It convicted the Paşas Midhat, Mahmut, and Nuri, and the Beys Ali and Necip, of complicity to the crime. The judges also found Seyyid Bey and İzzet Bey guilty of assistance to the crime. The court scheduled the pronouncement of sentences for the following day.

The court convened for the last time on Wednesday, June 29, 1881, at noon. The Istanbul summer heat was felt hard in the makeshift courtroom, which was actually a large tent. Tension in the tent reached a climactic point among the audience and the defendants. But the tension was an outcome of the entire drama and the excitement that came with it rather than a matter of unexpected consequences. The defendants and their attorneys, who stood up for the verdicts, knew that full condemnation could mean nothing less than capital punishment. The court had decided to issue two separate decisions, one for Midhat Paşa and the other for the rest of the convicts. Midhat was not present in the court when the sentences of the other defendants were pronounced. He was waiting for his turn that would follow.

The presiding judge, Sururi Efendi, started the session by saying that he had been absent the other day owing to illness and that his deputy Hiristos Efendi had served in his stead. As required by procedure, Sururi Efendi announced that the court would pronounce penalties after hearing the public prosecutor and the attorneys. The public prosecutor, Latif Bey, asked the court to apply clauses 45 and 170 on the three murderers and the convicted accomplices. Article 170 determined a death penalty for premeditated killers.[59] Article 45 stipulated that accomplices to a crime would be subject to the same penalty applied on a single perpetrator of the same crime. The prosecutor demanded to apply the punishment of penal servitude determined by clause 175 on the two beys who were convicted of assistance to the crime. Right after the presiding judge called for the responses of the attorneys, as the procedural code required, Mahmut Paşa cried out, "In my opinion Midhat Paşa had to be with us, but he is not here." The judge dismissed this comment by saying, "It is not related to you, it is up to the court to decide."[60] After hearing the defense attorneys, who asked for the court's mercy when determining the penalties, the judges left for the conference room. Leaving the bench for consultation was a mere formality required by clause 290 in the Code of Criminal Procedure. They came back to state the obvious, namely, full compliance with the requests of the public prosecutor.

The next session focused on Midhat. Once again, it was presided by Hiristos Forides Efendi and not by the presiding judge, Sururi Efendi. The ritual repeated itself. The prosecutor demanded to subject Midhat to the same clauses, which meant the death penalty. The prosecutor's speech was followed by this conversation:

MIDHAT PAŞA: Can I say something?

JUDGE FORIDES EFENDI: No doubt, the floor is yours.

MIDHAT PAŞA: Clause 45 addresses complicity. Who is the one who is performing the crime? Reportedly, Mustafa the Wrestler and Hacı Mehmet do. Am I with them? Did anyone see me together with murderers so as to indict me as an accomplice? They say that Mahmut Paşa and Nuri Paşa gave the order [to kill Abdülaziz] and that they had me involved in this matter. At least, if they could prove their claims. In fact, has it been proven that Nuri Paşa and Mahmut Paşa gave this order?

JUDGE: The legal meaning of the word *complicity* refers to cooperation in a criminal act. One cooperates by giving money and other things and by promising to give money, or by providing with means for committing a crime, and so on. . . . Your complicity in this case is about all of the above. The investigation and the hearings reveal that you were the one who organized, planned, and prepared this crime.

MIDHAT PAŞA: But I neither paid money nor provided a weapon.

JUDGE FORIDES EFENDI: You will make your objections before the Court of Cassation.

At this point, Midhat's attorney, Şehri Efendi, told his client, "Paşa Efendi, your objections will be raised at the Court of Cassation. The present discussion is aimed at pointing to reasons for mitigating the punishment."[61] Midhat, clever and educated as he was, was not a law practitioner.

In his objection, he was jumbling together procedural and substantive claims that were not supposed to be made at this final stage of the trial. The judge did not dismiss Midhat's claim the way Sururi Efendi hushed Mahmut Paşa in the preceding session. Either Hiristo Forides Efendi was more polite by nature, or Midhat, even if a person condemned to death, was too important a personality to be treated rudely. In any case, the judge's response was puzzled, revealing his embarrassment in the face of this digression from procedure. But the judge navigated the trial back to the safety of procedural correctness when explaining to the defendants about their right to appeal the decisions at the Court of Cassation. This explanation was not a matter of the court's goodwill; it was a procedural requirement dictated by clause 305 in the Code of Criminal procedure.

Midhat was the only convict who appealed the decision. One can only speculate why the others decided to put up with their dark fate without resorting to the last possible rescue board provided by the Nizamiye court system. But for the defendants in this showcase trial, there were no reasons to think about the Court of Cassation as a rescue board. There were too many signs that they could construe as evidence of a predetermined decision. The presence of the minister of justice in the trial, the swiftness of the proceedings, and the political circumstances at the time left little room for hope. On the other hand, Midhat could think of several good reasons to apply. For one, unlike the other defendants, he was a personage of international fame, like no other Ottoman statesman. He was the reason for the international attention that the trial had been drawing in the first place, evident in newspaper coverage around the world and discussions in the British Parliament.[62] A sophisticated and experienced politician, he was aware of the impact of public opinion, especially in Europe. Merely five years earlier, the violence that erupted in Bulgaria, a region he knew well from his term as governor there, had strategic impact on the relationships between the Ottoman state and the British Empire owing to negative newspaper coverage. He knew that appealing the decision to execute him could bolster his case in the field of public opinion. A former minister of justice, even for a very short term, and the architect of the 1876 Basic Law, Midhat was aware of the unique mandate given to the Court of Cassation, which, though an organ of the

Nizamiye court system, had a mission different from any other Ottoman court of law.

The highest appellate court in the empire was established twenty years earlier as part of the general process of legal reform, but it assumed its role as the guardian of procedural correctness in 1879, when it was named the Court of Cassation (Mahkeme-i Temyiz) and modeled after its French equal. The Court of Cassation was in charge of responding to appeals concerning the legality of court decisions from all over the empire. It possessed the authority to quash verdicts for procedural and substantive reasons, in which case it would return the quashed decision to the lower court for revision. Members of the Court of Cassation formed the highest echelon of the judiciary. The immunity of the judges from dismissal guaranteed the independence of the court, at least in theory.

Midhat's decision to seek redress for his grievances at the Court of Cassation was based on his familiarity with the legalist mentality of this court. In its daily work, the Court of Cassation preferred procedural considerations over substantive ones whenever possible. The position of this court as an institutional archetype of legalism found expression in its pedantic scrutiny of documents produced by the lower courts with the objective of safeguarding adherence to the procedural standards. Any minor violation of procedure could be a cause for quashing decisions in both criminal and civil cases. Committed to procedural justice as this forum was, it did not warrant a violation-resistant and flawless court system, as naive reformers might have expected. As with any other modern court system that structured around the principle of judicial review, justice was a costly product. Legalism was made possible by elaborate procedure, which rendered professional advocacy indispensable. Winning or losing a case in the Nizamiye courts was often a matter of the lawyer's skill in maneuvering through the procedural maze. Similar to any other modern court, legal representation meant higher chances for winning, and an experienced, skilled lawyer could increase the chances for a favorable court decision considerably. Yet skilled lawyers were expensive, and fees were high. In the final analysis, the sort of justice offered by the Court of Cassation was available only for litigants of means.[63] The cost was not a problem for Midhat, who hoped that the Court of Cassation would not ignore the apparent irregularities in the trial. Midhat Paşa presented his appellate petition on July 6. The Court of Cassation denied his appeal two days later. It confirmed the lower court decision and the sentence, arguing that it found no fault in the proceedings.[64]

This decision signified the end of the Nizamiye chapter in this saga. The subsequent events had nothing to do with the regular judicial venues or with the judiciary. It became a strictly political matter handled by senior officials in political rather than judicial forums. While there was no doubt that the execution of the murderers Mustafa the Algerian, Hacı Mehmet, and Mustafa the Wrestler, who possessed no political capital, would take place, the fate of the three paşas, Midhat, Nuri, and Mahmut, was a more complicated business. Once the matter was removed from the judiciary, legalism disappeared altogether, letting the political aspects of the trial come to light lucidly.

The day after the issuance of the Court of Cassation's ruling, the ministerial cabinet convened to discuss it. Clearly, this meeting was the doing of Sultan Abdülhamit, whose "interest" in the trial was all but covert. The grand vizier at the time, Sait Paşa, describes the discussion in his memoir.[65] Each of the fourteen ministers who composed the cabinet expressed their opinion. The consensus about the need to implement the court's rulings was no surprise. All of the ministers were aware of the sultan's political desires. Although in 1881 Abdülhamit was not yet the ruthless autocrat that he would become, the abolition of the Basic Law and the Parliament in 1878, and the way the trial had been handled, left no vagueness as to his taste about political opposition. Hence, there was no reason to expect that the ministers would risk career, position, and even life by questioning the trial's outcome. Their endorsement of the rule-of-law discourse is interesting, though, as well as few subtextual doubts that some of them raised. The minister of public works, Hasan Fehmi Paşa, said that since this matter was decided by the "formal courts" (*mehakim-i muntazam*), there was no point in considering it at the cabinet. He added, however, that the impact of this matter in Europe had to be examined. In this minor comment, he was merely giving an expression to a concern that was on everybody's mind, including the sultan. Others commented about the need to apply the law. The minister of commerce, Raif Efendi, for instance, said that the court decisions were issued in "the first, second and high instances, and objections were examined legally and rejected." Perhaps out of ignorance, he overlooked the trivial fact that the court of first instance never addressed this trial because of the severity of the charges. Nearly all the ministers stressed that the trial was conducted in accordance with the law, perhaps because they had no doubt that it might not have. Worthy of special attention was the response of the *şeyhülislam*, Ahmet Esat Efendi, who participated in that meeting in his capacity as a member of the cabinet. According to Sait Paşa, who recorded the discussion, the *şeyhülislam* stated that the court decision conformed with law and procedure and that the convicts harmed the community, the state, and the world of Islam and that they were to be held accountable in this world and the afterlife. This statement is interesting because convening a commission of ulema in order to examine the Shar'i validity of the decision was the sultan's next stage. Telling from the *şeyhülislam*'s statement at the cabinet, he had not demanded such a measure.

The sultan was determined to gather every bit of legitimacy that was available. Abdülhamit presented to the special ulema commission a set of "guiding" questions. The ulema commission convened on July 19. Like the cabinet, it was aware of the sultan's expectations. In its opinion, the commission wrote that it reviewed the documents of the trial and the report of the cabinet and that it concluded that all the convicts deserved a *tazir* (Arabic: *ta'zir*) penalty. In theory, this penal category referred to punishments that were administered at the discretion of the judge, as opposed to *qisas* penalties, which were fixed by the canonical texts, namely, the Quran and the Hadith. Mentioning the *tazir*/*qisas* distinction in this context seemed like an unnecessary casuistry. In any case, the opinion of the ulema commission made it clear that the crimes in question justified the execution of the convicted paşas.

The sultan's concerns (or doubts) persisted. So a couple of days after receiving the Shar'i opinion, he set up another special committee composed of senior ministers and officials, former grand viziers, and high military officials. He asked the committee to examine specific points that had been discussed in the trial. The matter of command responsibility bothered the sultan more than any other issue related to the affair. This problem appeared as the first question that he referred to the committee: "Was the murder of Sultan Abdülaziz an outcome of a compelling order that had been given by Sultan Murat? Or, alternatively, did the convicted paşas commit the murder or had other people commit it?" The sultan's questions to the committee dealt with the uncertainty of Murat's liability, considering his mental situation at the time.

To put the sultan's inquiry in its proper context, a summary of the events that preceded Abdülaziz's death is called for. On May 30, 1876, shortly before daybreak, military troops surrounded the Dolmabahçe Palace, the private residence of Sultan Abdülaziz. It was a well-organized coup arranged by Midhat; the minister of war, Hüseyin Avni Paşa; the director of the military academy, Süleyman Paşa; the grand vizier, Rüştü Paşa; Şeyhülislam Hayrullah Efendi; and some other senior officials. After fifteen years on the throne, Sultan Abdülaziz was deposed. The officers put the shocked sultan on a *kayık* (small boat) and shipped him to the Topkapı Palace. Roughly at the same time, Murat V, the son of the late sultan Abdülmecit I, was enthroned at the Ministry of War. A few days later, Sultan Murat consented to Abdülaziz's pleading and moved him together with his family and servants to Feriye Palace, a little more than a mile from Dolmabahçe Palace, on the European side of the Bosporus. Affected by the devastating news about Abdülaziz's death, the mental instability of Sultan Murat—referred to in palace circles as "madness"—became evident on September 7, 1876. Following a term of ninety-three days on the throne, Sultan Murat was dethroned by the decision of the ministerial cabinet, which accepted the recommendation of Midhat Paşa and Grand Vizier Rüştü Paşa. His younger brother, Abdülhamit, acceded to the throne.

In the question that Abdülhamit referred to the special committee that he convened after the trial, he wrote that if it were proved that Murat was giving the compelling order to kill Abdülaziz, the penalties of the convicts had to be mitigated. At the same time, if Sultan Murat was mentally sick, he could not be held liable and subjected to penalties, from both Nizamiye and Shar'i perspectives. I will elaborate on the legal problem of command responsibility in the next chapter.

These issues of liability were a strictly legal matter that required the expertise of jurists. The sultan's decision to set up a special committee for discussing these issues, most probably by the advice of his minister of justice, Cevdet Paşa, was a dubious move, from the perspective of legalism. Possibly, they aimed at convincing the public opinion—domestically and internationally—that no legal stone was left unturned before executing the paşas. The alternative explanation, namely, that Abdülhamit was truly worried about the possibility that innocent people would be executed, is less likely, bearing in mind his own involvement in the events that had led to the trial and in the proceedings themselves through his proxy, the minister of justice. At any rate, this measure was counterproductive in terms of the effort to indict the paşas by resorting to the courses of actions defined by legalism. Reopening questions that had been decided by the judiciary in an ad hoc committee was a motion of no confidence in the justice of the Nizamiye court. It was the sultan, no less, who raised doubts about the discretion of the judiciary by asking ministers and military officers to reconsider the legal issues. It is impossible to provide a definitive explanation for this strange conduct of the sultan, whose intelligence was noted by contemporary observers and modern historians. The wording of the queries that he addressed to the two committees reveals something of a confusion and stress. As the point of no return was approaching, he might have developed doubts about the entire scheme. In any case, legalism was abandoned altogether even though the legal questions kept nagging.

The committee did not need more than a day of discussions to issue its opinion, which it based on a scrutiny of the court decisions, the trial documents, and Midhat's objections. In its decision, the committee merely reiterated the court's position, namely, that an interrogation of Murat was impossible owing to his mental illness and that nothing could be done about the possible liability of his mother, who might have been the mastermind behind the scheme. The members of this committee, who found themselves in an embarrassing position, having to assess the legality of a judicial decision that had been justified by the Court of Cassation, revealed some integrity when concluding their opinion with the claim that since the committee had no legal authority, it could not pursue the matter any further.[66] The same committee was required to submit its opinion about the question of mitigation of the death sentences. Ten members voted for mitigation, while the other twelve voted for the gallows. It was foreign intervention, however, that saved the paşa's necks for the time being, and they were sent to imprisonment in the citadel of Taif.

This political trial had no impact on the overall fortitude of legalism as a legal culture exercised in the courts. In the years that elapsed since the trial, legal formalism defined daily practice in the Nizamiye court system across the empire. Every now and then, the government revised some clauses of the codes through addendums, but the codes remained the major instrument for providing the system with a sense of permanence, necessary for imagination of the entire system in terms of the rule of law. The durability of Ottoman legalism was salient when the empire deteriorated into a police state in the last decade of the Hamidian era. Even then, the courts remained committed to the codes. Neither had the 1908 revolution had any significant effect on the structure of the courts or the codes that defined the judicial discourse. The revolution, however, did offer a relief, temporary as it turned out to be, from years of Hamidian political oppression. Ali Haydar Bey, the son of Midhat Paşa, who had been dead for twenty-seven years, decided that the time was ripe to demand a retrial.

In 1910 a booklet of fifty-nine pages, titled *A Plea for a Retrial of Midhat and His Associates Including Necessary Reasons* (*Midhat Paşa ve Rüfekasının Muhakemesi Hakkında Esbab-ı Mucibeyi Havi İade-i Muhakeme Layıhası*) came out in Istanbul.[67] The author of the essay was the attorney Tomaidis Hirisantos (Chrisantos) on behalf of his clients Ali Haydar Bey, the son of Midhat, and Fahri Bey. Fahri Bey had been Abdülaziz's young chamberlain, who had served the sultan during the time he spent in Feriye Palace, following his deposition. The Yıldız court had found Fahri Bey guilty of complicity, sentencing him to life imprisonment in Taif. The government released him in 1908, following the revolution, and he returned to Istanbul, where he died a decade later. A retrial never took place. Ali Haydar Bey had accumulated enough experience in his long campaign to absolve his father's good name to believe that such a trial would take place, after so many years. Nevertheless, as I will demonstrate in the concluding chapter, this plea was part of a life project that had included lobbying outside the Ottoman Empire already at the time of Abdülhamit, instigation of critical coverage in foreign newspapers, and publication of a biography on Abdülhamit.

As far as Ali Haydar Bey and Fahri Bey were concerned, there could not be better timing. Two years after the revolution, denunciation of Abdülhamit's tyranny in the public sphere was welcome, and Midhat became a "martyr of freedom," as he was called in the plea and in newspapers. The exposition of the plea provides a sharp demonstration of the juncture of politics and law, which provides political trials with their unique hue, to be discussed in the next chapter. The author sets the struggle over constitutionalism as the exclusive context of the trial:

> In no time, Abdülhamit broke his promise and began to establish his despotic and imperious rule instead of a limited government. For example, although it is known that pronouncement of a constitution was one of the prerequisites of his enthronement, Abdülhamit delayed this announcement for four months, and his exchange with Midhat represented the first clash between freedom and tyranny. Abdülhamit created his own [network of] supporters while taking every possible measure to delay and prevent the announcement and publication of the constitution. During a cabinet meeting that addressed the constitution, the Minister of Justice, Cevdet Paşa, said that "since a wise Sultan like Abdülhamit was enthroned, there is no longer a need for announcing a constitution." Midhat Paşa intended to step down from his position as grand vizier, and the other ministers supported the constitution. The cabinet submitted to the Sultan the draft of the constitution.[68]

The initial decision to perform the Yıldız Trial as a Nizamiye trial had predetermined the nature of criticism that it invited in the following decades, also evident in the account of the trial provided by Turkish general İlker Başbuğ more than a century later. The plea for a retrial unfolded a long list of procedural infractions that could be referred to as such only within the particular discourse of the law's rule that had evolved since the beginning of codification. In other words, the plea illustrates the argument advanced in the present discussion with regard to Ottoman legalism through three layers of meaning. First, it is an illustration of Ottoman legalism by its sort of argumentation; second, a travesty of justice as the trial might have been, the authors of the plea could dispute the court decision only because they shared the same legalistic imagination of the law; and third, the plea provides a valid summary of the procedural violations in Yıldız Trial. The following list includes only a few of the many irregularities:

- The law stipulated that every action in the criminal court had to be initiated by a warrant prepared and presented by the examining magistrate (*müstantık*). Midhat, however, was arrested with no earlier notice or warrant.
- Once they arrested Midhat Paşa, the police had to hand him over to the officials circumscribed by the law, namely, the public prosecutor, the examining magistrate, or the gendarmerie officers, for interrogation. In practice, his interrogation took place on the steamship that was heading to Istanbul, in the presence of the minister of justice. Upon arrival to Istanbul, instead of detention at the appropriate "cradle of justice," Midhat was brought to the Yıldız Palace, "a place of imprisonment and brutality."[69]
- The composition of the court that tried Midhat and the other defendants did not meet the codified legal standard. The Law of the Judicial Organization stipulated that criminal courts for severe crimes (*cinayet*) would consist of a president and four members. The Yıldız court, however, consisted of six individuals, namely, five members and a president, an office that was divided in turn between Sururi Efendi and Hiristo Forides Efendi. Legally, so the petitioners claimed, a decision made by a court whose composition did not meet the standard was invalid.[70]
- The trial's protocol indicates that one of the witnesses, Hüseyin Husni Efendi, was not summoned to the court but had been questioned earlier through correspondence, and his written answers were read aloud in the trial. The petitioners argued that there was no law that legitimized such an action.[71]
- None of the witnesses who testified against Midhat Paşa spoke in his presence, as required by law, and he did not have access to their written depositions.[72]

The petitioners pointed to the unusual treatment by the Court of Cassation when reviewing the case, wondering how it could be possible that this court, which had quashed other court decisions for minor infractions, disregarded the long list of violations that came to its attention. They explain that palace officials managed to secure the submissiveness of the Cassation Court by threatening its president.[73] No less stern was the allegation made with regard to the court's impartiality. While impartiality of the judiciary was not a theme unique to modern legalism, these allegations were based on the specific clauses of the codes that referred to the independence of the courts and to the principle of separation of powers. The latter was one of the pillars of the rule of law the way it was imagined in the Ottoman Empire since the 1840s. The plea also mentions repeatedly the involvement of the minister of justice in the pretrial and trial proceedings. The petitioners argued that the palace had arranged a docile composition of judges. For one, a tenured member of the criminal court and an expert in criminal law, Bogos Şaşian Efendi, had been removed from office just before the beginning of the trial, to be replaced by Judge Tekefür Efendi, whose expertise belonged with civil and commercial law. The petitioners reveal that Judge Bogos Şaşian Efendi had exhibited courage and judicial independence when sitting on the bench in other cases, including a case where he was subject to threats from one of the palace officials. The judge who replaced him for the Yıldız Trial, by contrast, had a dubious record of bribe taking and dismissal from office. "After wandering around for three years, somehow he managed to return from the lowest stratum and re-enter the judicial ranks. Recently, he left the cadre due to objections."[74]

The plea unfolds additional concrete details about acts of injustice, also revealing new evidence. The sources of some of these pieces of information are obscure, referred to as "according to information that we have," and their validity is unclear, such as the claim that the sultan himself was present at the interrogation site. The author attributes other allegations to testimonies of individuals whose names are provided. For instance, the petitioners base their claim about the threats that were made against the president of the Court of Cassation on the alleged statement of one Ata Bey, "the former head clerk of the Imperial Accountancy."[75]

Although the petition for retrial was a solid manifestation of legalistic logic, it was not a typical legal document. It included passages that would never be part of a standard Nizamiye petition. Hence, in itself it was an irregular document, indicating the extraordinary nature of the political trial. For one, the petition lacked the aloof, highly technical style of Nizamiye petitions, court decisions, and documentation in general. These documents, sharing the discursive style of court decisions in the Continental legal system, were always devoid of normative statements or moral judgments that are customary in the common law system. Justice, in this formalist discourse, was a matter of a cold measure of human actions against codified clauses. The petition in question, by contrast, was infused with fervent statements about the wickedness of Abdülhamit, as revealed in his persecution of Midhat. The petition lacked references to specific legal clauses, an identifying mark of every Nizamiye document. Clauses 349–52 in the Code of Criminal Procedure, which regulated the proceedings in a case of retrial, were not mentioned in the plea. The petitioners bolstered their position with arguments that a normal Nizamiye procedure would deem irrelevant. For instance, they dedicated a long passage to a critique published by Namık Kemal, the famous author "adorned among Ottoman people and European authors with no exception," who wrote a piece about the duties of the just judge, in a critical response to the trial. The petitioners also mentioned the criticism that the trial evoked internationally.

To conclude, the petition illustrates the convergence of law and politics that form the context of every political trial. In the case of the Yıldız Trial, political action was framed in terms of a formalist rule-of-law discourse.

2
Political Trial

ON DECEMBER 12, 1909, the newspaper *Tanin* started serializing the verbatim protocol of the Yıldız Trial. Reactions from readers called for a special editorial response, which was provided by the famous translator and literary figure Selanikli Tevfik soon thereafter.[1] The justification for this response was stated at the outset: "Some opinion holders misinterpreted Midhat's trial, which has been published in our newspaper." The author reported that some readers wrote to the editors, claiming that instead of proving the persecution of Midhat and his friends, the trial's verbatim transcript demonstrated their culpability. In his reply, Selanikli Tevfik did not specify whether these reactions came from people who believed in Midhat's innocence and thought that the publication of the transcript was counterproductive in this sense or if, alternatively, these responses reflected the views of people who held Midhat guilty of conspiring to kill Sultan Abdülaziz more than thirty years earlier. In any case, Selanikli Tevfik dismissed such claims as "unacceptable." He agreed, however, that "those who come across the trial of Midhat Paşa by chance might not be aware [of the fact that] it was envisioned and contrived by Abdülhamit." The author, then, carried on to provide a succinct account of the constitutional hopes that had led to the accession of Abdülhamit to the throne in 1876 and their prompt miscarriage when it turned out that the sultan, who had been enthroned on the basis of his support in a constitution, was turning into a tyrant.

For all we know, the letters to the editor could be a straw man created by the editors in order to bolster their case. But even if these letters were fake, they nevertheless revealed the concerns involved with the newspaper's decision to publish the Yıldız Trial's transcript. The editors of

Tanin made a clever choice when recruiting Selanikli Tevfik for the task of educating their readers about the necessary distinction between the good and the bad guys. The prose of the proficient translator was characterized by clarity and confidence. He presented the story of failed constitutionalism as a process that started with the firm objection of the sultan-to-be to Article 13 of the Basic Law, which allowed Ottoman subjects to form any kind of association. It was at that point, according to Selanikli Tevfik, that Sultan Abdülhamit signaled out Midhat, the mastermind of constitutionalism, as the gravest threat to his rule and his main adversary. From then on, the author writes, Abdülhamit did everything he could to eliminate Midhat and the hopes (or threats) for constitutionalism that he represented. Resorting to trickery, thus Selanikli Tevfik explains, the sultan convinced Midhat to return from Europe by granting him the position of provincial governor. But it was really a trap, designed to bring about Midhat's arrest, trial, and demise. Selanikli Tevfik warned his readers that all the documents used in the trial were phony, arranged in advance in order to secure the annihilation of Midhat and the other politicians, under Abdülhamit's orders. He concluded his essay by claiming that only a retrial would prove that Midhat was not involved in Abdülaziz's death in 1876 and that the truth might be revealed to the public opinion, provided the documents were not destroyed.[2]

If the transcript of the Yıldız Trial could be understood as proof of both the culpability and the innocence of Midhat Paşa, as some readers argued, this editorial response raises a question concerning the reason for publishing a verbatim report of the trial in the first place. As noted before, we have no access to the actual letters that reached the editorial office of *Tanin* in Istanbul, to the extent that such letters were real, but the publication of a well-thought-out response indicates some serious concerns on the part of the editors as to the risk of misinterpretation of the transcript. Above all, it indicates that three decades after the trial, opinions about it were not a wall-to-wall consensus. This feature is typical of political trials; they are often scandalous and controversial, and they draw attention like no other type of trial.

The decision of *Tanin*'s editors to publish the transcript of a trial that had taken place thirty years earlier should be understood in the context of the precarious political situation that followed the 1908 revolution, also known as the Young Turk Revolution. The general euphoria that erupted in cities across the empire immediately after the overthrow of the oppressive Hamidian regime was soon superseded by uncertainties as to the next phase. The staggering achievement of the Young Turks in putting an end to the regime of Abdülhamit, one of the more enduring sultans in the six-hundred-year-old dynasty, was soon overshadowed by disagreements concerning the nature of the new regime. Discord was evident in both the military and the civil officialdom. While there was a wide range of opinions, two factions were discernible: unionists and liberals.

The unionist camp envisioned an election-based constitutional government, whereas the liberal camp supported a constitutional monarchy ruled by the senior bureaucrats. The military ranks were far from homogeneous as far as feelings about the revolution were concerned. The higher echelons in the military were overall in favor of the revolution but divided along the liberal-unionist camps. The officers who had led the revolution were inclined to allow the senior paşas of the Hamidian era to keep their political power and run the state. The division between unionists and liberals paralleled class divisions. Overall, the liberals, in both the military and officialdom, came from the upper class of Ottoman society, whereas the unionists belonged with the lower middle class, who had paid a price for decades of integration of the Ottoman economy into the world capitalist market. All sorts of agendas and concrete priorities in line with ethnic and religious identifications fueled the rift between unionists and liberals.[3]

On April 13, 1909, nine months of mounting tensions between conservatives and reactionaries in support of Abdülhamit and the senior officials who were supported by both unionists and liberals exploded through a series of events known in Turkey as the "31st of March Incident." An ad hoc partnership of rebellious soldiers and religious students managed to rule the capital for eleven days. They did not seem to have a clear program other than reversing the changes brought about by the revolution. They made the concrete demand to reinstall the deposed sultan and the more obscure call to implement the Sharia. The consequences of this episode were grave not because this coalition was successful; it was certainly not. The Third Army rushed from Macedonia to crush the reactionaries and protect the Young Turk government.[4] On April 27, Abdülhamit was formally dethroned and sent to exile, thereby removed forever from any position of political importance. Nevertheless, the perceived potential danger of similar events legitimized measures that were counterproductive in terms of the Revolution's initial objectives. The CUP government severely restricted freedom of expression in the press and in public meetings by legislation. Mahmut Şevket Paşa, the commander of the Third Army, now in command of the First and Second Armies as well and the martial law commander in Istanbul, capitalized on his success in the 31st of March Incident, turning it into political dominance in the cabinet for three years. From this point in time until the eve of the Great War, politics in Istanbul were a boiling pot of rivalries and provisional alliances involving military officials, liberals and unionists, rebellious ethnic groups, and foreign interests.[5] It was in this political context that interest in the trial of Midhat reemerged. Given this environment of unclear expectations and prospects, *Tanin*'s editor could only hope that their readers would not misinterpret the transcript of the trial. For them, Midhat had to be associated with constitutionalism. Nevertheless, political trials are destined to be the subjects of conflicting narratives, regardless of the aspirations of their designers.

THE CONCEPT OF THE POLITICAL TRIAL

Few theorists of law and society have taken up the challenge of clearing the conceptual obscurity of the political trial as a category of description and analysis. The assumed straightforwardness of this category masks its complexity; as noted in an oft-cited study on political trials, one can recognize political trials when one sees them.[6] The fact that intuition is helpful in distinguishing between political and ordinary trials does not mean that a definition is superfluous. On the contrary, conceptualization of political trials becomes all the more necessary in light of the growing impact of sociolegal scholarship, which has demonstrated the indivisibility of law and politics in every possible aspect of the law.[7] The conclusions drawn from the critical legal studies school thwart the distinction between political and ordinary trials. If modern liberal legal systems are imbued with social biases and there is a considerable gap between ideals of impartiality and everyday conduct dictated by mundane limitations and biases, as revealed by the CLS, is there sense in distinguishing political from ordinary trials? The distinction becomes even more puzzling if we accept the claim that all trials are political because all courts of law are organs of the state, thereby reproducing hegemonic perceptions, an argument made by several theorists.[8] Development of a comprehensive theoretical discussion on the meaning of political trials as a descriptive and analytic category is a task way beyond the objectives of the present study. Instead, this chapter is aimed at the much more modest objective of identifying a practical conceptual toolbox that might be helpful in illuminating the significance of the Yıldız Trial in the sociolegal history of the late Ottoman Empire.

Each political trial is a unique event through its departure from a certain norm of conduct. Trying to contain this feature of political trials, scholars have offered some typologies and distinctions.[9] In his typology, Ron Christenson takes up the concept of the rule of law as an acid test that allows differentiation between partisan trials and political trials that are committed to the rule of law. The former are guided by political agendas while veiled by a facade of legality, whereas the latter are committed to the principle of equality before the law.[10] Although he renders the rule of law a major standard for telling unfair partisan trials from fair political trials, Christenson does not tackle the fact that the rule of law in itself is a vague category that presents serious theoretical difficulties, as noted in the previous chapter.

A more nuanced conceptualization informed by sociolegal research is offered in Ken Kyle and Pat Lauderdale's survey of the theoretical literature on political trials. They argue that the existing attempts to explain political trials, typically focused on definitions, are based on limited conceptions of politics, on the one hand, and uncritical understandings of law, on the other. As a way out of discussions that are fixated on rigid definitions of politics, they suggest bringing in sociolegal perspectives when studying political trials. Doing so would mean, inter alia, awareness of concrete processes in which social definitions are created, transformed, and maintained.[11]

Once again, Judith Shklar's conceptualization of legalism provides valuable conceptual keys for the benefit of studying political trials. Oddly enough, later literature that has focused on these trials mentions her observations only in passing. A professor of political science, Shklar shared with legal realists the conviction that judicial performances of legal systems cannot be studied without reference to their concrete political contexts. For Shklar, there is no point is assessing political trials carried out in regimes that had abandoned all standards of justice, as was the case of the Stalinist and Nazi regimes, in terms of legalistic standards. However, these regimes are the easy cases, as far as the study of political trials is concerned, because where terror and persecution are institutionalized, sensible definitions of justice lose relevance to begin with.[12] It is the less intense contexts, whether constitutional, liberal, or nonliberal regimes, that call for practical differentiation between political and regular trials. Shklar provides a useful working definition of political trials: "What, after all, is a political trial? It is a trial in which the prosecuting party, usually the regime in power aided by a cooperative judiciary, tries to eliminate its political enemies. It pursues a very specific policy—the destruction, or at least the disgrace and disrepute, of a political opponent."[13] Most political trials, according to Shklar, abuse the principle of legality, or "scorn" it, in her own words. Abuse of legality, in this regard, is evident in trials that misuse the law or when the act made criminal by the law is not there in the sense that criminal acts are falsely charged; alternatively, acts that are legally legitimate are presented as criminal acts. The legalism applied in political trials, Shklar claims, is a continuum consisting of degrees, and since every political trial is unique by nature, to argue that legalism is resorted to in this or that case is far from enough. One needs to study the *sort* of legalism that is applied, the political goals at hand, and the nature of judges' commitment to legality.[14]

Yet even trials of infamous Nazis on account of cases of undisputable evilness that had to be eradicated through legal and nonlegal means present difficulties when considered from the perspective of intersection of law and politics. Hannah Arendt's report on the Eichmann Trial (1961) demonstrates the moral and legal difficulties that surround modern political trials. Specifically, even when the cause is just, the monstrous crime is there, and legalism is employed to certain degrees, political trials leave behind doubts caused by the politics that define the legal process. Arendt's irking conclusion illustrates this point:

> The irregularities and abnormalities of the trial in Jerusalem were so many, so varied, and of such legal complexity that they overshadowed during the trial, as they have in the surprisingly small amount of post-trial literature, the central moral, political, and even legal problems that the trial inevitably posed. Israel herself, through the pre-trial statements of Prime Minister Ben-Gurion and through the way the accusation was framed by the prosecutor, confused the issues further by listing a great number of purposes the trial was supposed to achieve, all of which were ulterior purposes with respect to the law and to courtroom procedure. The purpose of a trial is to render justice, and nothing else; even the noblest of ulterior purposes—"the making of a record of the Hitler regime which would withstand the test of history," as Robert G. Storey, executive trial counsel at Nuremberg, formulated the supposed higher aims of the Nuremberg Trials—can only detract from the law's main business: to weigh the charges brought against the accused, to render judgment, and to mete out due punishment."[15]

One cannot emphasize enough the immanent uniqueness of the political trial. Mentioning the Eichmann Trial in a study of an Ottoman political trial is not a matter of comparison, which would be awkward in every possible sense. Rather, the fact that two trials that cannot be more different in contents and contexts can be nonetheless qualified as modern political trials, thereby belonging to a single descriptive category, illustrates the single aspect of these trials that distinguishes them from ordinary criminal trials. In most cases, their immediate political context, a cluster of pressing partisan interests, hegemonic agendas, didactic objectives, and personal enmities find their way to the courtroom while either defying or resorting to legalism. Hence, an effective thick description of the political trial depends on a proper illustration of the related political contexts.

POLITICAL CONTEXTS

All political trials can be identified as such by the fact that each of them makes sense only when understood within a certain context of concrete political ambitions of members of the political elite. These ambitions and desires always "find their way" to the courtroom while cracking up the walls of legalism. In the Yıldız Trial, the mutual dislike of Minister of Justice Cevdet Paşa and Midhat Paşa was a mixture of ideological disagreements and bad chemistry. At the same time, the observers of the Yıldız Trial could imagine it as the final chapter in a story of collision between two political forces, one led by Midhat Paşa and the other by Sultan Abdülhamit. It was also the story that was told by Selanikli Tevfik twenty-eight years later. However, such a view would merely be a simplification of a complicate political beehive made of dynamic ad hoc alliances, personal sympathies and enmities, passion for power, and ideological convictions. The defendants in the trial did not form a coherent company, even if their ways had crossed in the past and would cross again in the grim future that they faced.

At this point in our discussion, I wish to direct our attention to the two defendants who had possessed the most significant political capital, Midhat Paşa and Rüştü Paşa. The defendants Damat ("son in law") Nuri Paşa and Damat Mahmut Paşa were men of substantial political power in their capacity as members of the imperial family. The rest of the defendants belonged to two groups. The suspects of the actual murder, Hacı Mehmet, Mustafa the Algerian, and Mustafa the Wrestler, were of no political importance. The third group consisted of six officials who had possessed some political power as officeholders, but they had played a secondary role in palace politics. On the other side of the divide, literally, there were the sultan and at his side Cevdet Paşa, the minister of justice. The three paşas, Midhat, Rüştü, and Cevdet, started their careers decades earlier as brilliant young men whose talents met the thirst of the Tanzimat state for men of skills and vision. Midhat and Cevdet were born at the same year, 1822. Rüştü was a decade older. When the iconic reformer and grand vizier Mustafa Reşit Paşa pronounced the Tanzimat in the Rose Garden of the Topkapı Palace on November 1839 (also known as the Gülhane Decree), Midhat and Cevdet were seventeen and sixteen years old, and Rüştü was twenty-eight. Their ascent to the highest positions in the country resulted from the usual blend of merit and luck, as will be shown in the following short summaries of their achievements up until their arrests.

"Translator" (Mütercim) Mehmet Rüştü Paşa (1811–1882)

Mehmet Rüştü was born to a poor family in Ayancık, a town on the Black Sea coast of northern Anatolia. When Mehmet Rüştü was three years old, his father, a boatman, left with his family to Istanbul in search of better life. The family sent the child to a school in the Tophane neighborhood, where they lived. In 1826, a week after the epic annihilation of the janissary corps, the fourteen-year-old boy joined the ranks of the local battalion of the new army, which was stationed in his neighborhood. During these years, the young soldier Mehmet Rüştü was tutored by a certain professor called Tanaş Efendi, who taught him French.[16] Rüştü belonged to a group of young people who benefited from the high demand for knowledgeable officers, some of whom would become key figures in the Tanzimat-state.

The historiography of the 1950s and the 1960s labeled the changes that took place in the first half of the nineteenth century as "the impact of the West," or in simplistic terms as "Westernization," describing it as a period of response to a "Western" challenge.[17] Revisionist historians, by contrast, have emphasized the selective and innovative adaptations that were characteristic of the reforms throughout the long nineteenth century. In addition, revisionist historians have demonstrated that many practices that past historians had identified as "Westernization" were in progress in the Ottoman state regardless of encounters with European "agents of change."[18] Nevertheless, the Ottoman ruling elite considered knowledge of French, the lingua franca of the time, as a sine qua non for joining the train of progress, in itself a concept that excited elites across the world. Command of French was one of the most valuable capitals in Istanbul of the nineteenth century's early decades, often paid off with rapid promotions. The dismissal of Greeks from state institutions following the Greek war of independence (1821–29), and the growing antipathy toward Armenians, both groups associated with command of French, made it all the more an asset for aspiring Sunni Muslims. The story (attributed to Rüştü Paşa's son) goes that when Sultan Mahmut II visited the citadel of Beykoz on the Anatolian side of Istanbul as part of his inspections of the preparation of the new army, he heard from Grand Admiral Hüsrev Paşa that there was a lieutenant stationed in Tarabya who had mastered French.

Tarabya, today a neighborhood of Istanbul, housed foreign embassies and residences of foreign diplomats. The sultan immediately summoned the young officer and was deeply impressed.[19] This encounter could only mean the beginning of a decadelong climbing up the ladder of officialdom. We should keep in mind, however, that rather than an à *la Turca* version of a Cinderella story, attachment to the "right" patronage network was a precondition for upward social mobility in general and advancement in officialdom in particular.[20] Hence, Rüştü's reputation reached the "imperial ear" primarily because he was a protégé of Hüsrev Paşa, an attachment that served him in the following years.

Rüştü became one of the country's leading translators, henceforth known as "the Translator," specializing in the technical and military fields. He served in various senior positions. In 1854 he was appointed a member of the High Council of the Tanzimat (Meclis-i Ali-i Tanzimat), which was a stepping-stone for the highest position in the government. On December 1859, the forty-eight-year-old Rüştü Paşa became grand vizier (a position equal to prime minister in Europe) under Sultan Abdülmecit (ruled 1839–61). It was the first of five terms in office, under four sultans. This position signified the roller coaster that Ottoman politics was. Terms were often brief, lasting months rather than years.

Ahmet Cevdet Paşa (1822–1895)

The legal brain behind the Yıldız Trial, Ahmet Cevdet Paşa, was the most important Ottoman jurist of his generation. He was present in the initial interrogations of Midhat Paşa and Rüştü Paşa, as well as in the trial. Ahmet Cevdet was born in 1822 to a notable family from Lofça (today's Lovech, in Bulgaria). The family seemed to earmark him for the career of an *alim*, a legal scholar. He arrived in Istanbul at the age of sixteen to learn with the most important *alims* of the time. During some fifteen years of intellectual incubation, it was clear that he was not the typical *softa*, the theological student. His intellectual interests went far beyond those of his peers, leading him to study with professors at the Military School of Engineering as well as educating himself in the fields of history and foreign law. His star started to shine when "Great" (*Koca*) Mustafa Reşit Paşa (1800–1858), the designer of the Tanzimat, was looking for an *alim* to teach him some Islamic law that would serve him in rationalizing and legitimizing the reforms. He was informed about the brilliant young scholar, whose broad horizons made him the perfect consultant for the statesman who was about to be appointed a grand vizier and change the Ottoman state from its roots. Cevdet thus became a protégé of Mustafa Reşit Paşa.

His appointment to *kadı* in 1844 marked the beginning of his career path in officialdom. Cevdet was a man of both letters and action. His career included administrative posts, such as governor of Aleppo (1866–67), as well as appointments that reflected his scholarly forte, such as his positions as a member in the Ottoman Academy of Sciences (1851) and the empire's formal historiographer (1853). In 1868 he was appointed minister of justice, a position that marked a new thrust to the project of legal reform that had started in the early 1840s. Cevdet Paşa's imprint was apparent in every major legal innovation of the period: the codification of civil law (*Mecelle*), the establishment of the Nizamiye courts, and the foundation of the Imperial Law School (1880). Cevdet was also a prolific author. His magnum opus was the *Tarih-i Cevdet* (*History of Cevdet*), notable by its original methodology and style.

Unlike Rüştü Paşa "the Translator," who came from the lower strata of Ottoman society, Cevdet Paşa belonged to the class of provincial elite. This difference in social backgrounds is probably a factor of significance when explaining differences in styles. Rüştü Paşa had the repute of a cautious and adaptive politician.[21] Cevdet, on the other hand, was a self-assured politician, confident enough to express sharp criticism on policies and on the morals of his peers in officialdom.[22]

Cevdet's writing often exhibits a didactic tone, calling bureaucrats to exhibit total devotion to the state while evading submission to self-ambition and favoritism.[23] The role played by Cevdet Paşa in the Yıldız Trial presents a blatant contradiction with his contribution to the rule of law, which he clearly imagined in legalistic terms. Neither was his commitment to destroy his political enemy, Midhat, a good example of the disinterested standards of the servant of the state for which he had been preaching. Nevertheless, when viewed from a sociolegal perspective, such contradictions are no surprise; rather, they are a banal fact of life.

3. Ahmet Cevdet Paşa. Photograph taken from Osman Nuri, *Abdülhamid-i Sani ve Devri Saltanatı Hayatı ve Hususiyesi* (Istanbul: Kitabhane-yi İslam ve Askery—İbrahim Hami, 1327 [1910]).

Ahmet Şefik Midhat Paşa (1822–1884)

Born Ahmet Şefik, Midhat shared several biographical features with his political foe, Cevdet Paşa. Like Cevdet, Midhat was born in 1822 to a notable ulema family. Unlike Rüştü Paşa, whose father was a simple boatman, Midhat's father was a *kadı* at the Sharia court, a position that brought the Istanbul-based family to the Bulgarian province of Vidin for a while. Years later, Midhat would return to Bulgaria as an ingenious governor.

The boy Ahmet Şefik was given the appellative "Midhat" when he started apprenticeship at the Imperial Council at the age of twelve. As was the custom for aspiring sons of the Ottoman elite families who did not follow the conventional educational path of the *medrese*, the early years of advancement in officialdom paralleled a somewhat eclectic acquisition of education. Midhat learned the classic subjects of syntax, Islamic jurisprudence, logic, and Farsi with several professors who taught in major mosques in Istanbul.[24] He did not belong to Mustafa Reşit Paşa's patronage network, which included most "men of the Tanzimat," but he possessed exceptional political instincts as well as talents that his superiors quickly recognized.

Following a few years of service at the offices of the grand vizier, the nineteen-year-old official was sent for civil service in the provinces, where he had the opportunity to gain firsthand administrative knowledge of life outside the political nerve center in Istanbul. Five years later, he returned to the Porte, where he made allies and enemies during fifteen years of service in scribal duties. Unlike Cevdet, Midhat was not a scholar; like Cevdet, however, he had a critical mind and a sense of duty that made him the ideal auditor. In 1861, at the age of thirty-nine, he was entrusted with the task of investigating cases of misconduct among provincial officialdom, a duty that cost him some new enemies.[25]

The achievements gained during the fifth decade of Midhat's life won him a reputation both domestically and abroad. The project of administrative centralization, which had been launched by Mahmut II (r. 1808–39), intersected with the trend of codification that gained momentum in the 1860s and the 1870s, and Midhat Paşa was at the center of both endeavors. As the governor of Niş (1861–64), he developed administrative and social concepts that the government codified and systematized in the groundbreaking Provincial Law of 1864. This law established new concepts of provincial administration, replacing the region-based laws in the form of *kanunnames*. The Provincial Law imposed a uniform structure and hierarchy over all the provinces, rendering them more legible and more governable by the central administration.[26]

Between 1864 and 1868, Midhat Paşa served as the governor of the Bulgarian province of Tuna (Danube), which was a model province for testing the Provincial Law. He returned to Istanbul with the aura of one of the state's leading reformers. If Cevdet was the face of legal reform, Midhat was the face of reform at large, leaving a trace of innovations wherever he served.[27] Following a short period in Istanbul, where he developed reforms in the fields of banking and taxation, Midhat returned to the provinces to serve as the governor of Baghdad (1869–72). This position was actually a punishment inflicted on him following continuing disagreements with Grand Vizier Mehmet Emin Ali Paşa, a famous reformer in his own right. Indeed, the Baghdad province presented a unique challenge owing to its tribal composition, which meant a complex political fabric of alliances and rivalries between chieftains. Midhat met the challenge with his typical zest, employing stick-and-carrot policies, settlement of nomadic tribes, and advancement of modernizing reforms in the fields of communication, transportation, and infrastructure, to name but a few.[28]

If the 1860s situated Midhat as the empire's foremost reformer in the field of provincial administration, the 1870s positioned him as the leading campaigner of constitutionalism. In 1873 he became grand vizier. A comprehensive history of the institution of the grand vizier in the long nineteenth century is yet to be written, but it might be the case that the highest position in the bureaucratic hierarchy was not necessarily the most influential one. Frequent rotation and pressures from sultans, on the one hand, and competition between political networks, on the other, sterilized much of the ability of grand viziers to advance comprehensive policies.[29] The camp of Nedim Paşa interpreted Midhat's passion for reform and rational conduct as a threat. A protégé of Sultan Abdülaziz and one of the more influential senior officials, Nedim Paşa managed to convince the sultan to dismiss Midhat after barely two months in office.

In the following years, during and in between brief episodes of ministerial terms, Midhat directed most of his energy to the promotion of constitutionalism. He discussed with Ottoman and foreign friends the nature of the constitution that he envisioned and the sort of federal regime that it would establish.[30] These discussions were an experimental balloon that provoked a considerable degree of unrest in the political beehive at the capital and beyond, which found its full expression in the eventful year of 1876.

The Crises of 1876

The Yıldız Trial was the most significant aftershock of the political earthquake that shook the Ottoman elite five years earlier. The astonishing events that culminated in the coup of 1876 could be nothing less than a fresh memory in the mind of every member of the political elite in Istanbul who had participated in or observed these events. Several developments mounted up to a constellation that generated a general sense of profound crisis on the eve of the coup.

Decades of mounting foreign debt resulted in an unprecedented financial crisis that placed the Ottoman state under an existential threat. A moratorium declared in October 1875 formalized the insolvency of the state, which was drifting speedily to the apocalyptic scenario of bankruptcy. On the eve of the 1876 coup, the ruling elite could not know that the sinking ship would be rescued and brought back to the course of economic growth with the help of the European powers, who felt the pressures of worried investors in the Ottoman markets.[31]

In addition to the financial ordeal, the government had to deal with revolts of Christian peasants that erupted in Bulgaria in April, backed by Russia, the nemesis of the Ottomans at the time. A chain reaction started with a massacre of hundreds of Muslims and the seizure of Ottoman strongholds by the rebels. The harshness of the Ottoman military response reflected the government's panic and loss of control. The Ottoman government employed ferocious irregular militias of Muslim volunteers (*Başıbozuk*) to put down the revolts, an unwise measure that led to a countermassacre of thousands of Christian subjects of the empire. The British press covered this bloody event intensively under the ubiquitous heading "The Turkish Atrocities in Bulgaria." The talk of the day in British politics, the crisis in the Balkans was about to turn around British longstanding support of the Ottoman Empire.

A collective sensation of imminent calamity was spreading in and around the imperial capital. News about massacres of defenseless Muslims in Bulgaria joined rumors about intentions of the pro-Russian grand vizier, Nedim Paşa, to open the city gates for Russian troops. The grand vizier's close relations with the Russian ambassador Nikolay Pavlovich Ignatiev nourished this word on the street. Sentiments transformed into political action led by the students of the *medreses*, the *softas*.

On May 8, the *softas* gathered in major squares and mosques to protest against the incompetence of the government. The standard pattern of negotiation between fuming rebels and the palace, which had happened so many times in the course of the city's Ottoman past, was the dread of every sultan. The strife lasted almost a week, resulting with the dismissal of Nedim Paşa and appointment of the moderate Rüştü Paşa in his stead. Sultan Abdülaziz appointed the two most popular senior officials at the time, Midhat Paşa and the general Hüseyin Avni Paşa to ministers.

The conventional narrative about the coup of 1876 in the historiography of the period is based on a few key sources, among them the interrogation of Midhat prior to his trial in 1881 and a detailed account of the events, written by Süleyman Paşa, the director of the Military Academy, who was among the planners and executors of the coup.[32] In the present discussion, both accounts can be used for putting together the context of the trial, but they can be also read as representations of the events that were discussed in the trial. As such, they no longer belong to the category of context, but rather serve as representations of the events in question. This comment is a reminder of the fact that reconstruction of political actions, whether in political trials or in history writing, is no more than a presentation of retrospective versions about the events. These versions are always tailored to fit the immediate circumstances at the time of their production.

The first question that Midhat was asked in his pretrial interrogation was "How did the enthronement [of Murat, who was installed in place of Abdülaziz] take place and by whom?"[33] Midhat's account of the events exhibited the situation in which he found himself immediately after his arrest in Izmir. After his miscarried attempt to escape arrest, he was fenced in. He did not know what to expect once the ship arrived in the capital. He knew that a trial was about to take place, and he was aware of the sultan's enmity toward him. However, he also had good reason to believe that his reputation in Europe might serve as a defense shield, saving him from demise. In his account of the coup during his interrogation, he delivered the message that changing sultans was an inevitable occurrence since the ruling elite reached the conclusion that the public was fed up with the sultan and his pro-Russian grand vizier, Nedim Paşa. Significant for the present discussion is Midhat's allusion to the threat that the sultan's attitude posed on the rule of law. Midhat told his interrogators:

> Because these pages will be too short to describe the reasons for the public's abomination toward Sultan Abdülaziz Han, there is no need to go in details. When he [Abdülaziz] has been informed that governing state without law is not possible, he began to denounce the law through and through. During Mahmut Nedim Paşa's second term as Grand Vizier, his [Abdülaziz's] thoughts and behaviors won him the people's hatred. Everyone was talking about the Padişah's misconduct.[34]

At the same time, it was important for Midhat to let his interrogators know that he was a passive actor in the coup. He pointed to the *serasker* (commander in chief), Hüseyin Avni Paşa, as the chief designer of the coup. Describing the overthrow of the sultan as an inevitable occurrence, Midhat presented himself as a mere observer of the events, who was informed about the progression of the scheme but did not contribute to its realization. The following quote from his answer in the interrogation exhibits his attempt to deliver a message about his inaction, on the one hand, and about the quality of the coup as a realization of the general will, on the other:

> Because military and naval forces were already organized by Hüseyin Avni Paşa, Kayserili Ahmet Paşa, Redif Paşa [President of the Military Council], and others, the presence of me, Rüştü Paşa and Hayrullah Efendi [the *şeyhülislam*] was considered sufficient. The decision to take action on Wednesday was made on a Saturday. Later, Hayrullah Efendi came to me and informed me that he met with Hüseyin Avni Paşa and they decided to reschedule [the coup] to Tuesday night. The decision was executed. The ministers, ulema and officials who came for the *biat* [oath of loyalty] showed their satisfaction, and obviously, joy was evident among the people in both the capital and the provinces.[35]

Midhat did not mention the central role played by Süleyman Paşa, the director of the military schools.[36] As noted earlier, both texts, Midhat's recorded interrogation and Süleyman Paşa's account, have served historians in reconstructing the events of 1876. Süleyman's account came out in Istanbul in 1910 under the title "A Perception of the Revolution or the Deposition of Sultan Abdülaziz and the Enthronement of Sultan Murat

V."[37] Based on his analysis of the essay, Robert Devereaux concluded that Süleyman Paşa wrote his account sometime before the pronouncement of the Basic Law (December 23, 1876), namely, a few months after the event.[38] In this detailed and vivid report, Süleyman Paşa, who writes about himself in the third-person form, unfolds the conversations and indecision of the conspirators before taking action, as well as the constant fear that these clandestine plans would leak and result in abortion. In his interrogation, however, Midhat Paşa did not mention Süleyman Paşa's role, but Süleyman Paşa appears in his own account as one of the three designers of the coup, together with the other generals, Serasker Hüseyin Avni Paşa and Redif Paşa. In fact, the reader of Süleyman's report gets the impression that the author was the most important link not only owing to the active role he had supposedly played in planning the deposition but also because of his influence in the barracks and ability to mobilize the officers. The role played by Midhat is the subject of yet another incongruity between Midhat's narrative in his interrogation and Süleyman Paşa's report. Midhat appears in the report as an active participant in the discussions and activities that led to the coup, a member of the immediate circle of plotters that also consisted of the three generals: Grand Vizier Rüştü Paşa, the relatively progressive Şeyhülislam Hayrullah Efendi, and Minister of the Navy Kayserili Ahmet Paşa. According to Süleyman Paşa's account, however, Midhat played a crucial role in exchanging messages between the conspirators and Murat Efendi, the crown prince, and his mother, who was about to become the "valide sultan." Possibly, in his interrogation, Midhat avoided mentioning Süleyman Paşa in order to protect him. Alternatively, Midhat did not want to relate himself with a senior official who had been convicted and sentenced to exile.

Just before dawn on Tuesday, May 30, 1876, two battalions encircled Dolmabahçe Palace, and naval forces positioned themselves on the waterside across from the palace. The heir, Prince (Şehzade) Murat Efendi, was led to the War Ministry, where he heard the *fetva* that sanctioned the deposition and received the oath of loyalty from the grand vizier and the other ministers who were present, including Midhat. Abdülaziz, now a toppled sultan, was taken on a *kayık*, a small rowboat, to the Topkapı Palace, having to hear his mother sobbing and shouting and having his clothes soaked by the pouring rain. Five years later, the disrespect displayed during these nerve-racking hours would be discussed in the trial. The coup was thus completed. The public content following the pacific coup was evident through spontaneous demonstrations of delight and instantaneous rise in the value of Ottoman bonds in the local market.[39]

Midhat's interrogators had no reason to believe him when he tried to diminish his role in the coup. The coup was not only about rescuing the empire from a careless sultan who had dragged it to financial disaster and overall feebleness. From Midhat's point of view and for General Süleyman Paşa, the deposition of Abdülaziz was meant to pave the way for the constitution that Midhat and other politicians had been envisioning for a while.

In his report, Süleyman unfolds in detail the discussions that preceded the coup. These conversations among the plotters give the impression that the desire for constitutional rule was a major motivation for the coup. Süleyman quotes himself saying to Hüseyin Avni Paşa, the *serasker* and individual considered as the mastermind of the coup, that without a written pledge of Prince Murat Efendi to constitutional rule, there would be no point in the risk that the plotters were taking upon themselves. Hüseyin Avni's response was somewhat restrained, but he expressed support in the constitution.[40] Not surprisingly, it was Midhat—according to Süleyman Paşa—who wrote the draft of Murat's enthronement speech, which was supposed to serve as a road map to the establishment of constitutional rule. It was at this point where the first cracks appeared in the ad hoc alliance between these powerful servants of the state, only a few days after their great accomplishment. Süleyman Paşa reports that the grand vizier, Rüştü Paşa, expressed objections to the draft to the point of sterilization of the constitutional message. Hüseyin Avni conveyed a similar lack of enthusiasm, asking Midhat and Süleyman to "be patient" and postpone their call for constitutionalism.[41] When Süleyman completed his report, the issue of constitutionalism had yet to be decided, and Murat was still the sultan.

Constitutionalism

Viewed in terms of Shklar's broad description of the political trial as an instrument for destroying political enemies, the Yıldız Trial was the last blow on the prospect of constitutional rule through its direct attack on the political standard-bearer of constitutionalism, Midhat Paşa. The success of this attack was evidenced by the fact that nothing less than a revolution, to occur more than thirty years later, could recuperate constitutional politics.

Terms used to describe political action during the modern era, such as *constitutionalism*, exhibit the problem of historicism as brilliantly outlined by Dipesh Chakrabarty.[42] When constitutionalism is discussed in non-European contexts, historians sometimes depict it in terms of its congruity with the stagist "development" of European constitutionalist thought within a historicist descriptive framework. Imagined in such historicist terms, constitutionalist initiatives outside "the West" can be but odd or otherwise relatively faithful replicas of a certain imagined Western "model," but they can never be equal or identical to this model. Similarly, historians of the modern Middle East often conceive constitutionalism as one of the embodiments of "Westernization." Hence, debates and actions related to the question of constitutionalism commonly take the form of the dichotomous convention of Westernizers-conservatives. The fact that non-Western thinkers have shared this historicist imagination does not refute its fictional foundations. For one, similar to the elasticity of the concept of the *rule of law*, the concept of constitutionalism does not possess an intrinsic meaning beyond the very general notion of limiting the power of the sovereign, a point that is demonstrated by the multiplicity of versions. Second, the world's political histories in the nineteenth and twentieth centuries defy depictions of constitutionalism in terms of linear development. These centuries, arguably the bloodiest in human history, teach us that constitutionalist forces are prone to repression, and constitutionalist rhetoric can be abused *ad absurdum*. At the same time, some of the most committed constitutionalist regimes have been involved in serial violations of constitutional norms domestically and in policies overseas. Considering that constitutionalism cannot and need not be subject to formal definitions, one can use it as an umbrella term for many versions of political action aimed at limiting the power of the sovereign, whether kings, sultans, or governments. As such, there is little sense in limiting constitutionalism to a single narrative about the development of any certain ideology. Rather, it can be thought of as a *discourse* that takes different forms in different historical circumstances.

Having in mind the risk of reducing the constitutionalist discourse in the Middle East to a matter of "reaction" to "Western challenge," we should avoid historicist depictions of constitutionalism too. As a political discourse, there was no constitutionalism in the Ottoman Empire prior to the nineteenth century, and there was no body of constitutional law that would equip political actors with conceptual tools for imagining constitutionalist orders.[43] As far as the intellectual sources of Ottoman constitutionalism are concerned, Aylin Koçunyan offers a dialectic analysis that transcends an either-or approach to the influences on Ottoman constitutional ideas, seeing it instead as an eclectic construction that resorted to domestic and European notions while responding to local and foreign circumstances. Hence, beginning from the early 1860s, European constitutional models inspired new self-regulatory texts of non-Muslim communities, such as the "constitutions" of the Armenian, Jewish, and Greek millets. These texts contributed to the harmonization of Ottoman legislation with communal structure, a notion that was apparent in the constitutional discourse.[44]

The group of exiled intellectuals known as the Young Ottomans, established in 1867, appears in the historiography of the late Ottoman Empire as the first Ottoman constitutional movement.[45] We can divide the writings produced by the Young Ottomans into two flanks. The first was criticism on particular policies of the ruling elite of their time, namely, the senior officials of the Tanzimat state. The second was a political theory that combined various constitutional ideas that had circulated in the European market of ideas along with Islamic concepts interpreted as constitutional in nature. Similar to European constitutional discourses, the entire corpus of writings produced by the Young Ottomans was far from uniform. Even the elementary notion of limiting the powers of the Sovereign was anything but self-evident. For instance, the hypothetical constitution envisioned by Mustafa Fazıl Paşa, the founder of the group, did not provide the government with any substantial restraining powers vis-à-vis the sultan.[46]

An additional example of the fluid meaning of constitutionalism is available in the theory of another leading thinker of the Young Ottoman group and probably the most celebrated one, Namık Kemal. Kemal developed a doctrine of representative government, which he called *meşveret*, thereby preserving the quality of this body as a forum for consultation. While favoring the constitution of the French Second Empire as a model for the legislative process, Kemal's position with regard to the question of the Sultan's powers was quite ambiguous.[47] This stand seemed to reflect the fundamental antipathy of the Young Ottomans toward the Tanzimat bureaucrats, whom they regarded as incompetent officials possessing excessive powers.[48] Given this antipathy, there could be no true political alliance between the Young Ottomans and Midhat, and other supporters of constitutionalism among the men of the Tanzimat.

Yet such an alliance was unnecessary to begin with, because the boundaries of the sultan's power were not an outcome of intellectual efforts. Rather, they were a matter of constant negotiation in the political field, based on power balance and changing circumstances. In the seventeenth and eighteenth centuries, for instance, the Ottoman political field was an arena of perpetual negotiation between interest groups that competed and bargained over social status, privileges, and autonomy.[49] The formalization of these negotiated terms through written agreements between the bargaining political groups, led by individuals of ulema, provincial notables (*ayan*), and military officers, was a development of the early nineteenth century, which started with the Hüccet-i Şeriye (1808). The latter was a pact contracted between the janissaries, the ulema, and the new sultan Mustafa IV (r. 1807–8) following the deposition of Selim III (r. 1789–1807), whose attempted reforms were perceived by these two groups as a menace. This text, which guaranteed a general amnesty to the rebels, represented the continuation of the preceding balance of power.[50]

The deposition of Mustafa IV and the enthronement of Mahmut II in 1808 were yet another demonstration of the *ayans*' potency and ability to tame unruly sultans while collaborating with other powerful groups. The coup resulted with another formal pact, much more famous, known as the Deed of Alliance (Sened-i İttifak). This written contract, signed in

Istanbul in September 1808, reiterated the preceding balance between the sultan, the janissaries, the ulema, and the *ayan*s. Recently, Ali Yaycioğlu has offered a subtle analysis of this document, its context, and its historiography. According to Yaycioğlu, it was a political watershed that redefined sultanic authority, turning it into a "supreme contractor."[51] The Deed of Alliance, which some historians view as "the Ottoman magna carta"—quite an overstatement—was the doing of provincial and central elites who "discovered" the potential of formal written agreements in keeping the Sultan under check.[52] The abolition of the janissaries in 1826 rendered the Sened-i İttifak and the Hücet-i Şeriye dead letters, when Mahmut II was laying the foundations for the new age of centralization, which became a defining feature of the Tanzimat state. In the course of the nineteenth century, the *ayan*s and the ulema lost much of their power as autonomous interest groups. Their fate was nothing like the janissaries', though, whom the central government managed to annihilate. Many of the leading ulema and *ayan* families across the empire integrated into the state apparatus, becoming part of officialdom in the provinces, thereby maintaining sources of revenue and status. This process eliminated the earlier drive for ad hoc alliances that meant to advance collective interests of *ayan*s or ulema as such. Nevertheless, negotiation between politicians and sultans over the boundaries of power remained a feasible course of action in the political imagination of the Ottoman elite.

As we saw earlier, Midhat Paşa and Süleyman Paşa eventually supported Prince Murat after casting about his intentions with regard to the constitution. Soon after his accession to the throne, it turned out that Murat was developing a mental condition that rendered him incapable of ruling, let alone advancing the revolutionary project of the constitution. The cabinet almost dragged the thirty-six-year-old sultan to the throne from his chambers after years of confinement by the former sultan, Abdülaziz. When Abdülaziz came to the throne (1861), Murat became the legitimate heir, being the son of the former sultan Abdülmecit, who had died of tuberculosis in the same year at the age of thirty-eight. Abdülaziz, who was Abdülmecit's brother, soon started advancing a scheme for changing the rules of succession in order to allow his son, Yusuf İzzettin Efendi, to become the legitimate heir to the throne.[53] Hence, for many years Prince

Murat had to endure the pressures and anxieties that derived from his precarious position, being both a threat to the sultan's schemes and the opposition's hope at the same time. These accumulating pressures, in addition to excessive drinking, seemed to result in a nervous breakdown.

According to Midhat's account in his pretrial interrogation, the senior ministers and Grand Vizier Rüştü Paşa decided to keep the sultan's "insanity" a secret. The palace staff was instructed to prevent foreigners from entering the imperial premises as a way of containing the crisis. The sultan missed four *selamlık*s, the old custom of public ceremonial procession to the Friday prayer. Midhat told his interrogator that when the sultan got better for a while, his mother convinced him to leave the palace in order to fulfill his duties, but "since his insane behavior was scandalous," he was instructed to avoid the *selamlık* processions altogether."[54] On August 25, British ambassador Henry Elliot reported to London about his meeting with Rüştü Paşa the same day. The grand vizier told the ambassador that he had lost all hope of the sultan's recovery and that the public was eager to hear about the enthronement of Prince Hamid Efendi (Abdülhamit II).[55]

The cabinet deposed Sultan Murat after ninety-three days of rule. Prior to the deposition, Midhat—on behalf of the cabinet—negotiated with the next in line, Prince Abdülhamit, the son of Abdülmecit, over the terms of his accession to the throne. Abdülhamit, who was eager to become a sultan, expressed his commitment to constitutional rule by making three promises: that he would promulgate the constitution promptly, that he would be attentive to the advice of the senior officials, and that he would appoint as palace secretaries some of the leading supporters of constitutionalism, among them Namık Kemal.[56] Midhat and Rüştü were not political allies, although five years later they found themselves on the same side of the divide as suspects in the murder of Sultan Abdülaziz. A few days before the enthronement of the new sultan, the British ambassador reported to his superiors that Rüştü "was determined to prevent the introduction of organic or constitutional reforms notwithstanding all the efforts of Midhat Pasha to bring them forward."[57] At the same time, Rüştü was not an ally of the prince, either. In another secret telegram to London, the British ambassador reported that Prince Abdülhamit "has been at pains to inform me confidentially of his general views and dispositions.

The prince revealed to the ambassador that "he had no confidence in any of the present or past ministers." Elliot, alarmed by this tone, told to the eager prince that "it would be impossible for him all at once to dispense with the services of such men as Mehemed Ruschdi Pasha, and Midhat Pasha both of whom were looked up to by a large section of the people."[58] In this atmosphere of mistrust and conflicting political desires, Abdülhamit assumed the throne on August 31, 1876, commencing one of the longest reigns in the history of the Ottoman dynasty.

The term *constitution* might be a misnomer when referring to the Basic Law (Kanun-ı Esası) promulgated by Abdülhamit, whose autocratic tendencies became evident in his insistence on the clauses of this law that allowed him to exercise absolute rule. The Basic Law was not a constitutional document in the liberal sense because it did not limit the sultan's power in any substantial way. According to this act, the government was responsible to the sultan and not to parliament, the sultan possessed the right to dissolve parliament at will, and he could send to exile individuals whom he considered a threat to the state. Nevertheless, it did include clauses that established the rule of law in the form of the exclusive authority of the courts in interpreting the laws and through the procedures required for modification of the Basic Law.[59]

The cabinet discussions that preceded the final text were a display of the fissure between the constitutional camp, led by Midhat, and the opposing camp, led by Cevdet. This chasm was not only ideological but also a reflection of personal enmity between the two giants of the Tanzimat, who were exchanging insults in these deliberations.[60] In the final analysis, the Basic Law of 1876 signified the failure of the constitutional camp, which was evidenced forcefully in the abolition of the law and the dissolution of parliament in 1878. In a sense, the Yıldız Trial marked the obvious next stage, namely, the physical annihilation of the symbol of constitutionalism.

Obviously, like all political trials, the actual motivations behind the proceedings in Yıldız were never stated as such; the desire to destroy political enemies was realized through standard legal procedure and translation to the language of legalism. Nevertheless, the elephant in the (court)room could not be simply wiped out, and at times it made quite an appearance. In his opening speech at the beginning of the trial, the public prosecutor could not resist linking the crime in question to the coup that had taken place five years earlier, although this move was unacceptable in legal terms:

> Given the illegal manner by which Abdülaziz had been taken down, it is only natural that the perpetrators chose murder. It is known that only four-five ministers decided on the deposition of Abdülaziz. . . . Whatever way you look at it, the officials [who ordered the deposition] had no right to depose [the Sultan]. To decide on such thing is to assume a serious responsibility. On the other hand, the obtained *fetva*, which resulted with the deposition, had a bad influence on the people. Actually, the army would not have intervened in the deposition, but it was deceived [by the perpetrators of the coup, who claimed] that they were going to protect the palace from the upcoming attack of the religious students (*softa*). These things intimidated Sultan Murat and the senior officials of the palace. Therefore, they [Murat and his camp] were convinced that Abdülaziz should be prevented from receiving the throne again, for their own safety. A committee that convened at the palace took the required decision [to kill Abdülaziz].[61]

All this was utterly irrelevant to the question that the court had to decide, namely, the criminal liability of the defendants. However, political impulses and legal performance converged and clashed at the same time when the question of criminal liability came up, especially with regard to the question of command responsibility.

COMPELLING SUPERIORS

The criminal procedure of the Nizamiye courts instructed the judges to hear the defense speeches before leaving the courtroom for discussing the judgment. For the defendants, it was the last opportunity to draw attention to the points that seemed to them the most crucial, the most convincing. The defense speeches in the Yıldız Trial differed in length and pathos. The case of command responsibility, which was raised in some of these speeches, begs for our attention for two interrelated reasons: first, this point was a focal one throughout the trial; second, the fact that it was a focal point in the trial signifies, among other features, its nature as a *modern* political trial. Let me present briefly the concept of command responsibility before I move on to demonstrate how it was used in the trial.

All modern legal systems endorse the principle that renders superiors accountable and punishable for misdeeds of their subordinates so long as the superiors are directly involved by abetting, directing, or aiding the immediate perpetrators.[62] Though this principle, known as command responsibility, has been widely debated in relation to military situations and in the context of international law, it is also applicable in nonmilitary cases addressed by municipal law. The two clauses of the Ottoman penal code that address the question of command responsibility are a simplification of the relevant clauses in the French Code pénal.[63] Nevertheless, we can view both versions as preliminary and rather crude attempts to deal with the question of command responsibility when compared to later legislations.

The boundaries of command responsibility would occupy the minds of criminal-law experts in the course of the twentieth century, especially when dealing with the horrors of World War II. The mass killings of civilians in the twentieth century pushed the question of criminal accountability of commanders and senior position holders to extremity. Whereas active participation of superiors in crimes committed by their underlings was a relatively straightforward case for reaching conviction, the question of omission was a knottier matter from a legal point of view. Postwar tribunals, for instance, convicted Nazi superiors for both their positive acts and their failure to act. The Geneva Conventions and international criminal tribunals have developed the legal mechanisms required for dealing with superiors' complicity when trying individuals accused of crimes against humanity.[64]

In all these cases, the courts had to establish the existence of mens rea, a basic principle in criminal jurisprudence that denotes "criminal intent" or "criminal thinking." In other words, for an act to be considered a crime, a certain level of cognitive intent to perpetrate the crime must be present. While case law systems differ from Continental systems in terminology and doctrine, both legal traditions acknowledge the need to establish mens rea when convicting an individual. The concept of mens rea encompasses a large variety of potential situations, the most complicated of which, and the one that is most pertinent to the problem of superior responsibility, is the intentional avoidance of inquiring into the truth about criminal conduct.[65] Timothy Wu and Yong-Sung Kang summarize this point: "Any adequate account of command responsibility must first confront the question of to what extent the superior should share the moral blameworthiness of the subordinate. This imprecise formulation raises two important doctrinal questions: what the applicable *mens rea* requirement is, and to which acts or omissions should the *mens rea* requirement apply."[66]

Obviously, the sophisticated doctrine on the place of mens rea in establishing superiors' liability was not available to the Yıldız court. In addition, being a political trial, getting to the truth of the matter regarding the senior officials' liability might have not been the objective of the initiators of this trial and the judges who were sitting on the bench. Nevertheless, there can be no doubt that they were eager to convey a scene of due justice, which required the judges to delve into the question of superior responsibility.

In his concluding defense speech, Refik Bey, the adept attorney of the three suspects of murder, argued that Mustafa the Wrestler and Hacı Mehmet admitted that they had slaughtered Sultan Abdülaziz. However, he argued, they did it under orders given by Mahmut Paşa and Nuri Paşa (the two members of the imperial family who bore the title *damat*, denoting a man wedded to the sultan's family). The attorney did not dispute the confessions of Mustafa and Mehmet to the crime, but he claimed that they were driven to action through a compelling order. This argument meant that given their low position on the social ladder, they had no choice but to obey an order given by people of immense political power. In this respect, argued the attorney, his clients were the victims of important men, whose culpability was evident in the bill of indictment. Actually, the attorney went as far as arguing that establishing the culpability of the senders of his clients would necessitate their complete acquittal.[67] This demand was not far-fetched in view of the applicable legal clauses. The bill of indictment defined the senior officials as compelling superiors, using the standard legal term *amir-i mucbir*. However, the attorney of the suspects of murders differed from the public prosecutor in his interpretation of the consequences of this definition. The prosecutor assumed that defining the senior paşas as compelling superiors would bolster the case of their culpability while not diminishing the gravity of the crime committed by the three actual killers. The prosecution demanded that the court would send all of them to the scaffold. For the attorney Refik Bey, however, the definition of the paşas as compelling superiors meant that his clients had no choice, that they acted out of fear and thus they possessed no criminal liability.

Indeed, according to clause 184 in the Ottoman Penal Code, if a person kills another under the order of a compelling superior (*amir-i mucbir*), the punishment had to be inflicted on the superior, not on the subordinate. The clause defines a "compelling superior" as a person who is able to kill his subordinate if the latter does not comply.[68] The question of command responsibility was one of the major legal battlegrounds in the trial. Midhat engaged in this battle as well, though using a different sort of argumentation.

The Question of Midhat's Accountability

In his defense speech, Midhat challenged the prosecution's argument that he was an *amir-i mucbir*, a compelling superior:

> Clause 184 stipulates that if a murder is committed due to the instruction of a superior who has means to apply pressure, it will be he who will be accused of murder. Since the Tanzimat, we do not have among us compelling superiors. Previously there were some. They can still be found in Yemen, Kurdistan, and among Arab Sheikhs. But here, even the Sultan cannot apply this title to himself. However, Nuri Paşa and Mahmut Paşa are defined compelling superiors. After accusing them in this way, the indictment committee infected me as well, as it did to Rüştü Paşa, like an epidemic. Why was the title of compelling superior used in the accusation? Probably to protect the precious assassins; because the nine individuals who will be found guilty will be put to death but the other ones will be discharged.[69]

In the idiom of the Ottoman elite of Istanbul, attributing any certain practice to the Kurds, the Yemenites, and the Arab tribes was equal to an Englishman designating a native's custom as "primitive." Hence, Midhat's point was that in the rule-abiding civilized Ottoman state, the very definition of a compelling superior had no validity, because no person of authority could kill his subordinate for disobedience. Midhat related to the part of the clause that stipulated that in cases where an underling kills a person under a superior's order while not being coerced in accordance to the terms of the clause that define coercion, he will be subject to the punishment of temporary penal servitude (*kürek*). The two clauses that addressed crimes committed on behalf of superiors (184, 185) distinguished between compelling and noncompelling superiors, acquitting the perpetrators in the former case and subjecting them to penal servitude in the latter case. While Refik Bey was trying to have his clients exonerated based on this distinction, Midhat used the same clause to contest the prosecution's claim that he possessed a compelling authority. This tortuous legal maneuver was a continuation of his line of defense throughout the trial. During the hearings, Midhat was arguing that he had not been involved in the sultan's death in any way. As we will see shortly, in this line of defense he meant to address the question of command responsibility.

Midhat's first hearing took place on the first day of the trial, following the interrogations of most of the other defendants. The opening question in Midhat's interrogation seemed neutral, but it implied the intention of the judge: "After the deposition of the late Sultan Aziz and immediately after the accession to the throne of Murat Efendi, was a cabinet of ministers established in the palace under the verbal order of Murat Efendi? And who were the members of this cabinet?"

That the sharp-minded Midhat immediately identified the intention of the judge is clear by his attempt to avoid a direct answer to this ostensibly simple question. The reporter of the *Annales judiciaires* tells his readers that Midhat was beating around the bush, unfolding at length irrelevant details about the coup and his advice to the ministers. Eventually, the paşa said that he had nothing to do with the crime. Judge Forides Efendi then told Midhat that he was required to answer the question and that he would be able to make his defense speech in due time. This request did not persuade Midhat to provide a straightforward answer, and he continued to evade the simple question that he had been asked. This time, the judge formulated his warning in a more assertive fashion, telling Midhat that it was the president of the court who directed the discussion, not the defendant. Midhat realized that there was no way to avoid the question about the composition of the ministerial cabinet, a question meant to open a discussion about Midhat's own involvement in the death of Abdülaziz. The subsequent exchange went as follows:[70]

JUDGE: Who were the members of the cabinet?

MIDHAT PAŞA: Me, Mehmet Rüştü Paşa, Hüseyin Avni Paşa, Mahmut Cellalettin Paşa, and Hayrullah Efendi.

JUDGE: What were the matters that belonged to the responsibility of this cabinet? Was it the cabinet's decision to transfer the late sultan to the Feriye Palace?

MIDHAT PAŞA: The cabinet dealt with all sorts of internal and external matters, with all that a regular cabinet deals with. The transfer [of Abdülaziz to Feriye] took place due to the request of the sultan [Murat].

JUDGE: Who was in charge of the sultan's safety, and who was the one who appointed the individual in charge of the sultan's safety?

MIDHAT PAŞA: There was no one person but several people. It was our interest to guard him well.

Through this exchange, the judge was able to establish the fact that Midhat had at least *some* command responsibility in his capacity as a member of the cabinet. Midhat, on the other hand, attempted to push the responsibility to the highest authority, namely the recently enthroned sultan, Murat. The logical next step for the judge was to have Midhat confront testimonies about his direct involvement in appointing the three individuals who later turned out to be the supposed killers, as servants of the deposed sultan, after his transfer from Topkapı Palace to Feriye Palace:

JUDGE: Nuri Paşa stated that it was after the decision of this cabinet that several individuals . . . attached to the house of Murat Efendi, namely, Mustafa the Wrestler, Mustafa the Algerian, and Hacı Mehmed, who are present here, were appointed to the service of the late sultan. Nuri Paşa also declares that you were a member of the cabinet that nominated them to this post. What do you answer to that?

MIDHAT PAŞA: We knew about the appointment [of the three individuals], and we were told that they were extremely devoted to the sultan so we had no reason to raise an objection.

JUDGE: Was it suitable to appoint men of this sort to the sensitive position of working for a sultan-caliph?

MIDHAT PAŞA: I did not know these men; I was merely aware of their nomination.

JUDGE: You say that you did not know these men, but numerous evidence proves otherwise, including the fact that immediately after the sultan's death, Hüseyin Paşa, who was a member of your cabinet, was seen talking to Mustafa the Wrestler. This indicates that your cabinet was the one that decided the death of the sultan.

MIDHAT PAŞA: Do you call this evidence?

At this point, the judge was aiming for demonstration of Midhat's mens rea as well as his command responsibility with regard to the murder:

JUDGE: In your interrogation, you said that you considered yourself lost if Sultan Aziz would return to the throne. Hence, it was necessary for you to place near the sultan a man whom you knew and trusted. This consideration, and your fear that the sultan would return to his throne, explains the murder.

MIDHAT PAŞA: This is a fine thought, but it does not constitute evidence that the murder was accomplished.

JUDGE: You drove away all the old servants of the sultan, leaving him only with [chamberlain] Fahri Bey, according to his own wish, you say. However, Nuri Paşa is saying in his statement that Fahri Bey was repositioned to the service of the sultan under the cabinet's decision.

The trust that the sultan had in him was an advantage for you, because the fact that he was near the sultan would make the project of the cabinet [that is, killing Abdülaziz] easier to execute. What happened, in reality, justifies this idea.

MIDHAT PAŞA: These are only deductions. Fahri Bey stayed near the sultan because the sultan wanted that. Fahri Bey told you that himself.

The judge moved on to discuss the disturbing matter of the sword, which Sultan Abdülaziz could use to save his life:

JUDGE: After his deposition, the sultan kept near him a sword in order to defend himself. You said that this sword was taken away from him under the decision of the cabinet. Doesn't this decision and its execution consist in itself of evidence proving that the cabinet had already decided to murder the sultan?

MIDHAT PAŞA: Immediately after the transfer of the sultan to Topkapı Palace, we gave the order to remove any kind of weapon from his possession. It was a precaution deriving from our concern that he might take his own life.

Midhat had a point when repeatedly dismissing the judge's explanation as deductions rather than real evidence. On the other hand, from a legal point of view, mens rea, being a cognitive situation rather than a positive action, is necessarily difficult to prove and therefore calls for a deductive process by the court. The court had to provide answers to the following questions: First, did Midhat and the other senior officials have command responsibility? Second, did Midhat and the other officials possess mens rea? Third, could the court categorize them as compelling superiors in accordance with the formulation of clause 184? Like any other Nizamiye trial, the judges came to the bench after having read the pretrial materials. Revealing conflicts between pretrial depositions and written testimonies was a major objective of the hearing in Nizamiye criminal trials, in addition to asking for clarifications on issues recorded during the pretrial stage. The question of how Midhat heard about the sultan's death was a critical one. Already in his initial interrogation, immediately after his arrest, Midhat emphasized that the news about the sultan's death in his chambers came to him as an utter surprise. Through this version, he meant to deliver the message that he had not been involved in the murder in any way, to the extent that it was a murder. He probably anticipated that the court would reopen this question in the hearing:

JUDGE: From whom and how did you learn about the sultan's death?

MIDHAT PAŞA: On Sunday, a little late, I went to the Bab-ı Ali to attend the council that convened there. I arrived there, and I did not find anybody. I was told that only Said Efendi, the undersecretary, was in his office. I went into his office, and I heard the news. It saddened me, and I started to think that people might suspect me.

JUDGE: The undersecretary Said Efendi states that you are not telling the truth.

MIDHAT PAŞA: It is of no importance; probably he did not have a choice; he had to say this.

In his response, then, Midhat reiterated the version that he had provided in his pretrial interrogation. However, he also added a stern allegation when implying that someone had forced the undersecretary to commit perjury, thereby disputing the court's integrity. The judge could accuse Midhat of contempt of court, but he chose to move on with the interrogation, a decision that made sense given that the conversation was progressing satisfactorily, from the judge's point of view. At this point, Judge Forides Efendi was heading to a wrap-up of the issue of Midhat's command responsibility by way of omission:

JUDGE: When you heard the news, did you go to the site [of the murder]? Whom did you find there, and whom did you inquire about the events? Did you initiate an investigation?

MIDHAT PAŞA: I left the Bab-ı Ali, and I went through Dolmabahçe Palace to the guard station of Ortaköy. I found there all the ministers, a considerable number of ulema, other dignitaries, and nineteen physicians. Everybody repeated, including Fahri Bey, that the sultan had committed suicide. I believed it as everybody else did.

The physicians conducted an autopsy and signed a report confirming the suicide.

JUDGE: You believed what Fahri Bey told you, and you did not order to open an investigation? Given your position, it was your duty to search for the truth. You tried to keep this event quiet, and this proves your complicity.

MIDHAT PAŞA: If this proves my complicity, then you will find all the other ministers guilty of complicity as well, but I do not see them by my side, taking blame for not having ordered an investigation.

JUDGE: Wasn't the cabinet obliged to examine the body of the late sultan?

MIDHAT PAŞA: The physicians did this better than us.

JUDGE: Did you ask the physicians if they had examined all the parts of the corpse? Moreover, was it not necessary that the cabinet would be with them while they examined the body? You did not do that. You only ran a superficial examination, which proves again that the murder was assigned by the cabinet, which you were a member of.

MIDHAT PAŞA: The report that the physicians signed answers the question.

JUDGE: The *fetva* that addressed the sultan's death was not written in accordance with the law since it was merely based on Fahri Bey's statements. In addition, the medical report opens the doors to many questions. Why is that?

MIDHAT PAŞA: I do not know. You will have to ask the ulema officials and the physicians.

Irrespective of the irregularities in this trial, and while not ruling out the possibility that Mustafa the Wrestler and his friends confessed for crimes they had not committed (a probability that we can neither prove nor disprove), there might have been something off beam in the functioning of the officials who had to respond to the shocking news about the sultan's death. The senior official Mahmut Cellalettin Paşa, who wrote the well-known chronicle of the period, *Mirat-ı Hakikat* (*Mirror of the Truth*), happened to be among those officials and ministers who were gathering at Feriye, right after the discovery of the sultan's body. In his account, Mahmut Cellalettin Paşa criticizes the lame conduct of the ministers, who rushed to conclude that their sultan had committed suicide. They based this conclusion, according to the author, on a hasty on-sight interrogation of Fahri Bey, the sultan's chamberlain. In his book, Mahmut Cellalettin Paşa complained that the ministers failed to interrogate the family members of the deceased sultan, who were living with him in the palace. The general air reported by the author was one of swiftness, when the ministers in charge were determined to conclude the religious ceremony and inter the sultan in the tomb of his father, Mahmut II, in no time, a message that was somehow delivered to the doctors who were summoned to examine the body. They were quick to conduct the examination and sign their report, which determined that it was a case of suicide.[71]

Mahmut Cellalettin Paşa's judgmental tone should be understood in the context of his antagonism toward Midhat. The chronicle came out in 1908, but Mahmut Cellalettin Paşa, who died in 1899, wrote it when Abdülhamit, his benefactor, was still on the throne, many years after the trial. Bearing in mind Mahmut Cellalettin's probable bias against Midhat and his inclination to please Abdülhamit, however, the same impression of urgency emerges from the testimony of Dr. Markel, one of the physicians who had examined the body and was heard at the trial. The Jewish doctor was sworn in on the Torah and provided his own account:

JUDGE: You are one of the doctors who signed the examination report, aren't you?

DR. MARKEL: Yes, sir.

JUDGE: What happened?

DR. MARKEL: It was twenty-three of May, 1875 [*sic*]. I was among the doctors summoned to the guard station in Feriye. I was among those doctors who were first to arrive there. Two hours later the other doctors came. *Damat* Mahmut Paşa invited us to examine the body.

JUDGE: Where was the corpse?

DR. MARKEL: It was placed on an ottoman in one of the rooms at the guard station.

JUDGE: What was the result of the autopsy?

DR. MARKEL: An autopsy was not carried out. We only examined the deceased's face, arms, and legs; we did not see anything else. It was expedited. It was said that no time was left until sunset and the body had to be transferred to the burial place. After we inspected the body with the other doctors, we investigated the room where the murder occurred.[72] Among the other things that we saw in the room where the examination took place was a junior officer, who addressed one of the paşas, saying, "For goodness sake, sir, I did not do it." The paşa answered him, "You silly man! Is there anyone who is blaming you for killing Sultan Abdülaziz?"

At this point, the defendant Ali Bey cried out, "I want to talk about it. He is wrong." The judge silenced him and ordered the physician to carry on:

DR. MARKEL: There was a lady present at the room with us. She described to us when and how Sultan Abdülaziz let himself into his room with a mirror and scissors in his hands, and how he put an end to his life.

JUDGE: Who was this lady?

DR. MARKEL: I would not know. After we finished our business at the crime scene, we returned to the guard station. We signed the report, which was written as soon as the physician of the British hospital Dr. Dixon and the physician of the French embassy Monsieur Marwan examined the body there once again. All these things were attended to in briskness. As I have just said, the government wanted to have the body buried before sunset.[73]

The Question of Rüştü Paşa's Accountability

Rüştü Paşa, who was the grand vizier in office when the momentous events of 1876 took place, was arrested in early May, interrogated in Izmir, released, and sent back to his mansion in Manisa owing to a medical condition. His intense interrogation lasted three days. The two police interrogators produced a verbatim protocol (*istintakname*) in line with the Nizamiye requirements. The protocol consists of 180 questions and answers. This record was meant to assist the prosecution in preparing the bill of indictment and the judges when interrogating the witnesses and plaintiffs and crafting their judgment. The protocol is yet another powerful demonstration of the fact that the political trial in question was embedded in the rule-of-law discourse. The times when grand viziers and senior officials could be executed out in the open and without a trial were over. The interrogators went out of their way to establish the liability of Rüştü Paşa, using sophisticated interrogation tactics. The former grand vizier, in turn, tried hard to avoid incrimination through fuzzy answers, alternative narratives, and "lack of recollection or knowledge" responses. Both sides, the interrogators and the interrogated, were aware of the fact that everything that was said was put on record for use in later stages of the trial, either by the prosecution or by the judges. As was the case with any other Nizamiye interrogation, both the interrogators and the interrogated signed their names at the end of each page, confirming the record's authenticity.

In a different time and a different place, Rüştü Paşa would probably "plead the fifth," but such a legal tool was not at his disposal. The best he could do to avoid self-incrimination was to argue consistently for lack of knowledge and involvement. The interrogators asked him scores of questions about the treatment of Abdülaziz following his deposition, the appointment of the three suspects of the sultan's murder, and various events that took place at the time. To many of these questions, Rüştü Paşa answered that he either did not know or could not remember. His general line of argument was lack of involvement because all the decisions that concerned the confinement and treatment of Abdülaziz were made by the palace's inner circle (*mabeyn*) and not by the government or the cabinet. Specifically, so he claimed, Sultan Murat and his mother, the valide, Şevkefza Sultan, had made these decisions. For instance, when asked about the reasons for the transfer of the sultan from Topkapı to Feriye, the paşa replied, "I have no information about it."[74] Similar was his answer to a simple question about the general details of Abdülaziz's family whereabouts following his death.[75]

Neither Uzunçarşılı nor other historians who mentioned the trial took notice of the fact that Rüştü Paşa was not telling the truth in his interrogation, a fact that is unmistakable through his claim of lack of knowledge. It is true that theoretically the former grand vizier could make the claim of lack of involvement to some extent, given the separation between the government, namely, the Bab-ı Ali, and the inner circle of the palace, the *mabeyn*. However, the emergence of the *mabeyn* as the exclusive center of political power was a feature of later Hamidian absolutism, and, at any rate, political networks and intrigues rendered the boundaries between both institutions rather obscure.[76] The dethronements of Abdülhamit's predecessors Murat and Abdülaziz were no doubt the working of senior officials who had possessed much power vis-à-vis the palace, among them Rüştü Paşa. A good number of Rüştü Paşa's answers made no sense in view of his seniority in officialdom. For instance, when asked whose idea it was to appoint Mahmut Paşa to a military position after the appointment of Sultan Murat, Rüştü Paşa, who was the grand vizier at the time, answered that he was not aware of this appointment.[77]

Using cunning interrogation tactics such as zigzagging between trivial and substantive questions, repetitions, and measured uncovering of information, the interrogators pushed the former grand vizier into a corner, causing the gradual collapse of his "lack of knowledge" strategy. On the second day of the interrogation, Rüştü Paşa was asked about the composition of the cabinet that was established in the palace for the purpose of arranging the coup and the enthronement of Murat. Rüştü answered, "I remember such a committee," as if it was a minor issue. He also said that the cabinet was established after the coup and that he was not involved, mentioning Nuri Paşa as one of the members of this cabinet. The interrogators replied that according to a statement of the palace official Seyyit Bey, the cabinet consisted of himself, Midhat Paşa, Hüseyin Avni Paşa, the previous *şeyhülislam* Hayrullah Efendi, and Damat Mahmut Paşa. Obviously, there was no way that Rüştü Paşa was ignorant about the existence of this cohort, and his reply could be nothing but an outright lie, when telling his interrogators, "If such a cabinet was established, I should have known about it, but it does not come to my mind." The interrogators continued, reminding the elderly paşa that regardless of the palace's involvement, every decision had to go through the cabinet, to be then sanctioned by an imperial decree. The former grand vizier simply replied, "I do not know." But the interrogators did not let it go, asking Rüştü Paşa who was responsible for executing the order to transfer Abdülaziz to Feriye, to which he replied that these matters were the business of the palace, and "we did not interfere." It was not quite a credible answer, taking into consideration the sensitivity of the matter at the time.

Using the tactic of gradually confronting the interrogated person with incriminating information, at this point the interrogators told Rüştü Paşa that Damat Mahmut Paşa was in charge of transferring Abdülaziz to Feriye. Yet again, the transfer of the deposed sultan was not a simple technical matter, and Mahmut Paşa was not a marginal figure in the political scene. Nevertheless, Rüştü Paşa claimed, "I do not know whether Mahmut Paşa was in charge there, or who [else] was in charge." Rüştü Paşa provided the same answer when the interrogators used the tactic of having the interrogated confront statements provided by former collaborators and fellow suspects. When told that statements from other officials, including Midhat, had confirmed the appointment of Mahmut Paşa, Rüştü replied, "I have no information."[78]

As the interrogation progressed, the interrogators were pulling additional cards, gradually unfolding their theory about the events in question, and using the tactic of presenting a general question followed by a more detailed narrative about any given situation, asking for Rüştü Paşa's reply. After two days of intensive interrogation, and after letting the record show that there was a serious problem with Rüştü Paşa's credibility, the interrogators presented to Rüştü Paşa their theory about the actual murder, also exposing one of their strongest cards, namely, the confessions of the individuals who supposedly killed Abdülaziz:

> Mustafa the Wrestler, who had been sent to serve the abovementioned Sultan, said: "I went with my companions to Feriye on Saturday. We stayed there for the evening. In the morning of the following Sunday we entered the room of the deceased in Feriye at around 1:30 [alaturka time]. Fahri Bey [the chamberlain of Abdülaziz] attacked [the sultan]; he held the arms of the abovementioned [sultan] tightly from behind. My friends Mustafa the Algerian and Hacı Mehmet held his knees. Using a white-handle pocketknife that Fahri Bey had given to me, I cut the veins of his left hand first, and then those of his right hand." What do you say about this?

To this crystal-clear description of the murder by its perpetrator, Rüştü Paşa replied, "I have not heard or known about this until this very minute."[79] The interrogators tried to manipulate Rüştü Paşa by offering him a sort of lifeline, deferring the guilt to his alleged collaborators. They told him that there were rumors that Midhat Paşa and Hüseyin Avni Paşa had intimidated him because they were eager to depose Abdülaziz. Rüştü Paşa, who must have been drained physically and mentally at this point, provided an obscure answer, arguing that he could not say anything about intimidation by Midhat because he forgot the details, but he did remember that Hüseyin Avni Paşa had threatened him.[80] Not before presenting to Rüştü Paşa more than a hundred questions, the interrogators conveyed their complete theory about his accountability, telling him that Murat, his mother, and Rüştü Paşa gave direct orders to kill Sultan Abdülaziz. Rüştü repeated his answer, which surely did not surprise the interrogators: "As I have stated throughout [this interrogation], I have no information about this charge."[81]

As the interrogation was concluding, the interrogators told Rüştü Paşa that since the beginning of the interrogation, most of the time he said that he did not remember the major events in question, but he went into details on marginal matters that came up in the conversation. It was the first occasion that the interrogators commented on Rüştü Paşa's conduct in the interrogation. He replied, "Five years have passed since then. I have been lying in bed for the last four years, afflicted by many illnesses. Since my memory is poor, I am unable to remember everything."[82] This answer, earnest as it was with regard to his medical condition, could not explain the paşa's selective memory, which was quite impressive when discussing matters that had little bearing on the investigation. The interrogators brought the conversation to a close by repeating their claim that Rüştü Paşa had been uncooperative and dishonest, also warning him that he would not have another chance to clear his name. Rüştü Paşa responded harshly: "This is a complete lie and an overt lie. Until now, I have answered to all the questions to the degree that my miserable memory could allow. I say that I don't know about matters that I had no information or awareness of, and things that I could not remember."[83]

From the prosecution's point of view, the interrogation of Rüştü Paşa was an achievement. The skillful work of the interrogators, who did not employ illegal means such as torture, produced the outcome that worked for the prosecution. Namely, Rüştü Paşa's version appeared on the record as unreliable, and he was not able to refute the suspicions against him, in terms of both command responsibility and direct involvement in the alleged murder of the sultan.

JUDGMENT

At the end of the trial's second day, after a half hour of deliberations among the judges, as required by the Nizamiye procedure, the head clerk pronounced the decisions. The court found Mustafa the Wrestler, Hacı Mehmet, Mustafa the Algerian, and Fahri Bey guilty of premeditated murder. It found Midhat Paşa, Mahmut Paşa, Nuri Paşa, Ali Bey, and Necip Bey guilty of complicity to the crime, and it declared the defendants Seyyit Bey and İzzet Bey guilty of assisting in the crime. The president announced that the court would pronounce sentences the following day. The court divided the last day of the trial into two separate sessions. It reserved the last one for Midhat and dedicated the preceding session to all the other defendants. In the first session, Mahmut Paşa was wondering why Midhat was not present. The president, Sururi Efendi, dismissed this critical comment by telling Mahmut, "It has nothing to do with you; the court is aware of its mission."[84] Nowhere during the trial had the judges explained the odd decision to separate Midhat from the other defendants.

As required by the Code of Criminal Procedure, each of the attorneys unfolded reasons for mitigating the penalties that were about to be declared. Most of them were general requests for mercy. The question of command responsibility came up again when Mahmut Paşa's attorney, Kostaki Sardinski Efendi, asked the court to take into consideration that his client did not act on his own initiative but rather obeyed his superiors. Mahmut Paşa interrupted his advocate's words by saying that clause 184 was the most suitable one for his case. After a half hour of deliberations outside the hall, the judges came back to the bench to declare the penalties. All the convicts, except for Seyyit Bey and Ali Bey, who were condemned to ten years of penal servitude, were sentenced to death. The judges uttered no word about the nature of complicity; was it a matter of command responsibility?

Midhat's fate was decided in the subsequent session. At this point, Midhat started arguing about his culpability in light of the pertinent clauses in the Penal Code (see chapter 1). His attorney, Şehri Efendi, who knew that there was no point in repeating substantive arguments once the court convicted the defendant, explained to the judge that Midhat's words were meant to have the court consider a more lenient penalty. The scene of the earlier session repeated itself. The judges left for deliberations, returning to the bench after thirty minutes. The president told Midhat: "As I explained earlier, you were found guilty of complicity and therefore the penalty will conform articles 45 and 170 of the penal code. Thus, you are condemned to the death penalty by the majority of voices; you have eight days to decide if you appeal to the Cassation Court or not." Midhat thanked the president, and the trial was over.[85]

The formal court decision (*ilam*), which has never been cited in the newspapers that published the trial's transcript, reveals an odd treatment of the question of command responsibility. In fact, it mentions this matter only when citing Midhat's response.[86] Why did the judges almost ignore the point of command responsibility in their written verdict although it had come up during the hearings and the pretrial interrogations? Here, the collision between legalism and politics became most apparent. When crafting their judgment, the judges faced a serious legal problem. Legally, defining the senior officials as compelling superiors (*amir-i mucbir*) would mean the innocence of the three perpetrators of the killing. On the other hand, defining the senior officials as noncompelling superiors would require a noncapital punishment. The latter judicial outcome was a harsh one, but it did not conform with the objective of the political trial to annihilate political enemies. The judges dealt with this problem by disregarding the question of command responsibility altogether.

This legal problem remained up in the air after the entire proceeding closed at the Court of Cassation, which justified the verdicts and the sentences. However, in the emergent Ottoman legalistic culture, this crude distortion of the letter of the law by the courts, which seemed eager to please Abdülhamit II, could not be simply overlooked. Settling this matter seemed to be the major motivation for the sultan when convening a special ulema cabinet to discuss the court decision, a measure that was extraordinary, not recognized by the codified procedure. Abdülhamit asked the cabinet to determine whether the former sultan Murat should be regarded as a compelling superior. There can be no doubt that Cevdet Paşa, the minister of justice, was the one who was bothered the most by this problem and the one who probably wrote the letter. A brilliant jurist and the leading figure behind the legal reform of his period, he knew that this distortion was counterproductive in terms of the trial's goals. The letter sent to the cabinet, which was formulated when having clause 184 in mind, displayed knowledge of the legalistic discourse. Hence, it asked the cabinet to determine whether disobedience of the killers would have exposed them to the risk of death by those who gave them the orders.[87] As mentioned in the previous chapter, the cabinet found the court decisions justified, but it did not really engage with the legal problem of compelling superiors, thereby not providing the goods that Cevdet and Abdülhamit were hoping for. So they brought the problem of compelling superiors to the discretion of a special cabinet. This time, the author formulated the questions addressed to the ministers in a more systematic way. Yet, once again, the cabinet could not solve a problem that in principle was the business of professional lawyers. This issue was doomed to remain a legal embarrassment.

This chapter opened with the letters—real or fake—that readers of *Tanin* sent to the editor, where they claimed that the trial's protocol proved the culpability of Midhat and his associates, a disturbing probability from the editor's perspective. Publication of the trial transcript aimed at reminding the wickedness of the *ancien régime* and educating the readers about the benefits of constitutional rule in a postrevolutionary period, when the political field was a stormy arena of many agendas. These letters, whose arguments are discernible through the forceful response of Selanikli Tevfik, reflected something that professional historians may have missed. The trial was confusing. It was no doubt a travesty of justice, as modern historians have claimed, but it was also a display of legalistic culture at the very same time. What made the trial a legal farce was not the fact that the court violated basic principles of justice; after all, practitioners of modern law witness the gap between ideals of justice and the judicial work on a daily basis in the form of structural biases, foot-dragging owing to case burden, and so on. What made the Yıldız Trial a sham was the fact that its enactment of legalism was collapsing into itself. Such an uncomfortable outcome has always been the risk facing modern political trials that have resorted to legalistic discourses.[88]

3

Performing a Show Trial

LIVING IN THE CAPITAL CITY of two bygone empires and the nerve center of the six-hundred-year Ottoman civilization meant that a new drama was always right around the corner. Generations of Istanbulis had to witness, evade, participate in, and sometimes be the victims of bloody coups, violent upheavals, and political unrest. Gruesome sights of beheaded viziers and hanged state officials had to be tolerated by city dwellers over the centuries, along with the constant fear of the next wave of violence to be led by furious janissaries who once again discovered that they had been paid with debased coins or were engaged with interfaction struggles in the streets of the city. The city, with its multitude of palaces and monumental buildings, provided its inhabitants with a continuous free show. From graphic spectacles of violent penalties inflicted on outlaws to spectacular processions of palace folks, alongside the frequent display of fireworks and canon fire celebrating weddings and circumcision fests of the imperial family, show was part and parcel of life in Istanbul.[1]

The administration of justice, however, had always been the business of professional judiciary, or officials of the highest ranks in administrative cases. Trials were conducted in courts of law, whether Sharia courts or—since the 1860s—Nizamiye courts as well. Trials of senior officials took place in the imperial divan and were not open to the public. The Sharia and Nizamiye courts were public forums, but the legalistic performance brought about by the Nizamiye legal culture, with its specialized legal jargon and tedious procedural discussions, rendered trials all but fascinating to laymen. Yet the Yıldız Trial was different, a sight the city had never witnessed before. The quality of the Yıldız Trial as a show was evident before it even started. Tickets to the trial were distributed to those individuals who were fortunate to obtain a seat among the audience. The Ottoman newspapers generated an atmosphere of excited anticipation when describing the trial as an unprecedented historic event. The standard ticket said, "This ticket provides entrance permitting [its holder] to view the trial at the Malta guard station [in the Yıldız Palace]."[2] The government gave out tickets to senior officials and military officers as well as members of the diplomatic corps. Everybody else (namely, anyone who was literate) could observe the trial through its coverage by the newspaper correspondents, who had been invited as well. This chapter reconstructs the performative aspects of the Yıldız show trial, which were ubiquitous not only in the site of the trial, in the hearings, and in the texts that it produced, but also in the public discourse that it provoked in the Ottoman realm and beyond it.

I wish to clarify how I use "performance" as an analytical tool. Performance possesses two meanings that are different and some would say contradictory yet interrelated to a certain extent: theatrical and linguistic.[3] Henning Grunwald provides a clear definition of the theatrical meaning of performance: "Performance involves the bodily co-presence of a spectator and a performer," whereas "'performativity' refers to the inherent and ongoing potential of specific cultural, discursive, or political configurations to generate social, aesthetic or transcendental realities." Everything that happens in modern courts is imbued with rituals and symbols meant to produce a sense of authority, objectivity, professionalism, and other attributes that form legal culture. In this sense, every trial is a performance.[4]

The court of law is one of the most performative institutions in modern and premodern societies, propped up by performative actions of both theatrical and linguistic quality. The conflation of these two meanings of performativity is easily evident by the codified rituals of the court personnel, by the interaction between spectators and performers (judges, attorneys, and even clerks) and by the fact that trials are infused with speech acts that create situations ("I sentence/acquit you"; "I object").[5] Though theatricality is somewhat more subtle in the inquisitorial legal system when compared to the adversarial one, where "show" is part of the rhetorical maneuvers of attorneys in their attempt to persuade juries and judges, it exists in both systems, and it is taken to its extreme in show trials.[6] In fact, hyperbolic emphasis on the performative aspect of the proceedings is a distinctive feature of show trials, differentiating them from "normal" trials. Performativity, in this regard, is apparent not only in the trial itself but also in the way it is represented, discussed, disputed, and remembered in the immediate and longer run.

CIRCULATING TRIALS

Members of political elites, whether sultans, grand viziers, dictators, or revolutionary juntas, who desire to eliminate their political enemies are always interested in more than annihilating an individual opponent; they are interested in eliminating the constituency that individual opponents represent, which form their power basis. Deterrence may play a part in regular criminal trials, but it is taken into consideration at the phase of sentencing and not in the preceding and perhaps more significant phase of establishing guilt. In political trials, the prosecutors' effort is restricted not to establishing guilt but to delegitimization of the defendant's very existence and with it the delegitimization of his constituency and the ideas that he represents. For this ambition to succeed, the trial must draw the public's attention. The unique meaning of show trials is immediately evident through the scope of public interest in these trials.

According to Leslie Peirce, the practice of preserving court records in Sharia courts throughout the Ottoman domains was an innovation of the sixteenth century, an outcome of Ottoman imperialization and administrative consolidation.[7] The registration type of the Sharia court record (*sijill*) was the summary of a completed case. According to Agmon, the purpose of the registration was twofold: providing the court with a reference to the decision and equipping the litigants with a formal document that they could use in future situations in or out of court.[8] Clearly, codes were produced for the use of those individuals who had direct interest in the proceedings, whether judges, clerks, officials, and litigants. Printing, however, rendered the judicial sphere a subject for the public gaze in unprecedented scale.

Printing technology first appeared in the Ottoman Empire in the late fifteenth and early sixteenth centuries through Jewish refugees from the

Iberian Peninsula, who had made the Ottoman realm their new home following the invitation of Bayezit II (r. 1481–1512). Until the early eighteenth century, however, printing was exclusively the business of Jewish and Christian subjects of the empire. The first titles in Ottoman Turkish came out in Istanbul by the printing press of the Hungarian convert to Islam, İbrahim Müteferrika, beginning from 1727. The crop of titles produced by İbrahim Müteferrika was quite modest, although the overall achievement of his venture had been far from the failure that modern historians have attributed to him.[9] Nile Green identifies 1820 as a defining moment when Muslim printing connected to "a global expansion of industrialized printing in Europe, America and Australasia" through printing activity in Iran, the Mediterranean, and the Malay Peninsula.[10] In the Ottoman domains, printed matter became a widely consumed product during the 1870s, together with the growth in the circle of the literates, who read novels and plays in Ottoman Turkish.[11]

In the Hamidian era, printing became a full-fledged "industry," amounting to thousands of books and hundreds of newspapers, supervised and censored by the government at all times. The publication of newspapers seemed to be ahead of the publication of books in quantitative terms, probably because the central government was quick to identify the potential of the press in shaping public opinion. Hence, following the example set by the governor of Egypt Mehmet Ali, who initiated the first official newspaper in Cairo, the Ottoman government launched its own official newspaper, *Takvim-i Vekayi* (*Calendar of Events*), in 1831. Nine years later, the first privately owned newspaper in Ottoman Turkish, established by an Englishman, William Churchill, launched *Ceride-i Havadis* (*Journal of News*). The following decades of the Tanzimat period witnessed an almost exponential growth in the number of titles and copies, both in the imperial center and in the provinces. Following the new sorts of religious and cultural freedoms granted by the state, the world of periodicals reflected the multiethnic nature of the Ottoman realm and the "cosmopolitanism" of its big urban centers, evident in the multitude of languages in which newspapers were published all across the empire.[12] Strict censorship was one of the Hamidian era's key features, evident in the disappearance of explicit criticism and oppositional discourse in the press. However, newspapers and periodicals continued in significant numbers. Some newspapers presented a long life span, even decades, while others were short-lived ventures.[13]

Interest in what was going on in the courts of law was shared by periodicals aimed for the wider public and a small number of professionalized journals addressed to legal practitioners. The legal journals belonged to a genre of Ottoman periodicals consumed by professional or semiprofessional communities, thereby signifying the onset of the professionalization age.[14] In the late nineteenth century, there were three law journals and reporters: the bilingual Turkish-Arabic *al-Hukuk*, a monthly journal published in Istanbul and owned by İlyas Matar, the famous Syrian intellectual and historian, a close associate of Cevdet Paşa, and a member of the court of first instance (*bidayet*) in Istanbul;[15] the French-language and short-lived *Annales judiciaires*, which came out in Istanbul beginning from 1880 and was owned by Georges Macridès; and the official *Ceride-i Mehakim* (*Journal of the Courts*), which was the most significant and lasting law journal.

The weekly and later biweekly *Ceride-i Mehakim* started to appear in 1873, addressing the large community of judges, prosecutors, lawyers, and officials who worked in the Nizamiye court system. It was a rich-in-content publication, a combination of official gazette used as an orderly communication channel between the Ministry of Justice and the community of legal professionals, also serving as a law reporter.[16] As such, the journal was a performance of the legalistic culture of the Nizamiye courts. Most of the cases derived from discussions held at the Court of Cassation. Presented in a standard, formulaic style, the cases transmitted the message of uniformity of practice and strict adherence to procedure. Most of the court decisions quashed by the Court of Cassation, which addressed cases from all over the empire, were sent back to the lower courts for correction, usually for reasons of procedural breaches. Each decision that was recorded in the *Ceride* was backed by citations of the related codified clauses. The Ministry of Justice used the journal as a professional tool for indoctrinating its legalistic vision. Obviously, there was a considerable gap between the ideal neatness exhibited in the *Ceride*'s form of presentation and the daily realities in the courts. Yet the journal, through its display of rationality, was meant to have the members of the Nizamiye community imagine the judicial work as a procedure-based legalistic ideal. As such, it signified a major change in the way the legal professionals imagined the law. In the past, a certain degree of unity of practice was made possible through the constant rotation of judges (and other public officials) across the empire, a practice meant to prevent them from developing local interests and possibly to reduce the risk of corruption.[17] But the *Ceride* took the overall tendency for coherence a giant step further, being an effective, unprecedented instrument in imposing a single set of standard practices and creating a sense of an imagined community of legal experts. Generations of legal professionals read the same trials published twice a week.

The mass circulation of specific trials, allowed by print technology, was not limited to the professional law journals. Newspapers in the imperial capital and the provinces reported on judicial cases as well. However, in contrast to the highly technical jargon of the law reporters and their emphasis on the civil and commercial cases (probably because they were more complicated procedurally than criminal cases), the popular press was interested in the drama of violence, reported in simple language and usually uninterested in the strictly judicial aspects.[18]

The Yıldız Trial was different. Unlike ordinary trials, its nature as a show trial was evident at the outset through the exceptional location of the trial, the organization of space inside the tent that was installed especially for the hearings, the distribution of tickets, and even the free buffet that the palace kitchens prepared for the visitors. As any other show trial, the judges, the attorneys, the defendants, the audience, and the readers of the newspaper reports imagined it as a historic event. As noted before, the meanings of performances are the outcome of the interactions between the performers and their spectators while these two respective roles are never cast iron. In every trial, participants exchange the roles of performers and spectators: Attorneys perform in their turn and become spectators when their colleagues perform, when the witnesses testify, and when the judges explain the verdicts. The judges play the part of spectators when the participants perform in front of them with the objective of persuasion. Similar exchange of performer-spectator roles can be attributed to the defendants. Even the audience might not always act as a "passive" spectator, when listeners interrupt or express emotions through gestures and sounds. In modern show trials, another layer of performativity is apparent through the media hype aroused by the trial. The reportage of the hearings is a continuous, serialized event exceeding the ordinary journalistic routine. Both the trial and its coverage in the media are ongoing events, whose participants are always aware of both. Newspaper readers are not only consumers of news; rather, they are spectators of journalistic performance that is always aware of the various expectations of their readership. Readership consists of various kinds of spectators who have various expectations: political stakeholders, ordinary readers who look for excitement, and fellow journalists.

In the authoritarian environment of the 1880s, a few years after the abolition of the Basic Law and the parliament, every Ottoman newspaper editor and correspondent was fully aware of the lines that were not supposed to be crossed, while some newspapers explicitly served as mouthpieces of the Hamidian regime. The reports on the opening of the trial, which appeared in June 28, 1881, set the groundwork and raised expectations through their festive statements about the trial's historic nature. The semiofficial newspaper *Vakit* promised its readers that "the moral effect of this trial will last forever," also guaranteeing a perfect spectacle of the rule of law. The normative law, usually a boring business from the point of view of the lay reader, was now celebrated as a symbol of Ottoman rule of law. The *Vakit* explained to its readers that the trial was implementing the newly promulgated Code of Criminal Procedure, assuring them that "benefitting from the advantages of the Code, the culprits used their right to defend themselves." It even provided its sharp-eyed readers with an unintended reason for suspicion, when hyperbolically making a statement that was supposed to go without saying: "All the interrogative measures were conducted in order to reveal the truth, and no other goal was present. Similarly, nothing was done outside the limits sets by the law."[19] Even more pompous were the celebratory formulations of the influential *Tercüman-ı Hakikat*, which presented the trial as the first event of its kind in the entire Ottoman history, not an incorrect statement, to be sure. Nevertheless, admiration of Hamidian justice exposed through the Yıldız proceedings was expressed unequivocally and hyperbolically, when the newspaper eulogized the sultan's achievements in the legal sphere, also praising the integrity of the judges.[20] Throughout its coverage of the trial, which was the most detailed account to be found in the popular press of the time, the *Tercüman-ı Hakikat* referred to it as "the public trial," emphasizing its alleged transparency and legal integrity.

Though the trial was covered by other newspapers as well, I wish to draw attention to the coverage offered by *Vakit* and the *Tercüman-ı Hakikat*, not only owing to the scope of their reportage and their broad circulation, but also because they can be considered as "performative extensions" of the Yıldız Trial. In other words, these newspapers, which no doubt represented the agenda of Cevdet Paşa and Sultan Abdülhamit in this trial, made an important contribution in the communication of the trial as a signifier of Hamidian justice through its application of the Nizamiye procedure and at the same time its exceptional value as a historic event. Hence, these newspapers were not only reporting about the trial; they were also facilitating its objectives. Paraphrasing the terminology of the Greek theater, these newspapers played the role of the chorus to a certain degree. Unlike the Greek chorus, however, they refrained from revealing the secret parts of the plot. On May 18, 1881, for instance, the *Tercüman-ı Hakikat* published a brief news report about the beginning of the investigation against Midhat Paşa in Izmir and his plea for asylum at the French consulate.[21] Two days later, it published a much longer report on the negotiations held with Midhat over the terms of his extradition. The newspaper did not attempt to conceal its hostility toward Midhat, beginning the report with the argument that "the public opinion" held Midhat's plea for asylum a hideous conduct that violated the sovereignty of the Ottoman state. The same report presented some of the telegrams that were sent to Midhat by Cevdet Paşa and the officer Hilmi Paşa, who was in charge of the arrest. There can be little doubt that Cevdet authorized the publication of these telegrams. The *Tercuman-ı Hakikat* provided minutes of the trial hearings, explaining this measure as a service to those who could not attend the trial, "such as women." It also complained about the reporting of other newspapers, which provided merely partial and inaccurate accounts, a harmful practice, considering the significance of the trial.[22]

The mission of the *Tercuman-ı Hakikat* in defending the justice of the sultan assumed further intensity when offering a polemical response to the coverage of the trial in European newspapers, a response that spread over several essays under the title "The Public Trial and Europe" (Muhakeme-yi Aleniye ve Avrupa). The author made efforts to deal with European criticism thoroughly, claiming first that there were no grounds to the argument that Istanbul newspapers did not enjoy freedom of expression when covering the trial. He then moved on to confront specific critical points made in the foreign newspapers, such as the claim that the minister of justice, Cevdet Paşa, took part in the judges' deliberations on the verdict, thereby violating the principle of judicial independence.

The newspaper also claimed that this accusation had no factual grounds, as the minister was sitting with the reporters behind the judges.[23] Clearly, this elaborate response to foreign accusations was a display of the Ottoman continuous effort, increasingly becoming an obsession, to contain the damage done by derogatory publications in the foreign media, a campaign described by Selim Deringil as "image management and damage control."[24]

Nevertheless, the entire coverage of the trial in *Tercüman-ı Hakikat*, with its display of unconditional faith in the Ottoman rule of law, was dictated by political alliances and a friendship that had grown sour. The newspaper's editor was Ahmet Midhat Efendi, who actually started his career as a protégé of Midhat Paşa when serving as the governor of Tuna (the Danube province) from 1864 to 1868. In fact, Midhat Paşa had given Ahmet Efendi his own name, appointing the twenty-four-year-old man to editor in chief of the provincial gazette. Ahmet Midhat Efendi followed the paşa to his post in Baghdad while simultaneously cultivating his own writing and printing career. In 1872 the sultan had Ahmet Midhat arrested and exiled to Rhodes following his collaboration with the Young Ottomans. After the deposition of Abdülaziz, he was pardoned and allowed to return to Istanbul, where he made the choice of supporting the new sultan, actually becoming a court historian of sorts through the publication of his book *Üss-i İnkilap* (*Origins of the Revolution*), which justified the coup and praised Abdülhamit's policies, including the abolition of parliament.[25]

Ahmet Midhat Efendi's loyalty to Abdülhamit while abandoning his constitutional inclinations, and his authority as a prolific author, won him prestigious state offices, such as the director of the Imperial Press and the editor of the official gazette *Takvim-i Vekayi*. In 1878 he became the editor of the *Tercüman-ı Hakikat*.[26] It is difficult to pin down a single reason for the abhorrence that Ahmet Midhat Efendi had been developing toward his former patron. In his interrogation prior to the trial, Midhat Paşa mentioned a slanderous essay that Ahmet Midhat Efendi had published in the *Tercuman-ı Hakikat*, accusing him of corruption and pro-Greek activity against the Ottoman state.[27] As is often the case, a mixture of the complex psychological aspects of patronage relationships and political opportunism dictated by changing circumstances was at play. In any case, the Yıldız Trial brought about a full-impact collision between Midhat Paşa and his ex-protégé, now serving the interests of the minister of justice, Cevdet Paşa, one of Midhat's greatest political foes. The collision was apparent not in the trial itself but in its representation on the pages of the *Tercuman-ı Hakikat* before and after the proceedings.

The newspaper *Vakit* provides yet another illustration of the performance of loyalty to the regime while serving the prosecutors' agenda, although exhibiting a gawky treatment of the performance of legalism. In its issue from July 4, 1881, the *Vakit* reported that the Court of Cassation was reviewing the Yıldız court decisions and sentences. The newspaper declared this procedure pointless, oblivious to the fact that the procedure of judicial review of trials addressing severe crimes was not only a legal necessity but also in the interest of the minister of justice, who could point to the spectacle of review as an indication of Ottoman rule of law. "It is known that there is no reason for the Court of Cassation to investigate the confessions of the perpetrators of the crime," the *Vakit* wrote. In fact, from a legalistic point of view, the wholehearted effort made by the newspaper in representing the case of the state against the convicts was self-defeating, when sharing with its readers information that had not come up in the trial. The author argued that after the coup of 1876, the accomplices participated in a corrupt debauch of daylight robbery. According to the report, the convicts Mahmut Paşa and Nuri Paşa had taken a bribe of six hundred liras in addition to taking over property and capital that belonged to the deposed sultan Abdülaziz. Nuri Paşa, so it was reported, had stolen from Abdülaziz the enormous sum of a million liras, which he transferred to Paris. Rüştü Paşa took from the palace of Abdülaziz money and even furniture, some of which had been given to him by Murat's mother.[28] None of it had been mentioned in the trial, and we have no way to determine how well founded these allegations were.

As noted in chapter 1, the Yıldız Trial took place in a time when a three-decade-long process of constructing a legalistic version of the rule of law was reaching a high point. The codification project had assumed a substantial degree of maturity, and so was the court system overall. In fact, major Ottoman newspapers praised the use of the new criminal procedure in the Yıldız Trial. They also celebrated the application of the principle of publicity of trials, seeing in these features a testimony to the firmness of Ottoman rule of law, safeguarded by the sovereign.[29] The flourishing of the printing press and the maturation of Ottoman legalism provided unprecedented boost to the performativity of the law.

The imprisonment of the Yıldız convicts marked the end of the Ottoman media's interest in the trial, although Ottoman journalists were not necessarily indifferent to the fate of the high-profile prisoners. Their readers were surely curious about the hardships suffered by those individuals who had used to be the most important people in their realm. Nevertheless, the Hamidian regime, gradually drifting to extreme absolutism, had no interest in allowing further excavation into the trial, all the more so following the condemnations it encountered overseas. As noted in the previous chapter, interest in the trial reemerged following the Young Turk Revolution, when the trial provided to the Committee of Union and Progress a story that signified the evilness and oppressiveness of the ancien régime. Through the serialized publication of the trial's transcript in the *Tanin*, the mouthpiece of the CUP, a new generation of Ottoman readers became acquainted with the show trial.

The trial equally fascinated the foreign press. By 1881 the Ottoman Empire was well connected to the global telegraph network. Cable communications created a global communication market and industries, allowing journalists to dispatch news reports in foreign parts almost in real time and with no trouble.[30] Most of the reports on the Yıldız Trial took the form of brief accounts, which was a standard form of presenting foreign news, both in the Ottoman Empire and in Western countries. Coverage of the developing story that was the trial started as soon as Midhat was arrested in Izmir. On May 17, 1881, *Reuters* reported, "Telegrams have been received by the Government from Smyrna [that is, Izmir] to the effect that Midhat Pasha was arrested to-day, the French and other consuls having refused to afford him asylum from the Ottoman Minister of Justice."[31] The narrative that Sultan Abdülaziz was the victim of an evil conspiracy, however, was evident in the foreign press as soon as the news about his death arrived. On June 5, 1876, the *New York Times* published a long obituary, praising the achievements of the dead sultan in the fields of administration, economics, and education, ignoring his colossal failures exactly in these fields. The last paragraph of the obituary reflected the conspiracy theory that five years later would turn into legal action:

> A favorite scheme of the late Sultan was the establishment of the succession of his son Youssouf Ezedin to the throne, instead of his nephew, the present Sultan Mourad V. The attempts to modify the laws in accordance with this plan caused more than one ministerial crisis, and ended uniformly in failure. This, with the intestine troubles of the empire, probably explains the forced abdication of the late Sultan, and leaves room for gloomy suspicion as to the mode of his "taking off," not wholly removed by the official announcement of suicide by the aid of a pair of scissors.[32]

There was no uniformity of opinion in the foreign press concerning the circumstances of Abdülaziz's death, however. The suspicion of assassination, implied by the *New York Times*, was not a consensus. The combination of a shadowy suspense melodrama that involved political schemes, and the ever-present curiosity about private lives in Oriental exotic palaces, was fertile ground for reporters eager to meet the demand for good stories. In the late nineteenth century, much like the early twenty-first, news reports about foreign events often reflected narratives provided by local newspapers, whose own sources were questionable, often giving voice to interested parties who hoped to spread around their own versions. Almost two months after Abdülaziz's death, the *Sydney Morning Herald* presented the "facts" that had been reported in the Istanbul-based French-language newspaper *Stamboul* on June 5. The report "revealed" the details of Abdülaziz's suicide, presenting them in a way that would allow its readers to imagine it as a theatrical scene. According to the report, the deposed sultan asked for a pair of scissors in order to trim his beard, the way he had used to do every morning. He managed to get hold of the scissors following the permission of his mother:

> He then commenced his toilette, and his old chamberlain, Fahri Bey, having been sent for by his order, Abdul Aziz commenced to talk to him, but in a very incoherent manner, referring perpetually to his idea of his enemies, and exclaiming, "why do not my guards protect me against my enemies?" His old friend attempted to calm his master's agitation, but not without weeping himself at the pitiable condition of the fallen Prince. Suddenly Abdul Aziz, opening his shirt sleeves, seized the pair of scissors with his left hand and gave himself a sharp stab with them in the right arm. Fahri then attempted to wrest the scissors from him, and a struggle ensued in the course of which the Prince passed the scissors from his left to his right hand. Fahri Bey, seeing that his efforts were useless, ran from room to room to give the alarm. At this moment, doubtless, Abdul Aziz inflicted the fatal wound, and severed the main artery of his left arm.[33]

Whereas the Ottoman press that covered the trial was emphasizing the integrity of the proceedings, taking pride in the transparency of the hearings and celebrating the application of the rational Nizamiye court procedure, the foreign correspondents were much less impressed. Ottoman journalists were clearly bound by both formal and self-censorship, but at the same time, some of them were truly committed to the patriotic project of image management vis-à-vis the world, particularly Europe, which they perceived as hostile overall. Yet for both Ottoman and foreign journalists, the scene of a court trial involving the highest-caliber statesmen, displayed right in front of them in a theater-like setting, was a new experience. Strong criticism about the court's integrity was raised by most, if not all, the foreign journalists who were present in the trial, paralleled by explicit sympathy to Midhat. Under the title "The Trial of the Pashas," the British *Tablet*, which summarized the three days of the trial, wrote:

> The public opinion of England was impressed, though by no means satisfied, by the evidence forthcoming on the first day of the trial of the Pashas accused of participation in the alleged murder of the ex-Sultan Abdul Aziz. The proceedings on the second day can only have deepened the feeling that elementary rules of evidence were violated, and that even the clear text of the Mahommedan law itself was set aside in the anxiety of the Tribunal to secure the condemnation of the inculpated dignitaries. It will be strongly felt that the promise given to the European Powers that the accused, especially Midhat, should have a fair trial has not been fulfilled in earnestness and good faith. Properly speaking there has been no evidence in the English sense at all forthcoming against Midhat Pasha, while the indications of prejudice and personal hostility in his regard were too clear to be denied. . . . From a strictly legal point of view, there is not a line or a scrap to connect the condemned Pashas with the alleged crime. The attitude of Midhat Pasha in the closing scene of the trial was especially dignified, touching, and calculated to enlist sympathy and belief.[34]

Some foreign correspondents were more thorough in their coverage of the trial, providing their readers with unmediated access to the proceedings. The *New York Times*, for instance, offered an excerpt from the public prosecutor's opening speech.[35] Reports on the trial and its aftermath continued in accordance to subsequent developments and circumstances. Midhat's death in his prison cell at the Taif citadel, three years after the trial, was another news drama that intrigued foreign media. The uncertainties, speculations, and inaccuracies that characterized the reports of Abdülaziz's death in 1876 were like a déjà vu when describing the death of the Ottoman famous reformer and constitutionalist. The *New York Times* attributed Midhat's death to a carbuncle, mistakenly writing that the paşa died in Constantinople.[36] The *Tablet* wrote in early July, "The suspicions that the sudden death of Midhat Pasha was not brought about by natural means has at length been most circumstantially confirmed, and it is now certain that Midhat Pasha and his fellow-prisoners were literally starved to death."[37] Other newspapers reported about the paşa's career while not going into speculations about the circumstances of his death.[38]

A new version about the trial came about with the publication of Ali Haydar Midhat's book on the life of his father, Midhat Paşa, which came out in London in 1903 by the title *The Life of Midhat Pasha: A Record of His Services, Political Reforms, Banishment, and Judicial Murder*. Ali Haydar included in the book some of the telegrams that the *Times* correspondent to the trial had sent to his newspaper throughout the trial, twenty-two years before. In addition to summarized descriptions of the arguments, counter-arguments, and statements heard in the hearings, the *Times* correspondent did his best to transmit the nonverbal dimensions of the trial, apparent in the physical setting of the court, body gestures, sighs in response to certain statements, and so on. Where the planners of this show trial wanted to transmit it as a performance of legalistic justice, the report of the *Times* correspondent was in itself a performance of justice, this time the correspondent serving as both an observer and a judge, gazing at an "interesting and picturesque spectacle," as he described the trial.[39] As an observer, the correspondent made it possible for the English reader of his telegrams (meant to be published) to be with the audience, to imagine the spectacle. Describing the confession of Mustafa the Wrestler, the correspondent reported:

> The first called upon to state what he knew, was Mustapha, the wrestler, a man of ordinary size and not presenting any signs of abnormal muscular development. His face was of common type and betrayed no symptoms of emotion as he related, in plain, unvarnished terms, how he had cut open the ex-Sultan's veins with a knife given to him for the purpose by Mahmoud Damad. His description, accompanied by slight and significant gestures, was brutally graphic, and made a strong impression on the spectators, more than one of the older men in the audience giving vent to their feelings of horror by audible exclamations.[40]

Thanks to the same report, the reader could also visualize Damat Mahmut Paşa, one of the alleged conspirators, as "a tall stout man, with regular and handsome features and large dark eyes . . . and his deep gruff voice showed more than once signs of great emotion."[41]

As the trial was ending, the *Times* correspondent committed himself to the mission of assessing the court's justice. He provided a list of evidence meant to leave no doubt in that respect. This evidence included a private audience that the court's president had with the sultan immediately before the trial had begun, receiving "from His Majesty certain instructions as to how the proceedings should be conducted."[42] In a telegram sent from Istanbul on July 1, the correspondent wrote to the newspaper that the palace had scrutinized his previous communications. Considering that the reporter was still writing from Istanbul, it is not clear why censorship was no longer a problem. In any case, his judgment was unequivocal: "I have now, fortunately, an opportunity of communicating with you freely, and I hasten to declare that the trial was little better than a parody of European judicial procedure, which has justly roused the indignation, not only of foreign observers, but also of many Turks, who have an elementary conception of justice and fair play."[43]

The list of evidence in support of this harsh judgment was considerable. The fact that the pretrial interrogations as well as the hearings had been taking place at the palace; the unceasing messages via messengers who "were constantly passing to and fro between the Palace and the tribunal"; the fact that foreign correspondents, most of them "ignorant of the Turkish language and judicial procedure," were not allowed to employ dragomans (translators); the violation of the principle of impartiality through the attendance of the minister of justice in the conference room when the verdicts were discussed, and perhaps the most incriminating evidence of all: "Raghib Bey, one of the Sultan's private secretaries, and Djevdet Pasha, the obsequious Minister of Justice, who is one of Midhat's personal enemies. These two personages sat behind the judges on a bench, and secretly gave directions in moments of hesitation and difficulty. I can state this without fear of contradiction, for during one of the sittings I was myself on the bench, and carefully observed what was invisible to the audience."[44]

To add credibility to the now strong evidence that supported the correspondent's judgment, he resorted to the old convention of Orientalist cynical ridicule, noting that the flawed defenses performed by the advocates of the defendants were yet another indication of Oriental ways. "Equally Oriental," the correspondent wrote, "is the fact that the learned gentlemen who undertook the so-called defense on such conditions, showed no signs of being ashamed of themselves."[45] Thus, all means were used to perform an unbiased reportage and justice.

PERFORMANCE IN THE YILDIZ TRIAL

The *Annales judiciaires* reported that the government decided to hold the trial near the imperial residence at the Yıldız Palace because the murder victim was a sovereign, also taking into consideration "the ideology and culture of the Muslim world." This symbolic decision about the location of the trial, according to the newspaper, was the only feature thereof that distinguished it from ordinary criminal trials. The *Annales judiciaires*, like any other Ottoman periodical, could not pass judgment on this decision, having to merely pass on to its readers this justification dictated by the trial's designers.[46] The decision to perform the trial as a regular Nizamiye criminal proceeding made perfect sense from the perspective of image management vis-à-vis the watching international community, especially Europe. However, the decision to hold the trial in the palace rather than using an ordinary courtroom was a dubious move in this respect. The setting of the Yıldız court, the entrance procedures, and above all its location could not leave any doubt among the audience as to the show that the producers of the trial had in mind.

For the audience, entering the site of the trial was like entering a temporary theater hall. For some of the individuals who received entry tickets (state dignitaries, embassy and consular staff, journalists), it was the first visit in the new residential palace, which was built a year earlier in imperial woodlands at the shore of the Bosporus, an area that had used to house mansions of the imperial family since the seventeenth century. The visitors were led to the huge tent erected on the ground behind the Malta kiosk, a neo-Baroque style, two-floor pavilion that was built in 1870 to serve Sultan Abdülaziz as a hunting lodge. The many soldiers who were crowding together all around the perimeter watched the viewers who were entering the high-ceiling green tent. The famous privacy of the imperial family was maintained through a canvas screen that separated the tent's perimeter from the Malta Kiosk and the other buildings of the palace, allowing access only to one of the kiosk's rooms, which was designated for the buffet. The visitors passed through the ceilinged makeshift corridor to enter a big space, elegantly designed to provide comfort. The frame of the tent was made of blue silk embellished with white fine arabesques. When raising their eyes, the viewers saw a nicely designed top of wide sheets joint together by poles and ropes. The space inside the tent was divided up into the section of the court and the audience's section, separated by a wooden barrier. The viewers were led to their assigned seats at the audience site, in accord with their position and rank.

The seating plan signified how the trial's planners hierarchized the audience. Right behind the barrier, three rows of leather armchairs were reserved for the diplomatic corps and their staff, in addition to Ottoman personages. Behind them, there were rows of chairs, the first of which reserved for foreign and local press correspondents. Overall, three to four hundred people could be contained, but most of the chairs remained vacant throughout the trial. Facing the audience, the area defined for the court was accessible on both sides by corridors saved for the prisoners who were about to march to their seats. The audience faced an elevated space on one of the sides of the tent, which contained the bench, made of luxurious seats occupied by three Muslim and two Christian judges, all dressed in the standard black frock coats and red fezzes, the "uniform" of Ottoman officialdom. They were presided by Sururi Efendi, a grey-bearded *alim*, who wore a black robe and white turban. At the sides of the bench, chairs were designated for the public prosecutor, the clerks, and other functionaries of the court. Imperial aides-de-camp and palace servants were standing behind the functionaries. A trench hollowed out below the bench was saved for the ten prisoners, who were seated on cane chairs, behind each of which stood a soldier.[47]

No doubt, upon occupying their chairs, the spectators of the Yıldız Trial expected excitedly to watch a show. Given their social status, most, if not all, of them had been in the theater before, and the similarity of the place to a theater could not escape them.[48] The way spectators and performers were separated, the elevated space reserved for the judges, and the trench designed for distinguishing the prisoners from both the court and the audience yet signifying them as an integral part of the performers—all of it was bringing to mind the classical proscenium arch stage, also known as the picture-frame stage. Living in the late nineteenth century and being the modern minds that they were, the viewers were used to conceiving their surroundings as a picture, in the Heideggerian sense of "the world as a picture." The modern mind, according to Heidegger, got used to thinking about itself as part of the picture that is always presented before him. The world is a spectacle to watch and at the same time be part of. The phrase "we get the picture" implies that the picture is intelligible not only through what it is but by what it stands for, "and all that stands together in it—as a system."[49] As far as those individuals who attended the Yıldız Trial were concerned, whether as audience, court personnel, attorneys, defendants, and palace staff, they took part in a performance that encapsulated a multitude of meanings. Among them was the drama of political rivalries; the tragedy of a victimized sultan, which was narrated once and again during the hearings; the concerns regarding the path that the Hamidian regime was heading; and the legal performance. The producers of the trial wanted to project it as a representation of Ottoman Nizamiye justice, a symbol of progress and rationality. Some of the spectators, however, experienced it as a parody of what they considered as the "the real thing," namely, European law, which was the impression of the *Times* correspondent and other observers.

As demonstrated in chapter 1, the performance of legalism was evident through adherence of the court to the standard Nizamiye procedure defined by the Code of Criminal Procedure. Yet performance was also evident in the rhetorical tactics employed by the judges, the advocates, and the prosecutor, who were eager to win over the viewers in the courtroom, as well as the "public opinion" and "the Europeans," reified categories that were ubiquitous in the Ottoman press. During the interrogation of Midhat, Judge Forides Efendi told him: "It appears from the investigation documents that the possible re-installment of Abdülaziz would be detrimental to you. Therefore, you had to place at his side people that you knew and trusted completely. Your malintent stemmed from the fear that Abdülaziz might ascend to the throne again."[50]

The judge when addressing Midhat during the hearing made this claim, which might have sounded to the audience an untimely judgment. Describing events without procedural modifiers such as *alleged* and *presumed*, or by presenting them as facts, as if they are not the open question that the court is supposed to address, is a typical tactic in litigation.[51] While the adversarial system might not put up with a judge who participates in the tactical games of destabilizing the opponent's credibility, a role reserved for the advocates and the prosecution, in the inquisitorial system the judge can employ such a maneuver in his capacity as the focal point of the discussion. Throughout the interrogation of Midhat, Judge Forides Efendi moved back and forth from an informative course of investigation to attempts at confronting Midhat with the accusations by presenting them as facts. At times, this attempt was pushed *ad absurdum*. When trying to establish the accountability of the ministerial cabinet with regard to the investigation of the cause of Abdülaziz's death, the judge asked Midhat, "Wasn't the cabinet responsible for examining the body of the Sultan in person?" To this question, Midhat provided the obvious answer, namely, that examination of the corpse was the duty of the medical doctors. The judge continued to pressure Midhat, asking him whether the cabinet instructed the doctors to examine the body thoroughly and whether the members of the cabinet were present at the time of the examination. The judge formulated the latter question as a taken-for-granted measure: "Weren't the members of the cabinet supposed to attend when the doctors examined the body?"[52] Of course, there was nothing obvious in the judge's expectation that the ministers, none of them a medical doctor, would watch the doctors doing their job.

On the whole, the conduct of the judges presented an odd blend of performance of legalism and continuous violation of procedure, demonstrated in the previous chapter. In addition, the judges presented a line of investigation intended to persuade the spectators in and outside the tent that Midhat was not worthy of their respect, in addition to the specific charges defined by the bill of indictment. The discussion on the circumstances of Midhat's arrest in Izmir, for instance, was entirely off base from a legalistic point of view. The judge asked Midhat why he sought the protection of the French consulate. Instead of refusing to answer this question on the grounds of its legal irrelevance, Midhat, who demonstrated assertiveness in other parts of the hearing, chose to meet the challenge. He did so because he considered the trial an opportunity to present his version with regard to the claim that he, a former grand vizier and minister of justice, expressed contempt toward Ottoman sovereignty by seeking foreign shelter. It was not a legal charge, but for Midhat this accusation was no less severe, casting doubt on his very patriotism. He explained that several weeks before his arrest in Izmir, he learned from letters and rumors that a scheme against him was progressing, covertly administered by two military officers who had been sent from Istanbul. A certain Colonel Ali Bey, Midhat told the court, arrived in Izmir and started to spread lies about Midhat, who considered arresting him:

> In fact, that night three-hundred soldiers surrounded my house. I was afraid to fall into the hands of the armed people of this Ali Bey. That is why I left through the garden door and got on the first carriage that I came across. The first gate that I found was the French consulate's; I passed through it. They said that I had anticipated all the options and that I had prepared in advance the backdoor and even the carriage. All these are lies. There was a backdoor, but it was meant to be used in case of earthquakes, and it was installed following my family's request.[53]

Through this explanation, Midhat wished to deliver to the spectators the message that he was a victim of conspiracy. Obviously, he knew that Ali Bey was merely carrying out the orders of his superiors in Istanbul, but blaming the sultan or his minister of justice for "spreading lies" was inappropriate and therefore not an option. Responding to this narrative, the judge did not miss the opportunity to convince the audience in and outside the courtroom that Midhat Paşa's behavior deserved all but respect:

> You are saying that you were afraid for your life and that is why you left through a secret door in your house and turned to the French consulate with a request for asylum. If that was your concern, you could turn to the officers of your country and its justice system. No one runs away from the justice of his country, searching for the shelter of a foreign flag because he is afraid of being scolded. You are denying and rejecting [the

> claims against you]. It does not serve you. On the contrary, it proves your guilt.[54]

Besides distorting Midhat's narrative by casting it into a different formulation, this response of the judge was exceeding the legitimate limits of the rhetorical tactics allowed for revealing the truth in a court proceeding. In fact, it was an outright violation of elementary professional standards of judicial impartiality, thereby defeating the cause of performing a show of legalism. Was the judge getting carried away? He might have been. Alternatively, Judge Forides Efendi was making a calculated move, suspending the show of legalism in favor of persuading the audience in and outside the courtroom that Midhat's behavior was unpatriotic and opportunistic. In this show trial, unlike normal Nizamiye criminal trials, the objective of winning over the spectators was no less important than the legal objective of establishing the charges defined by the bill of indictment.[55]

As noted before, all trials are performative to various degrees, while theatricality is typically subtler in the inquisitorial system. Nevertheless, in the final analysis, regular criminal trials in a functional court system are geared to establishing guilt on the basis of evidence and in conformity with the normative law. In political trials, by contrast, performance is hitched to those extralegal functions of the trial, defined by Awol Allo as a "normative ordering of a trial in the second degree," whereas the layer of the first degree refers to the sort of "show" that is part of the orderings that determine the criminal responsibility of the accused.[56] In his exchanges with the judges and the public prosecutor throughout the Yıldız Trial, Midhat exhibited confidence and at times aggression to the extent of disrespect to the court. In the morning session of the trial's third day, the paşa was asked for his response to the statements of the following individuals: the defendant Seyyit Bey, who was Sultan Murat's *mabeynci* (chamberlain); Nuri Paşa, who was charged with giving the orders to kill Abdülaziz; and the witness Said Efendi, the former undersecretary. Their statements contradicted some parts of Midhat's version concerning his lack of knowledge about the appointment of the murder suspects and his conduct at the day of the sultan's death. For instance, Said Efendi stated that Midhat Paşa was lying to the court when saying that he first learned about the sultan's death from the undersecretary upon arriving late to the Bab-ı Ali. In his answer to the judge, Midhat dismissed Said's statement as a lie, implying that the witness followed someone's order: "Perhaps telling the truth might expose him to problems," an insinuation that Midhat had already made in his pretrial interrogation.[57]

The judge carried on, asking Midhat for his response to the statement of one of the witnesses, Said Bey. Midhat answered that he would be able to respond if the written statement was read out before him. While the clerk was looking for the document, Midhat Paşa started to read aloud a paragraph from a report that reached the court. This report stated that when Abdülaziz was transferred to Feriye following his deposition, Midhat had asked for clarifications from Fahri Bey (Abdülaziz's chamberlain) concerning the appointment of Mustafa the Wrestler and his friends to the service of Abdülaziz in Feriye Palace, thereby indicating that Midhat was aware of the appointment of the three shady fellows. Reading from this document abruptly, without asking for the court's permission while totally ignoring its irrelevance to the question that the judge had asked him, was a surprising move that challenged the court as the exclusive authority in deciding the judicial agenda. In the legal culture of the Nizamiye courts, overseeing the strict observance of legal procedure was one of the major duties of the public prosecution.[58] The immediate fierce response of Latif Bey, the prosecutor in the trial, was therefore expected. He cried out, "I protest the defendant's words. He is insulting the justice authorities." Predictably, the judge followed suit and instructed the paşa to speak to the point. The audience must have been astonished to see that Midhat was utterly ignoring the judge's order, keeping on with his subject of choice:

> As to the report, one day I came across Seyyit Bey in the staircase at the palace. It was said that I asked him what kind of people were Mustafa the Wrestler and the other two. From this question, the Indictment Committee concluded that I was an accomplice to the murder, turning it into indisputable evidence. . . . It is very likely that I asked Seyyit Bey this question. At that time, I pulled out some inappropriate individuals from the palace. Maybe [I asked that question] to understand if there is a need to expulse these three, too."[59]

Midhat repeated his performance of assertiveness, often turning to sheer impudence. After having the court accept his demand to cross-examine each of the witnesses in accordance with procedure, he told the judge, "I will interrogate the witnesses." A former minister of justice, he knew that no judge in the Nizamiye courts could allow a defendant to interrogate the witnesses. In the Nizamiye courts, communication with witnesses was the exclusive privilege of the presiding judge, a point that was made by Judge Forides Efendi: "Here you are neither a judge nor an interrogator. You are a defendant and perhaps a convict. You will address questions to the court, and the court will interrogate the defendants."[60] The audience, which must have been stunned by this show of disrespect, saw Midhat commanding the judge: "Stop. First have the others leave the place." Forides Efendi disregarded this insolent exclamation and ordered Mustafa the Wrestler to carry on with his testimony. In a regular trial, such demonstration of audacity by a criminal defendant would result with a penalty. But this was not a regular trial, and the judge's relative toleration of Midhat's provocative conduct was perhaps a sign that Forides Efendi was losing his confidence in the power struggle that Midhat Paşa forced upon him. The performance of self-confidence and even aggression was in contrast with the paşa's real situation. A sober, experienced politician who possessed the most intimate knowledge of Ottoman politics, Midhat had no reason to cultivate false hopes about his future once the trial was over, a future that could not be grimmer. Exactly for this reason, though, he did not have much to lose, and the public opinion in Europe was the only card that he could play. His confident performance meant to convince the spectators, mainly the European ones, that rather than a prisoner devoid of any agency, totally at the mercy of the sultan, he was actually on a par with the court within the context of a political power struggle. In retrospect, this performance was effective in part, even if it did not eventually resuscitate the paşa from his premature death. The sultan had to mitigate his death penalty, following foreign pressure.

One does not need to be legally savvy to know that in judicial proceedings, clients should follow the orders of their attorneys, who "run the show" in the courtroom. The scene of the self-assured lawyer bursting into the interrogation room and commanding his client to keep silent in the face of the overwhelmed interrogators is well known to every television watcher. Often exaggerated for entertainment, these scenes reflect the obvious fact that performativity in court is dominated by attorneys because modern law talk is sustained by professional lingo and cultural codes that are hardly accessible to nonprofessionals, even more so on the procedural battlefront, which is often the main arena of judicial battles. In 1881 professional legal advocacy was a new trade, introduced into the Ottoman judicial sphere in the preceding decade. The concept of legal representation had existed in Ottoman law, but it was entirely different. For one, before the late nineteenth century, every individual could be empowered as a judicial agent (*vekil*) through a special contract and with no involvement of the state. Second, the duty of the judicial agent was limited to representing his client's interests rather than advocating his case in the court. Practices known as the bread and butter of modern attorneyship, such as procedural maneuvering, were not part of the classical Ottoman judicial agent's tasks, which were limited to providing the judge with the information required for reaching a verdict. The Ottoman professional attorney, known as a "trial agent" (*dava vekili*), was an invention of the mid-1870s, part of the evolution of the Nizamiye court system and its idiosyncratic discourse. The legalistic court culture and the emergence of legal formalism as the dominating discourse in the Nizamiye courts rendered legal advocacy almost a sine qua non in both civil and criminal trials at the end of the century.[61]

Nevertheless, in 1881, professional attorneyship was still a novelty of somewhat opaque worth. The procedural codes had been in existence for a mere couple of years, and legal professionals only started discovering their value as an arsenal of powerful legal weapon that could determine judicial outcomes. Those defendants in the Yıldız Trial who belonged to the leading political elite of the empire were reluctant to leave their defense to their professional attorneys. In addition, all of them complained that they were not allowed to spend sufficient time with their advocates to work on their defense, a protest that was not groundless. As far as the trial's designers were concerned, the employment of advocates was important for the performance of legalism, but they made sure to eliminate the risk stemming from a committed work of advocacy by limiting the time that the clients could spend with their lawyers, a complaint that Midhat raised repeatedly. As noted in the petition for a retrial, authored in 1909 by the advocate of Fahri Bey and Midhat's son, Ali Haydar Bey:

> The appointment of attorney to the accused is not meant to decorate the court or to gain fame by sitting next to the accused. The attorney's mission is to warn the court president from acting against the legal rules and bringing forward the secured rights. [However,] Midhat's attorney did not object to the way the court had been formed, the place it had been moved to, and to the presence of the minister of justice and other dignitaries. Let us say that [he did not object] because he was afraid.[62]

Procedure required that attorneys would make their defense speeches at the end of the hearings. A lawyer called Kostaki Sardinski Efendi represented Damat Mahmut Paşa. Like the other attorneys in the trial, Kostaki Efendi's contribution during the hearings was modest, his input reserved for the closing defense speech. The lack of communication between the advocate and his client was made clear through Mahmut Paşa's sudden intervention at the beginning of his lawyer's speech, a speech that did present a sincere attempt of the advocate to do his job properly:

> I will base my defense on three principles. First, I will explore whether or not there was a crime. Second, was my client an accomplice? Third, does this matter apply to the category of a compelling order (*amir-i mucbir*)? As to the first point, there can be some evidences for this. In addition, there are many details. I will not investigate these details one-by-one here. However, I can only say that the ministers at the time made a big mistake. Sultan Abdülaziz's body was in front of them. Instead of conducting thorough investigations, they were content with Fahri Bey's statement. Even minutes of the meeting were not taken. (So no one wrote down these dialogues there). If . . . [63]

Hence, the attorney took up the tactic of admitting a relatively minor misconduct, thus making the impression of credibility, while denying the graver accusations. But Mahmut Paşa hushed his attorney, telling the court that he was taking over and making his defense speech by himself because he had not been able to meet his attorney sufficiently. The truth of this claim was apparent by the fact that Mahmut Paşa had no idea of his attorney's tactic. When he was making his lengthy defense, leaving his attorney speechless and jobless, every now and then Mahmut Paşa told the court that he was not feeling well and about to stop talking, but then he carried on, responding to the prosecutor's interventions. Clearly, he was too nervous to notice his attorney's professional talents in addition to not having any good reason to trust him. Mahmut Paşa was neither a lawyer nor a politician of Midhat's caliber and experience. Forty-five years old, this member of the imperial family through his marriage to Cemile Sultan, the daughter of Sultan Abdülaziz, and a former minister of commerce, was not able to deliver the performance of self-assured restraint that Midhat Paşa did. Where Midhat reproached the court while playing procedural cards, aware of the court's legalistic culture, Mahmut Paşa was agitatedly and incoherently talking about his lack of involvement in the dramas discussed in the trial. He told the court that he learned about the deposition of Abdülaziz and the subsequent enthronement of Murat when these events were a fait accompli. In the same sentence, he argued that the coup could not be the doing of a group of four people (of which he had been accused of being part). Rather, it was the outcome of public opinion: "Yes, cannons were placed, swords were pulled out, but they were not intended to protect Sultan Abdülaziz. Perhaps they were meant to secure the new Sultan."[64]

Legally, Mahmut Paşa's contribution to the coup had nothing to do with the charges for which he was standing trial. Nonetheless, this was a political trial, and he was eager to convince the spectators that he was not part of the oppositional political camp that the present sultan and his minister of justice were interested in eliminating. The public prosecutor, who was quick to notice where Mahmut was heading, jumped in, saying, "The matter under discussion is not the enthronement of Sultan Murat but the murder of Sultan Abdülaziz." The tense paşa continued to talk about his lack of involvement in the subsequent events, denying the role that the prosecution attributed to him in the conspiracy against the dead sultan:

> It is also argued that I was appointed to guard the residence of the deposed Sultan. This is a lie. In those days, around Sultan Abdülaziz's

> death, I was appointed to search his chambers in Feriye, in order to place the ladies [of the Sultan's harem] in proper places and to secure documents and things related to the government, if there were any. Because of this, it is argued that I went to Feriye before Sultan Abdülaziz's murder. No, I went to Feriye only after his assassination. [But] I went there to carry out my duty. Since I had no business in Feriye and Ortaköy guard station, it was impossible [for me] to talk with Fahri Bey and İzzet Bey. The words that were attributed to me, as if I met with so and so workers and officers [when planning the crime] are all false.[65]

Mahmut Paşa was referring to the prosecution's claim that he had given to Mustafa the Wrestler the direct order to kill the Sultan: "I have to turn crazy to do something like this. Elhamdulillah, I am not stricken by madness." At this point, the protocol records an exchange between Mahmut Paşa and the public prosecutor, who was asking him questions while the presiding judge, Sururi Efendi, was keeping quiet. Once again, the performance of legalism was collapsing. The public prosecutor was not supposed to talk to the defendant directly but only through the presiding judge. In addition, the prosecutor, who—a minute earlier—had asked Mahmut Paşa to stick to the legal charges, was trying to position Mahmut in the camp of political opposition. The prosecutor asked Mahmut why he was absent from the gathering that was known to all as the "Çerkes Hasan incident," which took place on June 15, 1876, shortly after Abdülaziz's death. This enigmatic event occurred during a meeting of the cabinet at Midhat Paşa's mansion in the Fatih neighborhood, when one of Sultan Abdülaziz's brothers-in-law, a certain Çerkes Hasan, broke in and started to shoot around with a pistol. He killed the former grand vizier and prominent general Hüseyin Avni Paşa, who was probably one of the planners of the coup, as well as Foreign Minister Reşit Paşa. Few others were injured. The motives for this violent attack were said to be a combination of personal grudge and a desire to avenge the harms done to the deposed sultan. Çerkes Hasan was tried and executed by hanging three days after the killing.[66] The prosecutor's question concerning the absence of Mahmut Paşa from that disastrous meeting resulted with the following exchange:

MAHMUT PAŞA: [I did not attend] because I was not invited to this committee. At that time, they did not invite me to committees.

PROSECUTOR: Perhaps there was something else?

MAHMUT PAŞA: For what reasons? Specify.

PROSECUTOR: There were rumors that you were aware of Çerkes Hasan's intentions.

Mahmut Paşa rejected these accusations forcefully, addressing the prosecutor while the judge was keeping silent. Repeatedly exclaiming, "I did not kill anybody," Mahmut Paşa addressed a comment made by the prosecutor, referring to an alleged incriminating statement that was attributed to Rüştü Paşa, the grand vizier at the time of the deposition, who was accused of complicity but could not stand trial owing to illness. The prosecutor argued that in Rüştü's pretrial interrogation, the aged paşa said that Mahmut came to his beach house the night of Abdülaziz's death. Mahmut Paşa claimed that he did not remember reading this statement in Rüştü's interrogation protocol and that he could produce his servants to testify that he was staying in his house that night. The court had the interrogation protocol read aloud, thereby corroborating the prosecutor's claim. Mahmut Paşa, who was either truly surprised or trying to seem surprised, asked the court to look at Rüştü Paşa's signature on the document. Judge Sururi Efendi agreed to show the signature to Mahmut, but he also had to react forcefully to what the audience could interpret as Mahmut's explicit doubt in the integrity of the entire proceeding: "Sir, in fact, this kind of suspicions will damage [your] honor. Manipulating the contents of the interrogation document and falsifying other judicial documents are not things that conform with the court's dignity. This kind of behavior is considered a more serious crime than the one for which you are summoned to court."[67]

After the conviction of his client, attorney Kostaki Efendi had the opportunity to do his job, in line with the procedural requirement to have the defendants heard before deciding their penalties. Ignoring his client's denial of participation in the crime, the attorney argued that the law did not allow him to discuss the verdict once passed, but it did grant him the right to ask the court to take into account extenuating circumstances when deciding a sentence. Hence, he asked the court to remember that Mahmut Paşa was acting under the order of compelling superiors. To this, Mahmut Paşa added that "clause 184 is the most suitable for my case." At this point in the trial, it seems that the attorney and his client were more synchronized than before, understanding that once conviction was made, there was no point in pursuing the "not guilty" plea, and all that was left to do was saving the paşa's neck. The attorney performed his duty with considerable skill when presenting a colorful speech meant to warn the court not to make a decision that would position it in the category of uncivilized countries:

> With the court's permission, I wish to add a few words. Two thousand years ago, ancient nations had their own peculiar customs. When someone was murdered, his facial features at his last moments were drawn, and the painting was brought to the public yard. The murderer was led to the place with his head shaved, dressed in a red shirt and a rope wrapped around his neck. Walking in this shameful way, he was brought to his knees in front of the drawing that was lightened with a candle. His sentence was read aloud while he was waiting in this position. Then they divided the murderer's body into two, and tied each part to wheels of a gun carriage. Then they burned to ashes the fragmented body parts, and they hurled these ashes with the wind. However, the leaders of these savage nations have taken other paths. The penalizing treatment for elites and aristocrats was very different. They mitigated the penalties for these noblemen. Shouldn't one expect that mercy and benevolence be bestowed on my client, who is from among the noblemen? If you will show mercy to my client, you will be saved from a deep grief, both the Sovereign's and his subjects'.[68]

With its graphic images of dubious historical accuracy, insinuations about the analogy with barbarism, and the last ludicrous sentence about the possible regret of the present sultan, this melodramatic speech was nevertheless a clever way of putting pressure on the court in the face of the watching world. Whether this speech contributed to the outcome or not, later on the sultan mitigated Mahmut Paşa's death sentence to imprisonment. As was the case of Midhat, who might have been a fellow conspirer, Mahmut died prematurely in the Taif prison.

The obsession of the Ottoman elite with its international image, which was largely a response to the European fixation on "the Turks," was a major component in the performativity of the trial. One telling scene captured the interplay between performance of legalism and eagerness to win over the foreign spectators of the trial. At one point in the trial, when the public prosecutor was presenting the dead sultan's bloodstained shirt, one of the guards picked it up and asked the foreign viewers to take a close look at the shirt so they could see for themselves "how the precious Sultan Abdülaziz was killed." Obviously, this sincere gesture of the guard, moved by what he was hearing, thwarted the show of legalism. The presiding judge, therefore, immediately silenced the guard, saying that only the judges would assess the evidence.[69]

THE LANGUAGE OF JUDGMENT

The court of law is an arena where narratives about past events are presented, re-presented, and cast against each other. Court hearings often take startling twists and turns because litigants and their advocates modify their narratives in response to other accounts heard in or outside the court as the trial progresses. Narratives presented by witnesses often appear as fragmented, either owing to witnesses' meager rhetorical skills or because of challenges set by the opponent or the judge. Attorneys construct their narratives with the objective of winning their case regardless of "what really happened," so they employ rhetorical tactics accordingly. Ambiguity in law talk is a common rhetorical practice that allows litigants a good deal of flexibility throughout the judicial battle. Narratives tend to gain certain coherence just before the conclusion of trials, when the parties have a better idea about chances and risks and when ambiguity becomes a burden rather than a rhetorical asset.[70] We may paraphrase the colloquialism "It ain't over till the fat lady sings" when describing the use of narratives in ordinary trials. If the hearings sound like a cacophony of narratives, the act of passing the judgment is the moment where the lady sings and the game *is* over. The judgment is literally the moment of truth not necessarily in the sense that the objective truth comes to light—court decisions are subject to judicial review and courts make mistakes—but in the sense that there can be a single legitimate narration of the events in question. Perhaps too trivial a fact to mention, the exclusive status of this narrative is guaranteed by the unrivaled power of the court to enforce its decisions, for the court is the state. In both ordinary and political trials, the verdict is the ultimate narrative, but in political trials, it signifies the safe ground, from the point of view of the trial's initiators. The risk of unexpected developments during the hearings is over, as well as the need to contain embarrassing moments that stand in the way of legalist performance. The judges can either mute or contain these moments in the text of the verdict.

Every court decision is a performance of impartiality, justice, and sovereignty, though different legal systems exhibit differences in styles and tone. The text of the Yıldız court ruling makes sense when read as a Nizamiye ruling, with the performative features typical of this particular legal system. Similar to other legal systems of the civil law tradition, the French ideal inspired the legal culture of the Nizamiye courts. When designing the Nizamiye court system, the Ottoman reformers adopted the formalist discourse of the French legal system. Although the Nizamiye court system was to a considerable degree the outcome of a heuristic process that took place in the middle decades of the century in some of the provinces and the imperial center, it would not be incorrect to describe the final structure of this system as an outcome of "design." The codification of the late 1870s, especially the promulgation of the procedural codes and the Law of the Nizamiye Judicial Organization, allowed the reformers to impose a uniform structure and practice. There can be no doubt that the Ottoman reformers had in mind the French discursive style when envisioning the daily routines in the Nizamiye courts. This point is evident not only by the fact that chunks of the codes were translations and adaptations from the French equivalents, but also from the discourse evident in the documentation produced by these courts. Nizamiye court decisions were strikingly similar to the French model in their style, thereby representing an identical idea of how justice should be performed, even if the Ottomans never experienced something even close to the French historical trajectory, which resulted with this discourse. The French legal idiom that was generated by the Napoleonic codification of the early nineteenth century reflected the revolutionary desire to render law making a monopoly of the legislative body in its capacity as the exclusive manifestation of the people's will. The authority of the judiciary was therefore restricted to the mere task of applying the law.[71] Hence, the judge was ideally conceived as a sort of adjudicating robot who mechanically applied the codified laws with no heed paid to the accumulated case law. In fact, modern French law does not allow French courts to refer to past cases as a sole basis for their decision, and they rarely refer to previous rulings.[72]

This extreme formalist vision was (and still is) performed through the style of French court decisions, which has not changed since the Revolution. Court sentences are very brief; their structure always conforms with the formula dictated by the Law on Judicial Organization from 1790. As noted by Mitchell de S.-O.-l'E. Lasser, "The French judicial decision, in its paradigmatic form, possesses a univocal quality that denies the possibility of alternative perspectives, approaches or outcomes."[73] This characterization perfectly applies to the style of the Ottoman Nizamiye court decisions following the codification of 1879. Like the French model, they were highly formulaic, revealing neither the judge's voice nor the logical process that led to the decision or the uncertainties that had to be addressed when forming a decision. The numbered clauses of the code, specified at the end of the decision, formed its sole justification.[74]

John Dawson's *The Oracles of the Law*, published in 1968, remains the foremost criticism on the civil law system, viewed from a common-law perspective. Although Dawson did not use the terminology of performance theory, treating the discourse of the French law as a case of theatrical performance of legal rationality seems like a natural extension of his critique. According to Dawson, the formalistic discourse of French adjudication is a fiction, a masquerade of judicial discretion that is not, and cannot be, oblivious to decades of accumulated case law. The rigid formulas that dictate the formal style of the court decisions force the French judiciary to adopt cryptic modes of expression.[75] Considering the wholehearted adoption of the French discursive style by the Ottoman Nizamiye apparatus, Dawson's critique applies to the Ottoman case as much as it applies to other versions of the civil law tradition.

In his study of the "unofficial portrait of the civil judge," Lasser uncovers a whole sphere of French realist academic doctrine that provides a sober critique of the formalist performance, a dimension of French jurisprudence that Dawson seemed to miss or underestimate. Lasser traces this critical discourse as early as 1899, when a French legal scholar complained about "that fetishism of the written and codified statutory law."[76] I am not aware of an equivalent critical doctrinal discourse in the Ottoman legal literature of the nineteenth century. It seems to me that the Ottoman performance of mechanical adjudication was never challenged in Ottoman doctrinal scholarship.[77]

I wish to set the conventions presented above, which reflect "that fetishism of the written and codified statutory law," as a background for the following analysis of the ruling. The text of the Yıldız court ruling contained both typical and atypical features of the standard Nizamiye court decision, reflecting the tension between performance of legalism and at the same time the tendency to transcend the legalistic constraints that we can find in many political trials. I have already referred to the strange decision of the court to produce two verdicts, one addressing Midhat's case and the other referring to the rest of the defendants. The two texts are almost identical in structure. The following discussion will focus on the sentence concerning Midhat.[78]

In line with the standard Nizamiye style, the text reveals nothing about the interpretive effort made in every act of judicial discretion. Similarly typical is the absence of emotional expressions and personal opinions of the judge concerning the gravity of the crimes or the morality of the perpetrators, a rhetorical feature that is typical of common-law judgments. The related absence of any reference to the effect of the crime on the wider society, whether in terms of policy or mores, is equally distinctive of the Nizamiye judgment. Nevertheless, bearing these typical features in mind, the Yıldız court ruling is on the whole an extraordinary text, exhibiting attributes that are not to be found in standard Nizamiye verdicts.

For one, the text is unusually lengthy, spreading over eighteen pages of dense handwriting. It does not conform with the Nizamiye formula in terms of its organization. Rather than casting arguments raised in the trial into laconic formulaic language, the text appears as an assembly of the narratives that were presented throughout the trial, concluding with the definitive narrative of the court. The text is arranged topically as follows:

1. A detailed summary of the bill of indictment, which included the prosecution's response to Midhat's narrative, in addition to specification of the evidence (testimonies and circumstantial) against Midhat and the other accomplices.
2. A summary of Midhat's narrative as stated in the trial and presentation of some of his answers in response to questions presented by the judge.
3. The judge's response to Midhat's narrative, presenting his culpability.
4. A summarized presentation of the case made by the public prosecutor during the trial.
5. A summarized presentation of Midhat's response to the statements of the public prosecutor in the trial.
6. The decision of the court in response to Midhat's request to interrogate the witnesses.
7. The verdict and sentence.

One of the most salient performative features of this text is the linguistic register chosen by its author.[79] The prose of the verdict is closer to older forms of Ottoman Turkish than to the simplified linguistic styles of the late nineteenth century. Generally speaking, written Turkish prose during the Ottoman centuries was complex, accessible to only a small fraction of the entire society. Following the emergence of an imperial consciousness among the ruling elite in the late fifteenth century, a set of stylistic registers materialized, characterized by a considerable presence of Arabic and Persian vocabulary and morphological structures. Previously known as "Turkish" (*Türkçe*), in the mid-nineteenth century the term *Ottoman* (*Osmanlıca*) came to signify the official language of the state as part of the effort of promoting an Ottoman identity as a mass framework of belonging. In this period, attempts were made to simplify the style identified by modern historians and linguists as "Middle Ottoman," namely, the language used from the sixteenth to the eighteenth centuries. Middle Ottoman was complex, consisting of lengthy, and at times obscure, sentences with no use of punctuation.[80] Although newspapers and other publications from the late century started to use a simplified Ottoman (known as "New Ottoman"), some state officials continued to use Middle Ottoman in their daily tasks.[81] It seems that use of Middle Ottoman in the late nineteenth century, when other stylistic options were available, was a sort of mannerism, a marker of high status and good education. In the judicial sphere, both Middle and New Ottoman were in use, although the court decisions that were published in the *Ceride-i Mehakim*, the professional official gazette of the Nizamiye judicial community, used New Ottoman though phrased in a highly professional register. The Yıldız court ruling echoed a Middle Ottoman style, with extremely long sentences, no punctuation, and occasional digressions and repetitions, which is a typical stylistic feature of Middle Ottoman.

The reason for this stylistic choice, unusual for Nizamiye court rulings, can be only speculated. Considering the objectives of this political trial, Middle Ottoman is the perfect platform for narrative maneuvering favored by lawyers. The complex syntax, with the sudden change of topics and narratives and abrupt digressions, allowed the author of the verdict to emphasize certain arguments while marginalizing or concealing others. In addition, it seems that Sururi Efendi, the presiding judge who authored the text, plausibly under Cevdet Paşa's scrutiny, made an effort to screen the irregularities in the trial through this entangled narrative. Hence, the performance of standard Nizamiye legalism was compromised.

A considerable part of the text presents Midhat's version, the way it had been presented in the trial and during the pretrial interrogation. It begins with Midhat's version as to how he had learned about Abdülaziz's death when coming late to the Bab-ı Ali and discovering that all the ministers had left for Feriye Palace. From the court's point of view, starting the account with this event was an effective rhetorical move, since Said Efendi, whom Midhat described as the individual who had informed him about the sultan's death, was denying this account in court.

The author's manipulative play with the narratives is evident, for instance, when Midhat's account about his encounter with the situation in

Feriye is abruptly interrupted by a sentence representing the court's view, saying that Midhat Paşa argued that he did not remember that the medical doctors were paid large sums of money and were given boxes of jewelry in return for the service, as the prosecution claimed. This account is followed by a chronological digression that does not make sense in terms of the narrative flow, when Midhat's version as to the circumstances of his arrest in Izmir is presented in detail. Once again, his version is presented authentically, and then the digression ends when the text returns to the prosecution with regard to Midhat's accountability in handling the situation immediately after the sultan's death.

The paşa, so the prosecution claimed, did not see that Murat's family would be interrogated, being content with "the false statement" of Fahri Bey, Abdülaziz's chamberlain, in a way that was "unacceptable and unheard of both legally and logically." As noted before, this latter normative judgmental prose, typical of the common-law discourse, is unusual in the Nizamiye discourse. Describing how Abdülaziz's mother, formerly the most powerful woman in the dynasty, was taken to the guard station at Feriye after the discovery of her son's body, the prosecution's narrative, presented in the court decision, is not short of melodramatic expression: "The valide was treated with cruelty that would not be acceptable even among savages. When asked to board the ship heading to Topkapı Palace, the Valide cried out 'you killed my son. Will you kill me as well.' This was reported under oath by Lieutenant Ahmet the Bosnian from the *Asakir-i Şahane* [stationed] in Feriye and Asitaneli Reşit Efendi."[82]

The prosecution's long narrative unfolds the evidence against the three conspiring paşas, Midhat, Nuri, and Mahmut: the removal of the sword from Abdülaziz's possession a half hour before he was found dead. Also emphasized is the impossibility of Midhat's claim that he had not been aware of the appointment of Mustafa the Wrestler and his fellow murderers to the service of Abdülaziz given that "no measure could be taken without the decision of the commission that had been agreed upon in the *Mabeyn* following the enthronement of Murat." This and other evidence—all of which is circumstantial—led to the conclusion that Midhat Paşa was an accomplice to the principal crime. The narrative is oddly unsystematic, as if pieces of information were joined up in random fashion. This haphazard mode of presentation was plausibly designed to obscure the fact that all the evidence was circumstantial.

The prosecution's version is followed in the ruling by representation of the judges' discussion. Once again, the very existence of such details in a Nizamiye court ruling is atypical. This part of the text is actually a repetition of the prosecution's argument, including the occasional digressions. At a certain point, the text moves from a third-voice narrative to a representation of questions that were addressed to Midhat by the court and his respective sentence. For instance: "[Midhat] stated that since this word had not been written, he conditioned his coming [to Istanbul] on assurances. Upon this, he was asked [']now that you realized that you were in danger, why didn't you apply to the most senior commander in Izmir[?']. He admitted, saying [']I did not think of it there.[']"[83]

The prosecution's version is scattered throughout the text, making a clear distinction between the voice of the court and the voice of the prosecution a difficult task. Bearing in mind the objectives of this political trial, the voice of the judges and the voice of the prosecution were the same, reverberating the master narrative designed by Cevdet and his ruler, Sultan Abdülhamit. The conclusion in the text, nevertheless, was far from obscure. Midhat's culpability and his sentence were expressed in the laconic style typical of all Nizamiye court rulings, with the indication of the relevant numbered clauses. The last sentence was the Nizamiye formulation that concluded every trial of grave crimes, as dictated by the Code of Criminal Procedure, informing that the verdict and the documents of the trial would be sent to the Court of Cassation for review within a week.

On July 8, 1881, the Court of Cassation issued its ruling.[84] In stark contrast with the lower court decision that it reviewed, the Court of Cassation's ruling was standard in its style. It consisted of three brief paragraphs on a single page and bore the seals of eight judges. The prose of the text and its structure matched the standard formula that could be found in every decision issued by this court. The first paragraph reported that the Court of Cassation read the verdict of the lower court and the related documents; the opinion of the chief public prosecutor; the petitions of Midhat

Paşa, Nuri Paşa, and Mahmut Paşa; and the requests for mitigation of the penalties. In line with the standard structure of the decisions issued by this judicial forum, the second paragraph described the opinion of the chief public prosecutor, which was presented orally before the court. The prosecutor declared that no procedural fault was found in the proceedings under review and recommended the Court of Cassation confirm the verdicts. The third paragraph formed the conclusion, specifying the codified clauses that had dictated the penalties and declaring that the position of the chief public prosecutor was accepted. Hence, the Court of Cassation rejected the petitions and confirmed the lower court decisions and sentences. Nothing in this laconic text reveals the extraordinary features of the verdicts reviewed.

To conclude, the Court of Cassation's ruling was the final chord in the legal motion that started with the pretrial interrogations. The standard configuration of this text was a perfect performance of Nizamiye legalism. However, juxtaposition of this text with the style of the Yıldız court decision represents the pendulum movement that characterized the performative aspects of the trial, which I have sought to demonstrate in this chapter. Namely, the participants in this political trial moved between a performance of legalism and conduct that formed an infringement of the legalist code of conduct. Obviously, such infringements are to be found in every modern court. However, in show trials, participants often suspend their performance of legalism intentionally in order to transmit messages to the mass audience that observes the trial, in the Yıldız Trial through the reports provided by the journalists and the diplomats who were present in the hearings.

The "show" opportunities apparent in show trials are not the exclusive prerogative of the prosecuting party who supposedly "runs the show," a trap that it often fails to foresee. As Yoram Meital demonstrates in the case of the revolutionary tribunals in Egypt, the free officers used the court to rewrite the country's hegemonic narrative. However, defendants and witnesses were equally aware of the trial's mass publicity, taking full advantage of it in expressing their own views and criticism about the officers' narratives.[85] The Yıldız court was different in the sense that the political threat that Midhat represented was not discussed as such. In other words, the court did not discuss the question of constitutionalism or any other theme of broad political significance; rather, it concentrated its efforts on eliminating the threat through establishing Midhat's criminal guilt.

4

Legal Burdens and Political Legacies

IN 1903, the authorities in Bulgaria, at that time a vassal state of the Ottoman Empire, decided to place a statute of Midhat Paşa in front of the central branch of the Agricultural Bank (Ziraat Sandığı) in Sofia. In addition, they decided to send to each of the branches of the bank a portrait of the admirable paşa, whom they considered the founder of this important financial institution. Immediately after learning about this initiative, the Ottoman high commissioner to Bulgaria, Ali Ferruh Bey, did not save any effort in aborting it. In a report about the measures he had taken in this regard, he described the initiative as a hostile act by the local Bulgarian authorities. Eventually, he secretly managed to convince the bank's director to avoid hanging the pictures and placing the statute at the central branch. To be on the safe side, the high commissioner made sure to receive from the director all the copies of Midhat's portrait, also trying to get the master copy. In his report to the palace, the high commissioner described Midhat as a traitor and a murderer, repeating what he had told to the Bulgarian authority, namely, that Midhat had nothing to do with the foundation of the Agricultural Bank.[1]

The struggle over Midhat's legacy had started in the trial and continued long after his death. Two of the three paşas who spent their last years in the fortress of Taif since the summer of 1881 died in the first week of May 1884. Shortly after their demise, the palace instructed the officials to inform a few members of Midhat's family about his death and publish the cause of death in the newspapers.[2] The dry wording of the directive discloses nothing about the intensity of the story that started in the moment the Yıldız Trial convicts set foot on the imperial steamship that carried them off to Taif.

The history of the Ottoman ruling elite is replete with episodes that beg for dramaturgical emplotment. Bearing in mind Hayden White's well-known typology, some of them can be narrated as a romance, like the mesmerizing love story between Süleyman the Lawgiver (r. 1520–66) and Hürem (Roxelana); many more events in this history could be narrated only as heartbreaking tragedies, like the slaughter of nineteen princes by Mehmet III (r. 1595–1603) upon his ascendency to the throne. With these episodes engraved in the collective memory of the Ottoman elite, each of the senior officials who received from the sultan the grand vizier's seal was aware of the risks involved. Violent death had been the destiny of many grand viziers throughout the Ottoman centuries, to such an extent that this figure assumed a tragic shade in popular literature and chronicles.[3] The staggering experiences of the Yıldız convicts in the years that followed the trial are nevertheless an exceptional story when compared to earlier events of such melodramatic nature. For one, the entire episode of the Yıldız Trial was a display of new notions about the law.

The rule-of-law discourse in the late nineteenth century was not merely a series of performative legalistic practices and statements. It was also a new set of rules of the game that placed unprecedented types of constrains on political actors. Even if Abdülhamit II fantasized about following in the steps of his predecessors and simply having his political enemies perished and then presented in some gruesome way at the gates of the palace to create a deterring effect, he could not act out this fantasy. Deterrence and vengeance remained important elements of exercising political power, but they had to be worked out within the boundaries set by the rule of law. Even when Abdülhamit was drifting toward extreme absolutism at the turn of the century, he never abandoned the desire of some three or four generations of Ottoman reformers to belong to "the civilized world." In the Hamidian period, this desire of the ruling elite was embedded in an ultrasensitive awareness of its image abroad. In Deringil's words, "The Turks were concerned to the point of obsession with their image."[4] The rule of law, imagined in terms of legal formalism, was perhaps the most powerful quintessence of the idea of civilization, requiring the ruler to leave behind "traditional" forms of physical elimination.

Another (related) feature of this story distinguishing it from former cases of Ottoman political tragedies corresponds with the modern modes of communication and governance. Ottoman officialdom of the second half of the nineteenth century left a plethora of paper trails like no other generation of bureaucrats. This abundance of documentation was an outcome of the expansion in the size of officialdom (in itself an expression of new ideas about administrative specialization) but also the result of the revolutionary invention of the telegraph, which was used by officials and military officers throughout the empire with gusto. In the 1880s, for instance, the Ministry of Telegraph complained occasionally about transmission "traffic jams" caused by officials' disregard of the instructions to use the telegraph only for urgent and brief messages.[5] As we saw in the previous chapter, the newspapers, rendering geographic distances irrelevant to the flow of information, used the telegraph intensely. Printing rendered information a commodity to be sold to and consumed by the masses. The Y generation of the early twenty-first century tends to think about the information technology of its time as a technological revolution. But considering the available means of communication prior to the invention of the telegraph, the introduction of the Internet is one consequence, albeit a major one, of a revolution that had started with the placement of the first telegraph poles. Similarly, the feverish attempts of twenty-first-century governments to contain the damage and embarrassments caused by Edward Snowden echoes Abdülhamit's no less frenzied attempts to deal with the potential, imagined, or real damages caused by the upshots of the Yıldız Trial. The sultan discovered that sending one of the most valued statesmen of the century to exile, incarcerating him in one of the toughest parts of his realm, did not resolve the embarrassment. At the same time, physical elimination, however desired a solution, was not easy to execute, given the circumstances.

The present chapter, like this entire study, owes a great deal to the work of Uzunçarşılı, who collected and published the archival documentation related to the years that the Yıldız convicts spent in Taif. Committed to his Rankean perception of history writing, Uzunçarşılı believed that the documents spoke for themselves. Hence, the readers of his book *Midhat Paşa and the Taif Prisoners* (*Midhat Paşa ve Taif Mahkumları*), while offered a significant porthole to the captivating story of the prisoners, are left with no historical analysis and almost no contextualization. The purpose of the present discussion, then, is to take Uzunçarşılı's important endeavor one step further and at the same time offer a critical engagement with his approach and its legacy in Ottomanist historiography. In addition, the following discussion will unfold the aftermath of the Yıldız political trial while stressing the meaning of political justice when exercised in the context of the Ottoman "passage to modernity." It seems to me that had the details of this story been made accessible to English readers before, it would have been turned into a suspense movie long ago.

POLITICAL PRISONERS

The prisoners who boarded the imperial steamship on July 16, 1881, at this point unaware of their final destination, may have been too nervous to notice the ironic and coincidental symbolism. The elegant steamship carried the name of Prince Yusuf İzzettin Efendi (1857–1916), Sultan Abdülaziz's eldest son, who might have ended up a sultan himself, as his father had hoped, under different circumstances. The eight prisoners were silent when led to their cabins, each one of them lost in thoughts about the catastrophic developments of the passing month and the miserable future ahead. The captain was instructed to prevent the prisoners from contacting each other. The three paşas, Midhat (age sixty), Mahmut (in his early forties), and Nuri (age unknown), were led to their cabins on the ship's upper deck. The rest of the prisoners occupied smaller cabins on the lower deck. This latter group consisted of former palace officials Fahri Bey (age thirty) and Seyyit Bey (age forty-four); former military officers İzzet Bey (age thirty-three), Necip Bey (age twenty-eight), and Ali Bey (age unknown); and the convicted murderers Mustafa the Wrestler (in his early sixties), Hacı Mehmet (age thirty-nine), and Mustafa the Algerian (age unknown).

The telegraph network allowed the palace almost real-time monitoring of the journey. The steamship had to stop for fueling and supplies in various ports along the way. Each stopover was also used for reporting to

4. The imperial yacht, *İzzettin*, Istanbul, 1880–93. Courtesy of the Library of Congress, Prints & Photographs Division, Abdul Hamid II Collection, Reproduction Number LC-USZ62-82111.

the palace about the whereabouts of the ship and unusual developments. On July 31, upon stopping at the island of Rhodes, the officer Osman reported to the palace via telegraph that Nuri Paşa was displaying "signs of insanity and blackouts."[6] This condition, no doubt caused by extreme anxiety, would turn into full-fledged and chronic psychosis in the following years, routinely reported by his jailers. Actually, the fact that the other two paşas were not losing their minds already during the journey to Taif is something of a wonder, given that they were confined to their chambers most of the time, allowed to breathe fresh air on the deck only on arrival to Rhodes. After Rhodes, the ship crossed the Mediterranean to enter the Suez Canal. Following a brief stop at the port of Ismailia, the town that was founded by Khedive Ismail eighteen years earlier as part of the Suez Canal project, the ship arrived in early August in the city of Suez, on the north coast of the Gulf of Suez. Most probably, at this point in their voyage the prisoners had a good idea about its endpoint. The *İzzettin* sailed in the

Red Sea, arriving in Jeddah and then Mecca in early August. If the present account was part of a (historical) novel, the encounter of the paşas with the sharif of Mecca would have to be narrated as a foreshadowing, bearing in mind that the same sharif was arrested a year later because he was suspected of supporting the release of the prisoners.

Already before arriving in Taif, the paşas were aware of their grim situation. Upon arrival in Jeddah, Midhat had asked permission to withdraw money from his bank account in England but was denied. The paşas' request to make a pilgrimage to the Kaaba was also denied, no doubt by the direct order of the palace. Their visit to the sharif, immediately upon landing at Taif, marked the end of their journey and the beginning of their lives as inmates at the fortress of Taif. The officials who escorted them reported that each of the paşas kissed the hand of the sharif, who told them, "Make yourself comfortable." The jailers led them to the cells that had been prepared for them at the barracks.[7]

Telling from his title, the convict Hacı Mehmet had been to the Hijaz before as a pilgrim to Mecca, so at least he was not surprised to discover the overall wretchedness of the place. His fellow convicts, namely, Mustafa the Wrestler and Mustafa the Algerian, looked around them in despair, for Taif seemed like the antithesis of Istanbul. Some of the other prisoners, who had been part of officialdom, had come across godforsaken villages and towns before, but they had not lived there as permanent residents. In the eyes of the Ottoman elite, the Hijaz represented the ultimate exile. Living conditions were difficult by any standard of the late nineteenth century, dictated by recurring draughts, extreme heat and humidity in the long summers, and occasional floods in the winter. As noted by William Ochsenwald, "The overwhelming impression gained by visitors to the Hijaz was of bleak desert, bleaker mountains, and widespread poverty among nomads and townspeople."[8]

The Ottoman dynasty drew some of its legitimacy from its symbolic role as the protector of Mecca and Medina. Beginning from its Ottoman occupation in the early sixteenth century, the Hijaz had been a unique space within the imperial domains. The Hashemite sharifs, who had ruled Mecca in their capacity as descendants of the Prophet Muhammad, maintained much of their political power under Ottoman rule. Tax exemptions and occasional provisions indicated the emblematic importance of the Hijaz as a source of religious legitimacy to the Ottoman dynasty. Nevertheless, if sanitary and water conditions provide any indication of the central government's interest in a province, the fact that the holiest cities were also among the dirtiest in the empire is somewhat puzzling. Throughout the nineteenth century, cholera epidemics were like an incessant curse that befell the Hijaz, bringing extremely high rates of mortality among pilgrims and the local population through recurring outbursts of the disease, the most severe one occurring in 1865, claiming the lives of thirty thousand people. The authorities took some measures to cope with cholera, such as quarantine policies, but motivation to lead a comprehensive policy of improving sanitary conditions seemed to be lacking.[9]

Ottoman Taif, a small town on the slopes of the Sarawat mountain range, was a provincial center, but it was nothing like the modern Saudi city of 1.2 million people that it is today. Populated by a few thousand in the late nineteenth century, the town, which offered a relatively more comfortable climate in summer, served (and the Saudi city still does) as a summer resort for the notables of Mecca, although the journey from Mecca required almost twenty-four hours of horse riding. The town contained twelve mosques, some two hundred shops, a public bath, a barracks, and a fortress.[10] In 1862 the barracks was renovated, and the government mansion was built there. The special status of the Yıldız political prisoners was evident in the decision to settle them in a building affiliated with the government mansion. Troops of the regular (Nizamiye) army guarded this two-story structure, which was made of mud bricks.[11]

When entering their prison, the three paşas met an old acquaintance, a political ally really, former *şeyhülislam* Hasan Hayrullah Efendi. The forty-seven-year-old *alim* had served in the most prestigious positions that the religious career path could offer and was known for his relatively liberal inclinations. Hayrullah was among the personalities consulted by Midhat back in the mid-1870s, when crafting his constitutional designs. On May 1876, Sultan Abdülaziz appointed Hayrullah Efendi to *şeyhülislam* in an attempt to appease the protests of the religious students, the *softa*, who were demonstrating in the streets of the capital.[12] Hayrullah Efendi was one of the plotters who deposed Abdülaziz in the same year, also authoring the *fetva* that legitimized the coup. Ninety-three days later, he had to write another *fetva*, this time sanctioning the dethronement of Sultan Murat. His association with Midhat and the liberal circles in general turned him into a political risk to the new sultan. As part of his overall retreat from his commitment to constitutionalism, Abdülhamit dismissed Hayrullah Efendi on July 1877. Two years later, he sent the former *şeyhülislam* to exile in Medina. The Yıldız court convicted Hayrullah Efendi in absentia, sentencing him to imprisonment in Taif. As we will see later, he may have been the individual responsible for the fact that we have more than one account about Midhat Paşa's death.

Much of what we know about the life of the inmates in Taif emanates from routine correspondence between the local authorities and the palace. The local authorities reported regularly about the situation of the prisoners via telegraph and post. Every member of Ottoman officialdom was aware of the sultan's desire to get involved in the nitty-gritty details of everyday administration, an urge resulting from a combination of motivations: a sincere drive for reform and improvement of his realms, a workaholic personality, and an almost compulsive pursuit after real and imagined political enemies.[13] The senior officials who had to carry the burden of handling the prisoners knew that the sultan's interest in Midhat was exceptional even by the standards of Hamidian obsession for control.

The unique structure of political power in the Hijaz added another layer of complexity that had a bearing on the prisoners' lives. Ever since the Ottoman occupation of the Hijaz, the local authority had been a fragile equilibrium between the sharif of Mecca and the Ottoman governor, a power balance that was never institutionalized or codified. The nature of political power possessed by each of these two figures was determined by changing circumstances, Ottoman policies, and the personalities of sharifs and governors. When Ottoman rule in the Hijaz was restored in 1840 following some two decades of Egyptian rule, command over the military forces in the Hijaz was the governor's major source of power, in addition to the impact of his reports on palace decisions concerning the deposition of sharifs. According to Ochsenwald, in the nineteenth century, the sharifs possessed more power than the governors did.[14] In a recent study, however, M. Talha Çiçek argues that disagreements between sharifs and governors

5. Taif fortress, 1890s. Courtesy of Sinan Çuluk.

were an exception to the rule in the nineteenth century and that negotiations of the local authority with bedouin tribes were a demonstration of a relatively stable cooperation between the sharif and the governor. To be sure, the political status of both dignitaries was at the hands of the sultan, and the sharif was an integral part of the imperial bureaucracy.[15]

In any case, the political intricacies that were unique to the Hijaz determined daily lives of the Yıldız prisoners during their first year in Taif. Since the early 1840s, most of the sharifs were appointed from among two of the most powerful families of the sharifian circles: the ʿAwns and the Zaids. Sharif Abd al-Muttalib Efendi (1790–1886) was appointed in 1880 as part of the Hamidian divide-and-rule policy in the Hijaz, with the expectation that he would enforce Ottoman control and block British influence. Already in 1880, before the trial, Abd al-Muttalib had made sure to express before the sultan his hostility toward Hayrullah Efendi on account of his oppositional views.[16]

In addition to the issue of Zaid-ʿAwn politics, there was the rivalry between the sharif and the governors. The ninety-year-old sharif, who was appointed against the advice of Governor Naşid Paşa, had hawkish stands concerning the bedouin tribes and the British, whose interests in the region were expanding, and influence among the tribes was growing. During his two years in office, the sharif saw the dismissal and appointment of three governors. Meanwhile, the commander of the local troops, the war hero of the Siege of Plevna (1877), Osman Nuri Paşa, was building his own power base.[17] A seasoned politician, Abd al-Muttalib Efendi identified the Yıldız prisoners as a strong political card to be used for advancing political schemes. He used his authority over the prisoners to display loyalty to the sultan, taking harsh measures that included chaining them by their legs, an order that he annulled after a while, plausibly because of British intervention. On December 1881, he wrote to the palace, complaining about the lenient policy of the governor, Safvet Paşa, toward the prisoners. The sharif claimed that the governor provided Hayrullah Efendi with a concubine and funds and delivered to Midhat bills from the provincial treasury. These gestures, to the extent that they indeed took place, could be interpreted in Istanbul as an act of political resistance. Safvet Paşa was promptly dismissed.[18]

An associate of the sultan, who served as the commander of the Hijaz, Osman Nuri Paşa was now appointed governor of the Hijaz, entrusted with the task of restoring the power balance between the governor and the sharif and regaining stability, which had been waning under the sharif. In September 1882, Osman Nuri arrested Abd al-Muttalib, accusing him of corruption and oppression of the local population. The powerful war hero deprived the sharif from political power, clearly under the orders of the sultan, who had suspected for a while that the sharif had been cultivating warm relationships with the British.[19] When Osman Nuri Paşa assumed his new position as governor, he received from the palace clear instructions about his priorities.[20] The order to take every measure to prevent the Yıldız prisoners from absconding was equal in importance to the orders concerning the handling of the Sanusi tribe, one of the gravest political issues in the Hijaz at the time.[21]

How justified was the center's concern about a potential escape of the prisoners? Abdülhamit earned the reputation of a paranoiac, an image nurtured by his absolutist inclination, a hostile European media, vocal political opposition of exiled Ottomans in Europe, and his personal fostering of a huge network of covert informers. However, the circumstances of his enthronement and the several violent oppositional actions that occurred during his reign reassured the sultan that his concerns were all but irrational.[22] Personally involved in attempts to reform the Ottoman prison network, the sultan believed that an exodus of Midhat was a real possibility. In the most comprehensive study thus far on the Ottoman prison system during the late nineteenth and early twentieth centuries, Kent Schull reconstructs the institutional and ideological developments that transformed this institution. The Ottoman ruling elite of the 1850s adopted the notion that the state of prisons represented the level of civilization in every given country. While creation of a modern-style prison system was stated as a major task in Abdülaziz's Reform Edict of 1856, implementation on an empire-wide scale did not begin before the Hamidian era. In fact, until the late century, there was no prison *system*. When Abdülhamit ascended to the throne, the new "science" of incarceration had been in progress in France for several decades, reflecting new ideas about criminal justice.[23] Drawing inspiration from French and Prussian prison regulations and motivated by its passion to be part of the civilized world, the Hamidian regime invested some bureaucratic effort and capital in structuring a modern prison system. However, successes in this field were modest, limited to the establishment of few model prisons and production of regulations that set the administrative grounds for a future more humane system, which did develop under the CUP regime. Hence, in the early 1880s, when Midhat and his fellow prisoners served their sentences in Taif, there was some similarity between their situation and the conditions of most of the prisoners across the empire, who also lived in makeshift structures located in fortresses or military or government compounds, enduring the hardships caused by meager sanitary environments.[24]

However, there were also major differences between the prison lives of the Yıldız convicts and the lives of ordinary prisoners. For one, they did not have to share their spaces with the usual riffraff of criminals and convicts. As noted by Schull, the typical Ottoman prison was overcrowded, housing petty criminals together with felons, adults with children, convicts with suspects, and at times males with females.[25] In addition, each of the paşas was allowed to keep a servant to perform daily tasks such as cooking and laundry (except for times when servants were removed as a means of putting pressure on the prisoners). On the other hand, in contrast with regular prisoners, who could receive funds from family members, the Yıldız convicts totally depended on their jailers for food. Considering the fact that the three paşas were very wealthy individuals who still possessed properties and capital, this dependence was an additional source for frustration.

Given the provisional nature of Ottoman incarceration facilities, breakouts were common. Nevertheless, the potential damage of a possible flight of political prisoners, all the more so when one of them was a great statesman venerated in Europe, was incomparable with the consequences of regular inmates' breakouts. Correspondence between the palace and the local authorities reveals that this scenario was a concern as soon as the prisoners arrived in Taif, justifying direct communication between the local authorities and the sultan. But how likely was the risk of breakout in the case of Midhat and the other prisoners? As noted before, Abd al-Muttalib Efendi identified "his" prisoners as a political asset given the sultan's personal interest in their situation. In early September 1881, the sharif wrote a letter addressed directly to the sultan, informing him that an Egyptian newspaper published a report about the intentions of some Arab sheikhs to rescue the three paşas from jail. The sharif specified the precautions that had been taken, such as bolstering the military troops that guarded the prison and conducting investigations about "public and private opinions inside and outside." He asked for two additional squads of soldiers, also reporting about the need to cover the fortress's windows with metal. No less pressing was the need, according to the sharif, to banish from Taif a certain Arab family, who supposedly plotted to rescue the jailed paşas owing to enmity that had broken out between them and the governor. He also recommended the dismissal of the governor.[26] It is impossible to determine how much truth was in this account on the Arab tribe's intention to rescue the paşas, but similar concerns occupied the authorities in the following years.

Anxieties about British intentions to release the paşas by using military force reached a high point in the spring of 1883, when the British occupation of Egypt in September 1882 turned into a serious threat to Ottoman sovereignty in the Hijaz.[27] In February 1883, the governor informed the palace that the British admiral in Suakin, a port town on the west coast of the Red Sea, was planning to release Midhat Paşa and Mahmut Paşa. This word of warning initiated a rather nervous correspondence between the palace and the grand vizier, resulting with the Foreign Ministry summoning the British ambassador, Lord Dufferin, to express concern. The ambassador promised to confer on the matter with his superior, the minister of foreign affairs, Lord Granville. Reporting to the sultan about these developments, the grand vizier wrote that the ambassador asked for information about the prisoners' well-being and comfort. This request touched a sensitive nerve, as evidenced in a draft of an imperial decree written by the sultan, saying that the ambassador's request for information about the well-being and comfort of the prisoners had offended the sovereign, as the inmates were sentenced to death in court, in conformity with the law. In Uzunçarşılı's opinion, the sultan's fear of a British intention to liberate the political prisoners was the reason for his decision to have them killed.[28]

Ciphered telegrams exchanged between French diplomats and their government suggest that in January and February 1883, someone in the Hijaz indeed considered a rescue mission. In early January, the French vice consul in Jeddah, de Lastalot, reported to his prime minister that he had been asked to assist in extricating the three paşas. The consul wrote that he refused, but he also added that "contact [with the plotters] can be made again, in consideration of our interests," asking for instructions. The French prime minister accepted the opinion of the ambassador in Istanbul, ordering the vice consul to "refrain from participating in this project in any way."[29]

RECONSIDERING LEGALISTIC NARRATIONS OF HISTORY

Uzunçarşili was the last historian to offer a systematic study of the Yıldız Trial and its aftermath. His pedantic work in collecting and presenting the documents is perhaps the reason that his narrative has not been reconsidered in professional historiography. The documentary strength of Uzunçarşılı's work and his position as one of the forefathers of modern Turkish historiography provided his scholarship on the Yıldız Trial with the status of a definitive work. Later historians of the Ottoman Empire have never casted doubt on Uzunçarşılı's interpretation of the trial, accepting his verdict as the last word on the subject. It is exactly the status of "definitive work" that calls for reconsideration, for the impact of definitive works on the way history is imagined and reproduced is immense. Paraphrasing Michel Foucault (although not implementing his method devoutly), I am interested in the archaeology of the knowledge about the first legalist political trial in the Middle East. To continue the metaphor of archaeology, the event in question is not covered by many layers of historiographic earth. Actually, there were only a few layers, but quite thick ones, the thickest of which being Uzunçarşılı's scientific endeavor. I am interested, therefore, in highlighting the kind of historical imagination that guided Uzunçarşılı, arguing that modern-legalist consciousness constituted his work.

Legalism, since its emergence in the second half of the nineteenth century, has constituted both legal and historical imaginations. This argument owes to Paul Kahn's conceptualization of the law as a cultural phenomenon and the rule of law as a fluid idea that possess no intrinsic quality.[30] Quite frequently, interpreters of political events (historians, publicists, and others) reify the notion of rule of law while paying little or no attention to its conceptual obscurity. Reifications provide an effective means of advancing political action because they camouflage political positions, creating the impression of objective representation of reality. The Yıldız Trial was one episode in a chain of events that were political in nature. The trial attracted considerable public attention because it involved the most senior political figures of the time, including three sultans, making it an event of "historic magnitude." The Ottoman government's treatment of the convicts after the court decisions were issued was yet another indication of the fact that the entire saga was a matter of political enmities. Nevertheless, historian Uzunçarşılı reconstructed the events through a legalistic prism focused on evidence. In a way, he seemed to imagine his mission the way an impartial examining magistrate (*müstantık*, in the terminology of the Nizamiye courts) would think about his work. This fact is evidenced through the rhetoric he employed, including the use of cautious language in the introductions and conclusions of the three books that he published on the trial, while letting the documents "speak for themselves" in the rest of the books. Also telling is the rhetoric of "weighing the evidence" throughout the books as well as Uzunçarşılı's effort in rendering the question of fairness, a major theme in the entire discussion.

In the final analysis, then, the question that guided Uzunçarşılı and nearly all the historians who mentioned the trial in their works was the conformity of the trial and its aftermath with the rule of law. In a way, Uzunçarşılı's work, through the many endorsements of his verdict by way of references in historiography, became an integral part of the story of the Yıldız Trial. Uzunçarşılı's professional authority and the heavy Rankean burden carried by Ottomanist scholarship on the nineteenth century (especially but not exclusively in Turkish historiography) affixed his legalistic interpretation as the last word on Midhat's demise. But reducing this story to the question of its legality has not proven a fruitful course of historical interpretation, considering that the systematic study of one of the most exciting stories of the nineteenth century remained the province of a single historian more than a half century ago. As argued by Kahn, however:

> The rule of law is just one way of perceiving the meaning of political events. To see the event as an instance of law's rule is to suppress alternative perceptions of the same event. Those alternatives do not disappear. . . . Instead of attempting to measure legal meanings against an independent or objective truth, we need to measure legal meanings against alternative forms of organizing and understanding political experience. These alternatives are no more true than law's world: each is an historically contingent product of the imagination.[31]

In the previous chapters, I have tried to offer nonlegalistic interpretations of the trial, inter alia by rendering the performance of legalism a subject matter. In other words, I have tried to avoid the procedure of "weighing the evidence." By reconstructing the Yıldız Trial as a political trial constituted by Ottoman legalism, exhibited in the oscillation of the court between legal formalism and violation thereof, the interpretation offered in this study has sought to avoid the exercise of assessing political events against a reified rule of law. Reconstructing the trial's performative aspects in and outside the courtroom has allowed me to offer an alternative, nonlegalistic, interpretation. At this point in my discussion, I wish to focus on the competition between two narratives about the deaths of Midhat Paşa and Mahmud Paşa in Taif, a conflict decided long ago thanks to Midhat's historiographical and political advocates. It cannot be emphasized enough that determining which of the narratives reflects the true events is not an objective of the present discussion, although there can be only one valid narrative.

THE OFFICIAL'S NARRATIVES

On March 14, 1884, military physician Lieutenant (*Yüzbaşı*) Mehmet Naşid Efendi wrote the following report: "During an examination of the inmate Midhat Paşa several days ago, a big carbuncle was identified. The necessary treatment was applied. Today, the aforementioned carbuncle was diagnosed as [a symptom of] anthrax (şirpençe)."[32] Anthrax is a lethal bacterial disease known in the Mediterranean for centuries.[33] A skin lesion that deteriorates into an ulcer with a black center a few days after exposure is a common symptom of the disease. Given the lethal nature of this disease, together with the unsanitary environment in the fortress of Taif and the meager medical services provided in the village, the odds for recovery were extremely low. In early May, Governor Osman Paşa informed the palace that Midhat died on May 7, 1884, as a result of a carbuncle that had grown on his left shoulder and that he was buried in the Ibn 'Abbas cemetery. A few days later, the governor sent another note, reporting the death of Mahmut Paşa on May 13, due to typhus.[34]

Dr. Mehmet Naşid Efendi, who had determined the paşas' deaths, submitted detailed reports about the causes of death. The reports arrived in the palace along with accounts written by other military and civil officials concerning the functioning of the physician. The practice of officials reporting on the conduct of colleagues was typical of the Hamidian bureaucratic machinery. In his reports, the physician described the paşas' medical condition in earlier years and the treatments applied. The reports do not leave an impression of a cover-up. Rather, they read like a dry account by a doctor who makes an effort to carry out his medical duties in difficult circumstances. In the case of Midhat, for instance, the doctor described the development of a cyst on Midhat's eyelid, which he cured by applying a medication that he had managed to obtain from a colleague in Lebanon. He also described his attempts to help Midhat in dealing with the loss of teeth, a condition that resulted from digestion problems. The devoted doctor was trying to alleviate his patient's suffering by using sodium carbonate as well as a mixture of chocolate and condensed milk. Interpreting the entire detailed report as an attempt to conceal Midhat's deteriorating health condition makes no sense, and similar is the impression given by the medical report on Mahmut Paşa. The latter, according to the report, had suffered from chronic rheumatism, though he was less than fifty years old, an ailment that had worsened during the trial. The doctor described how he applied conventional medications sent from the imperial capital for helping the paşa with his recurring anxiety attacks. The description of the early stages of typhus, which eventually got worse and killed Mahmut Paşa, is similarly exhaustive:

> Mahmut Pasha was addicted to excessive eating; I heard him saying that once he had eaten a whole lamb on his own. On the evening of April 1, 1884, Mahmut Paşa called for me because he felt discomfort in his stomach. I asked him what did he eat and drink [before]. He said that suddenly he had felt an increased appetite and ate a soldiers' mess-tin of rice. He then entered the little residential *hamam*, but for some reason he fell down and a bruise appeared above his hipbone. The wound was bandaged with an alcohol-soaked flannel. He was offered a medication for his stomach, but he said that he already has this medicine, and rejected the offer.[35]

On June 6, the six officers who were in charge of the military units that guarded the prison wrote their own report. They confirmed the validity of the physician's report concerning Midhat. They testified that the doctor responded quickly to the emergency, removing the corpse to the infirmary, where the ritual of ablution was performed. Uzunçarşılı dates this report to May 7, 1884 (the Rumi date of 25 Nisan 1300), the same date that

Dr. Naşid Efendi authored his own report.[36] But it is an error, considering the actual date that appears on the officers' report, which is saved in the Ottoman archives.[37] The reason for mentioning this error is the suspicion arising from the date on which this document was authored in terms of the plausibility of a coordinated cover-up effort. The mistaken date might indicate such an effort, whereas the fact that it took the officers a month to author this letter might suggest that it was a response to an inquiry from the palace in an attempt to address uncertainties. Six days later, on May 13, the same officers sent another report, confirming that Mahmut Paşa died as a result of typhus.[38]

One can interpret the documents that sustain the officials' accounts as a well-orchestrated plot meant to paper over the murder of the paşas under the sultan's order, a crime that had been planned by employing covert communication, either verbal or written, perhaps by authoring documents that were intentionally destroyed. But this latter possibility is as plausible, and perhaps less plausible, when compared to the likelihood that the paşas' deaths were an undesired occurrence from the sultan's point of view, given the possible British response, which the sultan surely took into consideration. When he learned about the paşas' demise, Sultan Abdülhamit could not foreknow the relatively indifferent British response, certainly not after he had reached the conclusion that they were preparing a rescue plan. Arguably, the correspondence and the measures that were taken as soon as the news arrived in the palace seem like an effort to contain a situation before it got out of control.

The sultan read the medical reports with much interest, responding with an imperial decree that demanded from the governor further clarification. On May 27, the governor wrote an apologetic report, explaining that Naşid Efendi was the only permanent doctor in a village of three to four hundred households, responsible for the health of the soldiers and the inmates as well.[39] Meanwhile, the palace sent a ciphered telegram to the governor, informing him that "vicious suspicions" arose concerning Midhat Paşa's death, and since it would not be lawful to rely on the opinion of a single doctor in determining the cause of death, the governor was instructed to conduct a further investigation. The instructions could not be more specific. They also could not be more upsetting, as far as Governor

Osman Paşa was concerned: he was ordered to pick up some Meccan doctors as well as an "esteemed official," in addition to the sharif, and travel with them to Taif to supervise the opening of the paşas' graves and watch over the autopsies that were ordered. This procedure, so the palace had commanded, had to be observed by the local authorities in Taif, in addition to local dignitaries. According to this order, "The autopsy should be performed in conformity with procedure, in rigor, and in detail," resulting with a report whose copies would be sent to the sultan and the Bab-ı Ali.[40]

Shocked by this request, the governor wrote back to the palace, saying that everybody knew that illness was the cause of both deaths, and opening the graves would be an inappropriate measure. Even if performed, wrote Osman Paşa, decomposition of the bodies in such a warm environment would prevent an effective autopsy. The palace replied decisively that the sultan's order had to be executed in order to refute the suspicions. The governor complied, performed the horrid procedure, interrogated the related officials, and dispatched to the palace a report confirming that the deaths were an outcome of natural causes.[41] Later correspondence shows that the palace remained eager to gather information about the causes of death, asking the impressions of Meccan officials who were not directly involved. For instance, on July 21, 1884, the chief secretary of Mecca, Fikri Şerif Efendi, had to send a report, merely repeating the details that were already known, also emphasizing that he did not see what happened after the paşas' deaths because he had stayed in Mecca.[42]

These inquiries, along with the exchanges between the palace and the local authorities following the deaths of Midhat and Mahmut, while not refuting the possibility that the palace had ordered the killing of the inmates, do justify doubts with regard to this possibility, which later generations accepted as an indisputable truth. Doubts should also arise from the sort of effort made by the palace in gathering information about the paşas' deaths. Indeed, the Hamidian regime was known for the energies invested in managing its image, but the communication demonstrated above does not look like a predesigned performance. Rather, it seems like a frantic attempt at containing an event that could easily develop into a serious international political affair, from the kind that haunted the Hamidian regime. Uzunçarşılı's verdict, however, was not founded on the officials' correspondence, which he nevertheless presented. Rather, his conclusion that the paşas were killed under the sultan's order was based on another set of evidence, which can be identified as the life project of Midhat's son, Ali Haydar Bey.

THE LIFE MISSION OF ALI HAYDAR MIDHAT

Midhat's son, Ali Haydar, was nine years old when he had to witness the hasty parting of his father through the backyard gate of the family's mansion in Izmir, never to be seen again. In the blink of an eye, the family of one of the strongest men in the empire lost its patriarch and, for a short while, its sense of security. During the days that followed the arrest, Midhat's family, consisting of two wives, three daughters, a son, and Midhat's sister, was no doubt in a panic. The family sent Ali Haydar to the British consulate, where he stayed for more than two months. At the same time, they had some reason to remain hopeful, given the paşa's attempts to secure foreign protection. But the paşa's arrest, and the trial that followed, put an end to all hope. For a nine-year-old child, grown enough to absorb and remember the commotion and the trepidation, the events were no doubt a trauma that had an enormous impact on his later life. In addition to the anguish caused by the stunning arrest, the news that the family received about the trial in Istanbul, and the agony that resulted from the censored letters that their paşa sent from prison in Taif, the palace confined the family to Izmir for the years to come. Many years later, in the mid-twentieth century, Midhat's descendants told historian Fanny Davis that Abdülhamit's officers harassed the family long after the paşa was dead.[43] It is not entirely clear what they meant by "harassment," but clearly financial security was not a problem. Immediately after the paşa's arrest, the grand vizier assigned considerable stipends to each of the family members under the sultan's order, to be paid from the palace's treasury. The son, three daughters, and the sister of Midhat were made eligible for a monthly pension of one thousand *kuruş* each; his first wife, Fatma Naime Hanım, received a monthly pension of three thousand *kuruş*; his second, younger, wife (and Ali Haydar's mother), Şehriban Hanım, received a pension of two thousand *kuruş*.[44] In addition, the sultan never deprived the family of its wealth.

As the single male in Midhat's nuclear family, Ali Haydar grew up with the awareness that he was the one to carry the burden of vindicating his father's name. This task was not only a matter of honor, a sense of infringed justice, and the emotional attachment of a son to his tormented father, but also a matter of regaining social status. Patronage networks cemented Ottoman elite. Clearly, the banishment of the father, and his death in Taif, signified the risk of losing social position and laying bare the prospects for Ali Haydar in Ottoman elite. However, in the coming years, the family discovered that while restricted to Izmir and constantly monitored by the palace, it did not lose its weight in the Ottoman elite. Izmir of the late century, it should be stressed, was a metropolis of more than two hundred thousand, an important apiary of foreign and local interests, second only to Istanbul in dynamism and scope.[45] The family maintained connections with foreign diplomats and officials, as well as Ottoman elites who had remained committed to Midhat's political causes. These connections, as we will see shortly, would serve Ali Haydar in cultivating his own political career. The fact that Midhat's family maintained its position at the highest echelon of Ottoman elite was evident in the sort of education that Ali Haydar received. Though Izmir was a growing cosmopolitan port city, the family considered its educational opportunities inadequate. After Ali Haydar completed elementary school, the family asked for the palace's permission to send the boy to higher education in Europe. The palace refused, but it never thought that denying Ali Haydar from the venue of higher education in prestigious schools was an option, therefore allowing him to pursue it in Beirut, where he studied in French schools.[46]

In 1892 Ali Haydar returned from Beirut, to reunite with his family in Izmir. Upon arrival in Izmir, as soon as he left the steamship, he learned that his twenty-seven-year-old sister, Vesime, had died of tuberculosis. Lifting the body of his dead sister was an event that left a deep impression in him, as he wrote in his memoirs many years later, evoking feelings of revenge against the person whom he considered as the family's greatest foe, Sultan Abdülhamit.[47] The summer of 1893 was the point in time when Ali Haydar, then twenty-one years old, took his first steps as an adult. He petitioned the sultan, requesting to put an end to the family's exile of twelve years in Izmir and allow him and his younger sister to return to Istanbul. In his petition, he mentioned his mother's death as the reason for this request. It seems that Ali Haydar was encouraged by permission that he had received from the sultan some two months earlier to leave Izmir for a short trip to the province of Beirut in order to take care of the family's possessions there.[48]

In 1899, at the age of twenty-seven, Ali Haydar managed to abscond from the Ottoman territory and find safe haven in Europe, enjoying the support of European, specifically British, officials as well as Ottoman exiles. Very soon the news reached the palace, which sent scores of messages to Ali Haydar, mainly through Ottoman ambassadors and telegrams sent to the hotels where he stayed, trying to convince him to reconsider his treason and return to his homeland. The damage caused by Ali Haydar's absconding, from the palace's perspective, was only beginning to surface when Prince Hüseyin Kamil, the heir of the Khedivial throne, invited Ali Haydar to settle down in Egypt. The connection was made through a former personal secretary of Midhat Paşa, Vasıf Kılıçian Efendi, who was a close friend of the prince. The fact that Midhat's son was becoming a public figure of great importance was also apparent in a letter he received from the Prince of Wales, informing Ali Haydar that the British prime minister, Lord Salisbury, promised full protection.[49]

In his memoirs, Ali Haydar, who had added "Midhat" to his name at the turn of the century, writes that he first heard that his father died as a result of strangling when reading documents that a British friend handed to him in Egypt. Until then, his mother had hidden from him the details of his father's death. This discovery, so he writes, turned him into a full-fledged rebel through his publications against the sultan.[50] Ali Haydar set out on a political crusade aimed at clearing his father's name and challenging the version of the Hamidian regime concerning the cause of his father's death. At the outset, this campaign was not restricted to the business of Midhat's guiltlessness. Rather, he designed it as an act of general political opposition to the Hamidian regime. The opening shot for Ali Haydar's campaign was a handwritten essay that he sent to the sultan in 1900. Ali Haydar's ambitious political agenda, which went far beyond the objective of exonerating his father, was evident in the fact that the essay had nothing to do with the Yıldız Trial. Instead, it unfolded Ali Haydar's observations about the "Eastern Question," representing ideas that had been circulating among the Ottoman opposition in Europe. The only parts of the essay that included reference to Midhat Paşa were the introductory passages, where he accused the Hamidian bureaucracy for its persecution of Ali Haydar for the mere reason that he was Midhat's son.[51]

At the turn of the century, after more than two decades on the throne and years of detrimental publications in the international press, Abdülhamit had no illusions about his ability to stop Ali Haydar from embarrassing the Ottoman regime in Europe. In the following years, the sultan received routine reports from his ambassadors and agents on Ali Haydar's whereabouts, his meetings with foreign political leaders, and interviews that he gave to foreign newspapers.[52] Abdülhamit was aware of the major role played by Ali Haydar in the vibrant opposition of the CUP in Europe and Egypt, leading the pro-British camp in the organization and donating money to the movement.[53] However, there was nothing the palace could do to stop Midhat's devoted son from spreading his own chronicle on the Yıldız Trial and its aftermath. Against the background of the waning image of the Hamidian regime in Europe, and encouraged by European politicians and Ottoman exiled opposition, Ali Haydar showered the sultan and his ministers with letters demanding the annulment of the trial and acquittal of his father, as well as recognizing the injustice that he had suffered a quarter of a century earlier.

In January 1901, unusual bundles of letters arrived in Istanbul from Cairo. The bundles were addressed to the palace, the Ministry of Justice, the Office of the Şeyhülislam, the sultan's aides-de-camp, and the grand vizier. French translations of the letters arrived to the Russian and British ambassadors in Istanbul. The bundle sent to the palace contained supposedly original letters that Midhat's family had received from the prisoners Midhat Paşa and Hayrullah Efendi sixteen years earlier. The other packages contained handwritten copies of the same letters. All the bundles that were addressed to the Ottoman officeholders included the same cover letter, bearing the name and signature of "the son of Midhat Paşa."[54] In the cover letter, Ali Haydar presented a direct attack on the justice of the sultan, defining the trial as a violation of the law and demanding reconsideration. He wrote that he received the letters from a friend in Egypt, who had received them from a certain Kurd. The cover letter sent to the foreign embassies was shorter, but no less austere: "I take the liberty of having the honor to transfer to you the autographed letter of my father on his suffering and the translation of the other letters concerning the horrible murder that was committed in the presence [of the witnesses] in Taif."[55]

The bundle that was sent to the palace included an allegedly original letter written by Midhat in his prison cell on May 6, 1884, namely, one day before his death. Midhat begins the letter, addressed to his wives, daughters, and son, by warning them that it might be his last. He describes several attempts to poison the inmates' food, which failed thanks to the alert and loyal servant Arif Ağa. The paşa reported that dangerous people surrounded him, and thereby he was facing the "darkest schemes."[56]

An English translation of the letter was included in Ali Haydar's biography of his father, which he published in London eighteen years later. There are some minor but odd differences between the letters that Ali Haydar sent to the sultan in 1901 and their English translations. For one, in the "original" letter, Midhat addressed his wives, Naime and Şehriban. In the published English translation, it was addressed to "my dear wife."[57] It seems that in an attempt to win the sympathy of the English readers, Ali Haydar obscured the fact that Midhat had two wives (a typical feature of an Ottoman elite household), while his mother, Şehriban, was originally a slave of Circassian origins, purchased by the paşa for two thousand gold coins.[58] There is another, more significant, difference between the two versions, though. The letter sent to the palace in 1901 (and its many copies that reached position holders in the capital) ends with Midhat granting his family the permission to return to Istanbul. In the letter, Midhat asks his family to take care of his sister and make sure that she receives a certain share from his inheritance. For some reason, Ali Haydar decided to omit this part in his English translation of the letter. Some of the copies sent to the various Ottoman offices and foreign embassies in Istanbul were written on official papers bearing the logo of the famous Shepherd's Hotel in Cairo, a luxurious hotel that belonged to the international hotel network Palace Hotels.[59]

The bundles that Ali Haydar sent to Istanbul in 1901 also contained a letter that had been allegedly sent by Hayrullah Efendi to Midhat's family, informing them of the real circumstances of his death. The copy of this letter also appeared on a formal sheet of the Shephard's Hotel. According to the letter, Midhat did not die because of the anthrax that he had suffered, as the newspapers reported, but was actually strangled to death together with Mahmut Paşa "at the same night and the same hour." The former *şeyhülislam* also reported the stealing of some of the paşa's possessions by the local officials. The letter concludes by informing the family that Midhat left a hundred liras to his faithful servant Arif Ağa.[60]

The publication of Midhat's biography in 1903, authored by his son, formed the apex of Ali Haydar's international campaign. Telling from the letters sent a couple of years earlier to the British embassy and other private correspondence, Ali Haydar was fluent in French but not in English. Hence, he must have written the manuscript in Ottoman Turkish or French and had it translated to English.[61] The book was a direct attack on Abdülhamit, an objective made clear in the preface:

> There can be no doubt that at the present time Turkey is suffering from a Reign of Terror, and is in a state of anarchy. . . .
>
> My readers will learn how the Sovereign of the Ottoman Empire, in order to carry out his own system of Government, has suppressed every effort for reform, and has removed those men, who by their force of character, by their uprightness, and by their popularity, seemed capable of thwarting his designs, and amending the condition of the country and of the people.
>
> I wish to state here that I have a profound respect for the Imperial Throne, and it is this consideration alone, I repeat it, and the honour of my country, which makes me regard it as a duty to humanity to expose the nefarious system of Sultan Abdul Hamid.[62]

This biography unfolds Midhat Paşa's political life in a flowing narrative combined with scores of translated documents and notes attributed to Midhat. The two last chapters, surely the most disconcerting ones from the perspective of the Hamidian regime, were Ali Haydar's narrative about the Yıldız Trial and the murder of Midhat and Mahmut in Taif. The entire version is based on an account that Ali Haydar attributes to Hayrullah Efendi, who supposedly witnessed the execution of the two paşas in their prison cells. Ali Haydar does not specify how exactly this letter had reached to him. After presenting the long account, he writes, "Thus ends the faithful translation of the document sent by Hairoullah Effendi, the ex-Sheik-ul-Islam. We have preserved all its originality."[63] A close look into this particular text and its other versions that were in circulation at the time, however, must raise some doubts.

There are some editorial differences between the English version of Hayrullah's report and the version that appeared in the Turkish edition of the biography, published six years later.[64] The details and the general structure of the narrative, however, are identical. The following description refers to the English version, which was the first published edition. Given the objectives of the present discussion, I can provide only a summarized description, which cannot do justice to the exhaustive, vivid report that is available in the biography, offering a captivating narration of scenes from prison life. The narrative begins with the emergence of a carbuncle on Midhat's right shoulder during his third year in prison, diagnosed by Dr. Naşid as a symptom of anthrax. The prisoner Mahmut Paşa, who suspected that Naşid Efendi, a recent medical school graduate, was incapable of treating Midhat, sent a telegram to the governor, asking for a more experienced doctor, "but Osman Nouri had not even the politeness to reply to him."[65] The lesion healed after a while, despite the "rudimentary treatment" provided by the doctor. In the following weeks, the officer in charge, Major Bekir, pressured the inmates following the orders he had received. He dismissed the paşas' personal servants and appointed soldiers in their stead, who "were completely ignorant of the Pasha's habits."[66] In addition, the officer informed Hayrullah that his wife and baby, who were living in the village, would be banished to Istanbul. On April 8, according to the report, Major Bekir was about to travel to Mecca with the mission of transferring the servants, the cooks, and Hayrullah's family to Istanbul. Before departing Taif, the officer came to see Midhat. This encounter included an extraordinary exchange between the two. After asking Midhat for any messages to deliver, the paşa conveyed a sharp monologue, which left the young officer speechless:

> You are not ignorant of the distinguished posts I have successively occupied. Now, you see how I am treated; I see nothing before me but the most gloomy prospect, and it is through you that they will get rid of me. You will be the instruments, and each of you, most probably, will be promoted; the officer will become colonel, the colonel will be gazetted as a general, and so on; but remember that you may die after Abdul Hamid. If you die before, your titles will be inscribed on your tombs; but if the contrary occurs, then I am convinced it will be quite otherwise. Pause now, examine your consciousness, calculate your own moral and material interests, and without looking so far ahead, whilst His Majesty is still alive, just think for a moment what has become the Chief President of that arbitrary tribunal which condemned me in so cowardly a manner, without any tangible proof. It is quite true that Sourouri Effendi was appointed *Cadi Asker*; but was he not exiled soon afterwards, under the title of Governor of Manissa. As to Djevdet Pasha, the second president, he is, as everyone knows, deprived of his functions, and is now at home—a disgraced man.[67] Think of these events, and you will form a correct idea of the situation. I see that some crime is overhanging me. Remember the verse of the Koran which says: "Whosoever kills shall be punished with hell and eternal tortures." . . . [W]e are all deserving of chastisement at the hands of Divine Justice. And now that you know my opinion, will you communicate it faithfully to the Vali?[68]

Bekir returned from Mecca a week later, bringing back with him the servants, cooks, and Hayrullah's wife and baby. This entire episode, supposedly reported by Hayrullah, is quite awkward. Given that the palace was involved in every measure taken with regard to the inmates, it is quite unlikely that the governor would overturn the decision to remove the servants and banish Hayrullah's family—a decision that had been surely made in the capital—only because he was moved by Midhat's observations.

The author of the report describes several attempts to poison the paşas. The prisoners detected these endeavors beforehand by the color of poisoned milk, the strange taste of tainted food, and the residue of a suspect material in the saucepan they used for food preparation. The author writes that after the assassination of Midhat and Mahmut, two guards confessed to him about their attempts to poison the paşas. On another occasion, the officer Bekir tried to persuade the servant Arif Ağa to cooperate in another poisoning initiative, promising him an enormous fee of six thousand liras, an offer that the servant turned down decisively. Following these recurring failures, the perpetrators moved on to plan B. The captain called for Arif Ağa to inform him that the palace ordered the elimination of Midhat and that the servant had been instructed to open the door of Midhat's cell at night. According to this account, the servant started to shout frantically, saying that he would never betray his master. Midhat overheard the cries of Arif Ağa, who also warned him not to leave his room because the officers were contriving his murder. The servant was taken to the barracks, while the officer went to the prison cells to calm down the inmates. Midhat shared his room with the inmate Ali Bey. At 1:30, the door of their room was forced open, Ali was dragged from the room, and the assassins strangled Midhat to death. At the same time, several assassins broke into Mahmut's room and strangled him as well, using a soaped cord. They used this method because unlike Midhat, Mahmut "possessed considerable muscular strength."[69] They wrapped the corpses and transported them to the infirmary. The two paşas were interred at dawn, with no religious ceremonies.

This narrative is engaging through its style and vivid descriptions, but it raises some questions that have remained untouched in historiography. For one, why would the guards need the help of Arif Ağa to open the door of Midhat's cell? After all, it was a prison, whose doors were subject to the guards' control. Second, why did the assassins need to use the poisoning stratagem when they could simply execute the paşas by strangling, as they eventually did, according to Ali Haydar's narrative? Third, the author of the report provides a complete list of the assassins' names, consisting of seventeen individuals, also specifying their military units and regions of origin.[70] How could the author of the account, a prisoner, possess this sort of detailed information? Fourth, considering the author's familiarity with these and other specificities, why does the report say nothing about the reopening of the graves about a week later and the autopsy conducted under the palace's direction? To be sure, we can provide speculative yet reasonable answers to each of these questions. For instance, those individuals who schemed the assassination sought Arif Ağa's help in order to minimize the chances that the whole affair would leak and become a scandal. Similarly, one can suggest that Hayrullah Efendi possessed detailed information about the guards because small talk between guards and prisoners was not an inconceivable scene. However, the point I wish to make refers to the validity of the historian-as-judge approach. Uzunçarşılı's, who presented "the evidence" in a legalistic manner, neither doubted the authenticity of this narrative nor raised these questions, which have remained buried under the layers of historiographic reproductions of his verdict.

Additional uncertainties arise from the fact that there is more than a single version of this account. The Ottoman archives possess two versions of this account, which somehow reached the palace.[71] Both documents bear neither signature nor date. The slightly shorter version bears the seal of the Committee for Investigation of Documents (Tetkik-i Evrak Komisyonu). According to Uzunçarşılı, in 1905 the very same text came out in Egypt as a pamphlet. It is impossible to tell with any certainty whether the handwritten versions saved in the archive are copies of the published version, or, alternatively, if they form the original texts supposedly written by the eyewitnesses to the assassination of the paşas. Uzunçarşılı acknowledges the existence of two versions: the shorter one, which appeared in Ali Haydar's biography of his father, and the one published in Egypt in 1905. How exactly did the handwritten version find its way to the palace? According to Uzunçarşılı, the palace possessed the two versions. The shorter version was found in the prison by officers in Taif and was forwarded to the palace. The more detailed version was sent to the palace by a certain "Said the Kurd," who had supposedly received it from a certain Cemil Paşa. The latter was the governor of the Hijaz in 1886, who happened to be the brother of Ali Bey, one of the prisoners. According to Uzunçarşılı, the governor started to investigate the deaths of Midhat and Mahmut as soon as he arrived in the Hijaz. He discovered the text and handed it to Said the Kurd, a former member of the local Committee of Shar'i Investigations, asking him to translate the text into Arabic and Farsi. Said the Kurd, who refused to comply, forwarded the writing to another official in Istanbul, who delivered it to the palace.[72] Uzunçarşılı does not provide references in support of his description of the circumstances in which the two accounts reached the palace.

Who was the author or authors of these texts? Uzunçarşılı was confident that one or two of the prisoners in Taif who had witnessed the events wrote them, but he was less certain about the exact identity of the author. He believed that either Hayrullah Efendi or Ali Bey wrote them or perhaps both. That other prisoners contributed was yet another possibility. As mentioned earlier, Ali Haydar expressed no doubt that the author was Hayrullah Efendi.

Uzunçarşılı chose to transliterate the longer version, which was written in Ottoman, into Turkish and include its full text in his book.[73] There are some nuanced differences between the two versions, also noted by Uzunçarşılı. For instance, in the shorter version published by Ali Haydar, the author complains that when Mahmut Paşa sent a message to the governor, asking for a more experienced doctor to treat Midhat's lesion, the governor did not bother to answer. In the more detailed version, the governor replied that it was impossible and there was no reason to send another doctor from Mecca, as Dr. Naşid Efendi was a certified physician.[74] Why did Uzunçarşılı choose to publish the longer version of this narrative? Besides the fact that this version is a bit more detailed and therefore more informative, it also seems somewhat more "authentic" to the historian's eyes. The shorter version (which Ali Haydar published) is neater in its configuration: there are no erasures or corrections, and the handwriting appears uniform and well ordered. The longer version, by contrast, contains some corrections and erasures, which Uzunçarşılı identified as Hayrullah Efendi's.

What could be the reason for the existence of two eyewitness narratives of the events in question? The shorter version reads like an edited version of the longer account, rather than a different narrative written by a different person. In other words, the similarities between the two texts, in terms of formulations and structure, are too substantial to be regarded as two different accounts written by two different eyewitnesses. Assuming that one of the inmates was the author of these texts, interested in duplicating the narrative to be smuggled out of prison, what would be the reason for preparing two different versions rather than preparing two identical copies? The difference in some factual details, as in the example of the governor's reply to Mahmut Paşa's request, renders the possibility that both texts were written by the same individual quite unlikely. If these accounts were written almost in real time, as Ali Haydar and Uzunçarşılı were confident, the discrepancy makes little sense. The oddity does not allow even speculation, let alone an explanation. If we continue to play the game of "weighing the evidence," a feature of the legalistic-historical approach favored by Uzunçarşılı, we must reach the conclusion that there is a possibility, however slight, that the scripts, which served as the basis for the narrative about "the real story" of the paşas' deaths, are not authentic eyewitness testimonies. A legalistic approach to this historical episode would have to consider this possibility, which has never been done.

The above discussion is highly speculative, of course; every explanation is as good (or as weak) as the other. Rather than adopting a philological methodology, my purpose in discussing the readings of the archived scripts is to highlight the weaknesses of the legalistic approach to the story of the Yıldız convicts. Bearing in mind Ginzburg's observations concerning the differences between the judge and the historian, a legalistic approach to history seems to be doomed to collapse into itself, regardless of the performance of academic apparatus. This outcome is not only a derivative of the trivial fact that witnesses cannot be summoned for interrogation and cross-examination because they no longer exist, but, more profoundly, because historians and judges ought to ask different questions. This statement might be a banality, but the fact remains that Uzunçarşılı's narrative about the aftermath of the Yıldız Trial, a narrative crafted through the prism of legalistic history, has never been questioned.

When Abdülhamit was dethroned and the revolution was under way, the narratives ascribed to Hayrullah Efendi had been circulating in published forms for several years in Europe and Egypt; an imperial decree had prohibited their distribution in the Ottoman Empire. On August 1908, roughly a month after the revolution, Ali Haydar returned to Istanbul. Three months later, and several months before the publication of Ali

Haydar's biography of Midhat in Istanbul for the first time, the government instructed the Ministry of Justice to have the public prosecution look into the option of initiating legal action against the soldiers mentioned in the pamphlets that described the murder of Midhat and Mahmut.[75] In July 1909, the military command in Aydın reported that it seized two of Midhat's murderers, who also gave their statements.[76] There is no evidence of a subsequent criminal course of action. After all, twenty-five years had elapsed, and there were many more pressing matters to which the CUP regime had to attend. In addition, there was no political need for a retrial, because Abdülhamit was defeated and Midhat Paşa's legacy was secured. Midhat's work in the field of constitutionalism, and his record as a great patriot and reformer, turned him into an obvious hero of the revolution. The story of his persecution by the despotic sultan made him the ultimate political martyr, whose fate symbolized the evilness of the ancién regime. In the previous chapter, we saw how this rehabilitation of the paşa's image was noticeable in the representation of the trial by the revolutionary press.

The political victory of the CUP, Ali Haydar being one of its leaders, signified the victory of Ali Haydar's narrative about the trial. In his memoirs, he describes his first and last audience with his greatest foe, Abdülhamit, shortly after the revolution, when Abdülhamit was still sitting on the throne yet completely deprived of his political power. According to Ali Haydar, the sultan wanted to meet him from the day he set foot in Istanbul, but Ali Haydar did whatever he could to avoid such a meeting. Eventually, however, he agreed to meet the sultan after the insistent pleadings of the British ambassador, who told him that such a meeting would be the perfect revenge.

The audience took place in Yıldız Palace, after the ceremonial Friday prayer. Ali Haydar was received in accord with the protocol, ushered into the room where the sultan was about to enter with his entourage. Ali Haydar described the person that he held accountable for the murder of his father: "He had an extremely lean face, dyed hair, a big and asymmetric nose, sharp mind with a fiery pair of eyes, and skeletal hands restrained in white gloves."[77] Ali Haydar's account of the audience transmits the drama encapsulated in the encounter between the vanquished despot and the triumphant son of the sultan's alleged prey. These words were the first that Ali Haydar heard from God's shadow on earth, as the sultans used to be called: "Sorry to have kept you waiting. Before [this meeting] I received the British ambassador. . . . Now I ask you, Ali Haydar Bey, why did you send me such telegrams from Europe?" Ali Haydar writes that following these words, the past suddenly came to life in front of his eyes, and he had to reply, "I am in the presence of His Highness in order to forget the past." Abdülhamit, according to Ali Haydar, was embarrassed by this unforeseen answer, but he maintained a facade and carried on: "May the enemies of Allah get blind; all those who brought about the disaster of your father. I regarded your father [Midhat Pasha] as my own. The Basic Law was made for the peace of this country and nation. But the traitors were envious; they deceived me!" Ali Haydar writes that the sultan's eyes filled with tears while pretending innocence. The sultan continued: "Ali Haydar Bey! Today I am committed to your father's policy. All our future hopes are at the hands of the British policy. I am thus convinced. When you were very young, I received you and your mother for an audience. I remember it as if it happened today. I told you that I will rise you to the place of your father and that the palace's gates are always open for you and your family." Hearing these preposterous words, Ali Haydar wondered to himself whether he was daydreaming, but in the final analysis, "as far as I was concerned, no greater revenge could be possible in this world."[78]

In 1912 a tomb was erected in Taif to venerate Midhat, under the responsibility of the sharif. The government created the position of the tomb's caretaker, assigning it to a local official, Vasfi Efendi, who received a monthly salary of 150 *kuruş*.[79] Either Vasfi Efendi did not do his job properly or the funding waned, for in May 1914, the newly appointed governor, Vehib Paşa, complained about the tomb's desolate condition, asking for its transfer to the imperial capital.[80] Vehib Paşa, who participated in the Gallipoli Campaign, lived to see the demise of his empire and the emergence of the Turkish Republic (which revoked his citizenship following his escape from prison owing to charges of abuse of office). However, he did not live to see his request fulfilled, when the Turkish Republic brought Midhat Paşa's remains to Istanbul in great pomp in June 1951, to be interred at the Monument of Liberty (Abide-i Hürriyet). Symbolically, Midhat rests there for eternity with the company of seventy-one soldiers who had participated in the events of May 31, killed by the pro-Abdülhamit reactionaries, as well as the leaders of the CUP, who had overthrown Abdülhamit.

Conclusion

Imagining the Law's Rule

IN 2015, a well-known Turkish journalist and author, Hasan Cemal, posted on an Internet newspaper a satirical poem that commenced with the following lines:

> In Turkey, the supremacy of law is no longer valid.
> There is neither rule of law!
> Nor state of law!
> If that is so, what is there?
> There is an Erdoğan State![1]

Reverberating the "emic/etic" distinction in anthropological research, Roger Brubaker and Frederick Cooper differentiate between categories of political and social practice and categories of analysis. The former are "categories of everyday social experience, developed and deployed by ordinary social actors, as distinguished from the experience-distant categories used by social analysts."[2] The rule of law is a handy category of political practice, especially in democratic or semidemocratic regimes that allow at least a certain degree of freedom of expression. Politicians slate their opponents by criticizing their lack of commitment to the rule of law, and commentators criticize their governments for abusing the rule-of-law principle or for developing authoritarian dispositions. Cemal's satirical lines quoted above reflect the anxieties that are always associated with the notion of the rule of law as a category of social and political practice. For one, as a category of political practice, the rule of law imposes an either-or discourse that does not recognize the option of "partial" rule of law.

Any peculiar failure in the application of the rule of law, real or assumed, is presented in public discourses as a harbinger of dictatorship or violent chaos. Employment of the term in public discourses is rarely accompanied with clarifications about the actual meaning of the "the rule of law," for there is no need or demand for such an explanation when advancement of a concrete political agenda is the objective at hand, rather than understanding a phenomenon. In any case, political agendas are best served by an either-or rhetoric. The simple black-and-white scenario that sustains rule-of-law talk echoes Montesquieu's understanding of the rule of law as the only possible armor that ordinary people can wear against the belligerence of rulers and officeholders. Nevertheless, his *Spirit of Laws* offers an exceptionally rich interpretation consisting of philosophical reflections and concrete prescriptions that convey the complexity of the law's rule, a convolution that is absent from modern public discourses.[3]

The notion of the rule of law seems to carry the burden that Brubaker and Cooper identified with regard to other key terms in the interpretive social sciences and history, such as *class*, *democracy*, *tradition*, and *identity*. Scholars often miss the distinction between categories of analysis and categories of social practice.[4] Namely, similar to "identity," "the rule of law" is often used analytically as a "thing" that may or may not exist. Like all reified concepts, often it loses touch with concrete realities. In a succinct essay exhibiting her typical razor-sharp style, Shklar pinpoints the weakness of the rule of law as a category of analysis the way it is used in political theory. While published more than a decade before Brubaker and Cooper's essay, it touches on the same fundamental problem: "It would not be very difficult to show that the phrase 'the Rule of Law' has become meaningless thanks to ideological abuse and general over-use. It may well have become just another one of those self-congratulatory rhetorical devices that grace the public utterances of Anglo-American politicians. No intellectual effort need therefore be wasted on this bit of ruling-class chatter."[5]

Nevertheless, as a category of analysis, Shklar *does* deem it worthy of consideration, which nevertheless brings her to the conclusion that the way some of the iconic social theorists of the twentieth century had used the term, the rule of law is just as meaningless. She argues that this concept has become an obscure category, "reduced into incoherence" in political theory, because it has been stripped from the historical and political contexts that gave the original archetypes of the concept its actual meanings. Specifically, she refers to the two distinct rule-of-law theories that were developed by Montesquieu and Aristotle, both reflecting the realities of their times. Shklar concludes that the rule-of-law notion can be meaningful only when "recognized as an essential element of constitutional government generally and of representative democracy particularly."[6] A similar conclusion, albeit devoid of the harsh critical tone favored by Shklar and embedded in a much more systematic methodology, is evident in Tamanaha's conceptualization of the rule of law.[7]

Both Shklar and Tamanaha, however, like most if not all the theorists who tried to abate the inherent analytical and descriptive obscurity of the concept, to the extent that they referred to concrete historical evidence, drew almost exclusively on the historical experiences of Europe and North America. As argued in chapter 1, the resulting theoretical discourse is rather narrow in terms of history and geography.[8] Nevertheless, some of the world's greatest civilizations—China, Japan, and the Ottoman Empire are good examples—were rule-bound entities, where law was a constitutive force in social and political life.[9] While the concept of liberal constitution was unknown in the Ottoman Empire prior to the nineteenth century, there were legal mechanisms that provided ordinary men and women with considerable—though imperfect like everywhere else—protection from aggressive officials, most notable of which were the Sharia courts and the petition institution. In addition, a good number of scholars specializing in the study of Ottoman court records identified a degree of predictability and commitment of Ottoman *kadı*s to state-made positive law.[10] However, an attempt to read the modern ideology of legalism into early modern Ottoman law based on these findings might lead us to a context-resistant, anachronistic characterization of this legal system. As demonstrated by Boğaç Ergene for the early-modern period, judges were equally committed to promoting legal solutions through the practice of arbitration and negotiation between the parties, and extrajudicial conflict resolution may have been quite a widespread practice. Agmon identified the same commitment to arbitration (to be distinguished from normative law-based adjudication) in Ottoman Sharia courts of the late nineteenth century.[11]

In this study, I have adopted Kahn's interpretive framework with regard to the law's rule. To consider the rule of law as a cultural phenomenon imagined differently in diverse contexts, as Kahn suggests, is to cast off any attempt to subject the related multiple world-historical experiences into abstract "models" or lexical definitions. Conceived as a cultural phenomenon, the rule of law is a matter of neither a functional or dysfunctional model nor a successful or unsuccessful application of any certain ideal type. Rather, it is a mode of thinking about the law, which we can describe and analyze in relation to concrete contexts and historical circumstances. Legalism, the way Shklar defines it, is a case in point. It became a defining feature of legal cultures around the globe in the nineteenth century, also evident in the Ottoman Empire, to the degree that it epitomized the rule of law.

I have tried to show that the Yıldız Trial can be best understood in the context of the emergent culture of legalism, with its strict observance of legal formalism. If legalism had a far-reaching impact on common-law countries, it became the foundation of civil law countries. The Ottoman project of codification was an offshoot of a global codification movement that had started in the second half of the eighteenth century, a process that is still in progress in some parts of the world. In the "long nineteenth century," codification was much more than a technicality or a new method of ordering the legal and administrative spheres. Rather, it was a new mode of imagining social relations in the public and even in the private sphere, an imagination dominated by legal formalism. The Ottoman jurists of the late nineteenth century, like their peers in other Eurasian countries, associated legal formalism with the standard set of values that demarcated "progress." Namely, procedure-centered legal discourse was supposed to turn law into a science the way science was conceived in the nineteenth century: a procedure whereby real-life realities were translated into generalized formulas through the power of reason. The Ottoman legal sphere of the long nineteenth century consisted of various forums: Sharia courts, local councils with certain judicial powers, consular courts, and communal courts.[12] Nevertheless, the Nizamiye court system was the institutional and ideological engine that set the tone and defined the actual meaning of Ottoman legalism through its day-to-day practice in and outside the courts.

Sultan Abdülhamit's decision to have Midhat Paşa and the other senior officials tried in a Nizamiye judicial forum was an obvious one. In fact, he did not have any other reasonable way of eliminating Midhat, the individual whom he was truly after, considering the latter's domestic and international prestige. The question of whether Abdülhamit believed that his uncle, Sultan Abdülaziz, was the victim of murder in 1876 rather than committed suicide is an open one. Equally enigmatic is the question of whether he believed that Midhat and the other suspects were responsible for the assassination, to the extent that there was an assassination. I have advanced the argument that intriguing as these questions are, they are not only unanswerable but also beside the point, from the perspective of sociolegal analysis. Abdülhamit was a sophisticated ruler whose sharp political instincts kept him on the throne for thirty-three years. There can be no doubt that he considered Midhat a political nemesis, and after 1877 there was no question about Abdülhamit's abhorrence toward constitutionalism, which he perceived as a direct threat to his rule and perhaps to the well-being of his empire. His campaign at debunking constitutionalism as a political force of significance started with the abolition of the Basic Law and parliament. Elimination of constitutionalism's political figurehead, Midhat Paşa, was the obvious next step. While there was some flux between the Nizamiye and the Sharia courts in civil matters, the Nizamiye courts possessed exclusive jurisdiction in criminal matters, and therefore the sultan had no choice but to have Midhat and the other suspects prosecuted in this forum.

Indicting an individual of Midhat's high caliber in the Nizamiye court was a dicey business, from Abdülhamit's point of view. The Nizamiye court's legalistic procedures and discourse were an opportunity and a risk at the same time. On the one hand, it provided the sultan with a civilized way of getting rid of Midhat, thereby smiting the constitutionalist camp hip and thigh. On the other, the risk of acquittal through fair process was too grave to be taken. In such circumstances, assigning the task of managing the case against Midhat to Cevdet Paşa was yet another obvious decision made by the sultan, and not simply because Cevdet Paşa happened to be the minister of justice at the time. In a sense, Cevdet was Midhat's alter ego. A scholarly giant and the chief architect of legal reform in his generation, Cevdet possessed prestige, an intimate knowledge of the judicial nuts and bolts, as well as an eagle-eye view of the legal system. If Midhat was one of the sultan's unruliest oppositionists, Cevdet was one of his most appreciated confidents. Paradoxically, however, Cevdet's personal involvement in the proceedings was meant to eradicate the risk of acquittal, a menace that emanated from resorting to the legalistic Nizamiye justice. Still a paradox, Cevdet's presence at every important phase of the proceedings was a far cry from the ideals of legalism, as was the decision to perform the trial in Yıldız Palace. Ironically, if we understand legalism as an ethical attitude that established a causal connection between rule following and moral conduct, the massive procedural infringements throughout the trial rendered it an immoral project.

The decision to perform the trial in Yıldız Palace turned it into a full-fledged political trial as well as a show trial. As such, we can no longer assess it in terms of the standard Nizamiye trial, although it was definitely performed as one. Similarly, it cannot, and should not, be studied as an acid test for the overall integrity of the Nizamiye legal system. As I demonstrated elsewhere, the Nizamiye court system was a successful project when measured against the standards of its designers and in terms of the legal ideals at the time. Its shortcomings were typical of modern legal systems everywhere.[13] Like all political trials, the Yıldız Trial was a unique presentation of immediate political circumstances and agendas expressed in a standard legal idiom. While unique in terms of their concrete contexts, many (though not all) modern political trials draw legitimacy from the performance of legalism, which they often abuse.

There were a good number of procedural irregularities in the Yıldız Trial. However, the point to emphasize is that we can identify these infringements as such because the trial was a performance of standard legalism. More specifically, its performance was defined by the Penal Code and by the Code of Criminal Procedure, and the professional judiciary carried it out. As such, the trial was bound to a certain imagination of the rule's law. This trial was a different case from the Stalinist show trials and their various versions in the communist satellite states during the twentieth century. The latter were an industry of extremely violent political purge that rejected legalism altogether. Stalin, for instance, was furious to learn that legalist procedures were resorted to in Czechoslovakia.[14] It was also different from the special revolutionary tribunals in Egypt, which did not consist of professional judiciary.[15] The Yıldız Trial, by contrast, was an enactment of legalism.

Emphasizing the performative aspects of the trial in this study, most notably the performance of legalism, is not the same as arguing that it was a caricature of justice or a mock trial, as historians have typically depicted it. It may have certainly been a colossal compromise of justice, and it was surely a flawed performance of legalism, but in terms of sociolegal analysis, it was also much more than that. As I have tried to demonstrate in this study, the trial provides keys to understanding the Ottoman imagination of the law's rule following the passage of the legal system to the phase that Kennedy described as classical legal thought. The logics of codified clauses dictated the interactions between interrogators, judges, attorneys, and defendants in terms of tone and contents. A salient example discussed in this study was the matter of command responsibility, which was a legal card played by both the prosecution and some of the defendants, who discussed it in conformity with the provisions set by the relevant codified clause. It is true, however, that once the argument of command responsibility failed to serve the prosecution's objectives, the judge removed it from the table by omitting it in the text of the ruling. This brutal legal act manifested the clear power equation evident in political trials. Namely, defendants can use the court to expose the cracks in the prosecutors' performance of legalism, but the prosecutors possess the means and power for silencing these voices. In the same way, the interrogation of Rüştü Paşa was a vivid demonstration of the professionalism of the legal staff recruited for the trial. Employing effective interrogatory tactics, the interrogators of the former grand vizier during the pretrial phase were able to evoke serious doubts concerning the integrity of his version, and thereby the integrity of the entire bunch of senior officials who pleaded innocence.

For a show trial to be considered as such, ambitions for political elimination must be the essential motivation of the trial. Additionally, show trials are devised to teach the public a lesson. As such, their producers always display them as "historic" events even before they are set in motion, creating a general drama. As noted by Allo: "The trials of Socrates, Jesus of Nazareth, Joan of Arc, Galileo, the Nuremberg defendants, Eichmann, Barbie, Milosevic, and Saddam Hussein are all remembered not just for the interesting discussions their indictments raised in the court of law, but also for what they have performed in the court of public opinion and for the consequences they had far beyond the courtroom."[16]

The Yıldız Trial was not the first political trial in Ottoman history. In 1494, for instance, the scholar Molla Lütfi was prosecuted, convicted, and executed on the charge of unbelief, following years of leveling harsh criticism against the ulema and state officials of his generation.[17] Quite similar was the case of Molla Kabız in 1527, who was acquitted from the charge of heresy, but following the intervention of Sultan Süleyman the Lawgiver (r. 1520–66) he was convicted again and eventually executed.[18] Nevertheless, I argue that the Yıldız Trial was the first *modern* political trial not only because it was embedded in a legalist imagination of the law's rule but also through the sort of performativity allowed by real-time press reports. From beginning to end, the designers of the trial, the participants, and its observers domestically and internationally, knew that the proceedings were an open book through their publication in the press, in the form of either verbatim reports or summarized minutes. This awareness, which pervaded interactions *in* the trial and discussions *of* the trial, signified a new sort of diffusion between law and society, which was obviously unknown in earlier periods and that has gained momentum in the twentieth and twenty-first centuries, with the emergence of new forms of mass media. Ottoman newspapers, bounded by Hamidian authoritarian restrictions, and at the same time guided by patriotic sentiments, expressed unreserved pride in the recently adopted penal codes that dictated the proceedings. Aware of the ruler's expectations, they "marketed" the trial as a victory of the law's rule while keeping silent about the many procedural infringements that were evident since the trial's first day. As I argued in chapter 3, the newspaper coverage of the Yıldız Trial, titled in one of the major newspapers as "the Public Trial," allowed a mass circulation of the legal show, way beyond the fabric walls of the makeshift courtroom. The Hamidian regime also used the new medium to respond to unfavorable coverage in European newspapers, some of which were quick to recognize the cracks beneath the performance of legal formalism. The foreign press's close attention and the opportunities that the regime saw in the local subdued press turned the dynamic dialogue between performers and spectators into a pivot, at every level of the trial. As I demonstrated in the third chapter, in this environment, which is taken for granted in our digital era but was an uncharted experience in the Ottoman society of the late nineteenth century, the assumed presence of spectators outside the trial deeply affected performances in court.

The performance of legalism was dropped altogether once the Court of Cassation confirmed the Yıldız court's decision. The sultan convened ad hoc committees aimed at discussing questions that had already been decided judicially, such as the matter of command responsibility, a nonstandard course of action as far as Ottoman criminal law was concerned. Nevertheless, if performance of legalism is never a security for justice, the lack thereof is not necessarily a carte blanche for unrestrained arbitrariness, especially when the world's most powerful government was watching from London. Abdülhamit convened these committees as a means of legitimizing the unsurprising harsh punishments inflicted by the court. Eventually, however, he had to mitigate the death sentences and send the convicts to the Hijaz.

Unlike the death of Abdülaziz in 1876, the deaths of Midhat and Mahmut in Taif eight years later did not turn into a court case. When the CUP eradicated the Hamidian absolutism, replacing it with a short-lived semiliberal regime, the circumstances of the day as well as the limitation period made such a scenario impossible, although the ex-con Fahri Bey and Midhat

Paşa's son, Ali Haydar Midhat, did request a retrial. The paşas' deaths, however, became a case of judicious historiography. Uzunçarşılı's thorough work in gathering and presenting historical evidence was not very different from the task of the *müstantık* (examining magistrate) of the Nizamiye courts. Uzunçarşılı understood his historiographical duty in a similar way that Nizamiye judges and prosecutors understood theirs when working on run-of-the-mill judicial cases. Namely, they were required to produce documents, and eventually a ruling, which were devoid of normative assessment or references to complex extrajudicial contexts. Thanks to the development of elaborate procedures of legal review in the nineteenth century, which established the genre of the case file, as well as the elaborate newspaper reportage, Uzunçarşılı enjoyed access to a multitude of evidence. However, with it came also a multitude of versions about the events that came up in the trial and more than a single possible version about Abdülhamit's responsibility to the deaths of Midhat and Mahmut in Taif.

Obviously, working in a Kemalist environment where the project of negating the Ottoman past—especially the Hamidian one—was still in motion, there was no question that Abdülhamit was the archvillain in the story of the Yıldız Trial and its aftermath in Taif. Nevertheless, similar to the legal positivism of the nineteenth century, performances of historical positivism have their considerable limitations. Specifically, they tend to collapse in terms of their own procedures and ideals. I have tried to show that Uzunçarşılı, regardless of his pedantic work with the evidence, overlooked some "reasonable doubts" stemming from both the documents and the contexts of the events in question. This claim, however, can be relevant only to the genre of judicious-legalistic historiography.[19] I cannot overemphasize that exoneration of Abdülhamit from the charge of responsibility to the deaths of Midhat and Mahmut has *not* been an objective of this study. Similarly, exonerating or indicting Midhat Paşa and the other Yıldız convicts from the charge of killing Sultan Abdülaziz is a task that has not been part of this study. In a way, my discussion of "conflicting evidence" (discussed in chapter 4) was an exercise intended to make a point about the essential flaws in the conventional treatment of the Yıldız Trial in historiography. This treatment is weak not only in terms of its conclusions but also in terms of its legalistic pretensions.

In more than one sense, this book offers a dialectical dialogue with Uzunçarşılı's work on the Yıldız Trial. I have offered an alternative interpretation of the trial in the form of sociolegal analysis anchored in a microhistorical mode of description and analysis. The watermarks of microhistory are apparent throughout this study. Namely, I have considered the untypical episode no less telling than the typical one. Similarly, I have employed thick description of the small unit of observation as a means of offering observations about big changes. Both sociolegal analysis and microhistory were not in existence when Uzunçarşılı published his studies on the trial. Regardless of the generational and methodological gap that separates this author from İsmail Hakkı Bey, I wish to conclude the book with a word of gratitude, cherishing the timeless contributions of one of Turkey's greatest historians.

NOTES

BIBLIOGRAPHY

INDEX

Notes

PROLOGUE

1. The bills of indictment are accessible at "Ergenekon İddianamesi."

2. At the outset, the proceedings that led to the Ergenekon trials raised expectations for bolstering Turkish democracy by subjecting the military to the government and eliminating the option of a military coup, until then a constant, even if shadowy, probability in Turkish politics. However, the trials and the related public discourses ended up contributing to the existing cleavages between pro-Islamists and seculars. See Yaprak Gürsoy, "Turkish Public Opinion on the Coup Allegations: Implications for Democratization." For an interpretation of the trial that emphasizes the conspirational imagination that pervaded it, see Başak Ertür, "The Conspiracy Archive: Turkey's 'Deep State' on Trial."

3. "İbretlik Midhat Paşa Davası ve Bugün."

4. An example of what Pierre Nora defines as the "push and pull that produces *lieux de mémoire*" is provided through the history of the first modern football stadium in Istanbul. It was inaugurated in 1947 on the space that previously served as the stable of the Dolmabahçe Palace, originally called Dolmabahçe Stadium. In 1950 Turkey's one-party regime ended when the moderately right-wing Democrat Party won the elections. In 1952 the ruling party renamed the stadium after Midhat Paşa, probably as a way of emphasizing the party's commitment to the legacy of the Kemalist founding fathers, who had embraced Midhat as one of their heroes, following the steps of the Young Turks. In 1973, during the coalition government shared by the Republican People's Party and the National Salvation Party, the stadium was once again renamed, this time after İsmet İnönü, the second president of the Republic. In 2013, under Erdoğan's AKP government, the stadium was demolished and a state-of-the-art multipurpose arena constructed in its stead. This time it was named not after a political icon but rather after the sponsoring multinational telecommunications company, Vodafone. For Nora's discussion on sites of memory, see Pierre Nora, "Between Memory and History: *Les lieux de mémoire*." For an employment of Midhat's name in legitimizing leftist economic policies, see the popular history written by the popular leader of the Democratic Left Party and four-time prime minister, Ecevit. See Bülent Ecevit, *Mithat Paşa ve Türk Ekonomisinin Tarihsel Süreci*.

5. Başbuğ actually claims here that the Ergenekon case was a fiction originally invented by Güney. Tuncay Güney, a Jewish Turk, is one of the most mysterious individuals involved in the Ergenekon trials. Formally a journalist by profession, he was allegedly recruited in the early 1990s, at a young age, by the Turkish internal security apparatus, assigned at a certain point with the task of infiltrating the Turkish Gendarmerie Intelligence organization (JITEM) and the Ergenekon network. The Ergenekon investigation resulted with the exposure of his alleged secret identity in 2008, and he is mentioned many times in the bill of indictment as a suspect. In 1999 he left for the United States after being arrested and indicted for fraud and released on bail. Later, he moved to Canada, where he has served as a rabbi under the name Daniel Levi.

6. İlker Başbuğ, *20. Yüzyilin En Büyük Lideri Atatürk.*

7. İlker Başbuğ, *Ermeni Suçlamaları ve Gerçekler.*

8. http://www.ilkerbasbug.com.tr/?p=1887.

9. İsmail Hakkı Uzunçarşılı, *Midhat Paşa ve Yıldız Mahkemesi*, 307.

10. The Ottoman title "paşa" is still used in Turkey as an informal title of generals and admirals.

INTRODUCTION

1. Iris Agmon and Ido Shahar, "Theme Issue: Shifting Perspectives in the Study of Shari'a Courts: Methodologies and Paradigms," 7. In this article, Agmon and Shahar explain the growing scholarly interest in the Sharia courts.

2. On the sweeping change that Ottoman state and society underwent during the long nineteenth century, see Ehud R. Toledano, "Social and Economic Change in 'the Long Nineteenth Century'"; and Donald Quataert, *The Ottoman Empire, 1700–1922.*

3. Omri Paz, "Documenting Justice: New Recording Practices and the Establishment of an Activist Criminal Court System in the Ottoman Provinces (1840–Late 1860s)."

4. Boğaç E. Ergene, "Evidence in Ottoman Courts: Oral and Written Documentation in Early-Modern Courts of Islamic Law."

5. The pre-nineteenth-century *sijill* does not easily lend itself to microhistorical interpretations. Peirce's work on an Anatolian court of the sixteenth century is an exception. See Leslie Peirce, *Morality Tales: Law and Gender in the Ottoman Court of Aintab.* Iris Agmon showed that beginning from the 1870s, new procedures for recording cases in the Sharia courts yielded detailed protocols. She used this documentation for microhistorical studies of late-Ottoman legal culture. See Agmon, *Family and Court: Legal Culture and Modernity in Late Ottoman Palestine*; and "Recording Procedures and Legal Culture in the Late Ottoman Shari'a Court of Jaffa, 1865–1890." For the possibilities and limitations of this source, see Agmon and Shahar, "Shifting Perspectives."

6. Milen V. Petrov, "Everyday Forms of Compliance: Subaltern Commentaries on Ottoman Reform, 1864–1868"; Ehud R. Toledano, "Shemsigul: A Circassian Slave in Mid-Nineteenth-Century Cairo"; Omri Paz, "The Usual Suspect: Worker Migration and Law Enforcement in Mid-Nineteenth-Century Anatolia."

7. *Annales judiciaires de l'Empire Ottoman: Revue hebdomadaire de la jurisprudence, de la legislation et des débats judiciaires*, no. 42, July 9, 1881.

8. Uzunçarşılı, *Midhat Paşa ve Yıldız Mahkemesi*, 254.

9. *Tanin*, nos. 279, 282, 283, 284, 286, 287, 288, 289, 291, 292, 293, 295, 296, 298, 299, 300, 303, 305, 307, 309, 316, 320, 323, 324, 325.

10. Midhat Paşa, *Mir'at-ı Hayret*. Osman Selim Kocahanoğlu transliterated the book to modern Turkish and added an introduction. See Kocahanoğlu, *Midhat Paşa'nın Hatıraları: Yıldız Mahkemesi ve Taif Zindanı*.

11. Ismail Kemal Bey embarked on a promising career in Ottoman officialdom in the late 1850s, but his benefactor's downfall marked his own gradual marginalization in the Ottoman civil service, until his flight to British asylum in 1900, where he started his life project, which won him the title "founder of independent Albania." Ismail Kemal Bey, *The Memoirs of Ismail Kemal Bey*.

12. Ali Haydar Midhat, *The Life of Midhat Pasha: A Record of His Services, Political Reforms, Banishment, and Judicial Murder, Derived from Private Documents and Reminiscences*; Ali Haydar Midhat, *Midhat Paşa'nın Hayatı Siyasiyesi, Hidematı, Menfa Hayatı*.

13. Fahri Bey, *Ibretnuma: Mabeynci Fahri Bey'in Hatıraları ve İlgili Bazı Belgeler*.

14. Tomaidis Hirisantos, *Midhat Paşa ve Rüfekasının Muhakemesi Hakkında Esbab-ı Mücibeyi Ilavi İade-yi Muhukeme Laythası*.

15. Dror Ze'evi, "The Use of Ottoman Shari'a Court Records as a Source for Middle Eastern Social History: A Reappraisal."

16. "Cela m'a attristé d'autant plus que j'ai pensé immédiatement que le monde pouvait concevoir des soupçons." *Annales judiciaires*, July 9, 1881.

17. "Şu haberden ne kadar müteesif olduğumu tarif edemem. Çünkü irtihalın vukundan herkes şüpheye duçar olacak idi." *Tanin*, June 25, 1909.

18. *Annales judiciaires*, July 9, 1881.

19. BOA (Başbakanlık Osmanlı Arşivi, Turkish Prime Minister's Ottoman Archives, henceforth BOA), Y.EE. 19/50.

20. Buşra Ersanlı, "The Empire in the Historiography of the Kemalist Era," 147.

21. For instance, İsmail Hakkı Uzunçarşılı, *Bizans ve Selçukiylerle Germiyan ve Osman Oğulları zamanında Küthaya Şehri*.

22. İsmail Hakkı Uzunçarşılı, *Midhat Paşa ve Rüştü Paşaların Tevkiflerine Dair Vesikalar*. Uzunçarşılı is also known for his effort in preserving primary sources, especially epitaphs from the Seljuk era. He used to walk around in the old cities, registering,

transliterating, and translating epitaphs, originally written in Arabic or Farsi. Some of these sources were either stolen, broken, or lost and are known only from Uzunçarşılı's work.

23. İsmail Hakkı Uzunçarşılı, *Midhat Paşa ve Taif Mahkumları*.

24. Uzunçarşılı, *Midhat Paşa ve Yıldız Mahkemesi*. Locating the related files was not an easy task, considering the absence of orderly catalogs and the fact that many of the documents were kept in Yıldız Palace rather than the standard archives at Topkapı Palace and the state archive (BOA).

25. Ibid., xii.

26. Ibid., xiv. In Turkish the word *hüküm*, used by Uzunçarşılı when describing the works of Abdurrahman Şeref Bey and İbnülemin Mahmud Kemal İnal, means "conclusion," "judgment," "ruling," and "judicial sentence."

27. Ibid., xv–xvi.

28. İbrahim Halil Kalkan, "Between Medicine and Honor: The Legal Ban on Torture in the Ottoman Empire, 1840–1858."

29. Previously located at the historic site of the Bab-ı Ali, recently the Prime Minister's Ottoman Archives has been moved to the Kağıthane Valley in Istanbul. This change, probably meant to promote AKP's project of urban development, provoked a controversy in Turkey. Many argue that the decision to move the archive to its new location is a catastrophic one, considering the constant humidity of the ground, which had repeatedly flooded in the past fifty years. Critics mention the poor quality of the new building, which does not meet elementary standards. See, for instance, Patrick Adamiak, Jeffery Dyer, and Michael Christopher Low, "The End of an Era: The Less than Grand Opening of the New Ottoman Archives"; and Barın Kayaoğlu, "Has AKP sacrificed Turkey's Ottoman Heritage?"

30. Kaan Durukan, "Ideology and Historiography: State, Society and Intellectuals in Modern Turkey," 54–55.

31. For a harsh criticism of Ottoman studies as practiced in Turkey, see Halil Berktay, "The Search for the Peasant in Western and Turkish History/Historiography." This criticism is still valid, twenty-five years after it was published. The term *document fetishism* as a way of capturing the historical positivism of the nineteenth century was coined in E. H. Carr's canonical *What Is History?*, 15.

32. Fahri Bey, *Ibretnuma*, ix.

33. "Sultan Abdülaziz Han'ın Katli Ağlatan Sahne." I am grateful to Yener Bayar for his assistance with locating these sources.

34. "Talat Paşa Mithat Paşa Yeter Artık Bıktık Bu Yalanlardan."

35. See, for instance, a news report broadcast on the television channel Kanal 7, showing Abdülaziz's bloody shirt and other pieces of clothing, which are kept in Topkapı Museum. Director of the museum and celebrity historian İlber Ortaylı provides strong support to the murder thesis in an interview. See "131 Yılık Yalan Sultan Abdülaziz

İntihar Etmedi Öldürüldü." For a documentary consisting of interviews with Turkish historians, broadcast on TRT2, see "Ahmet Cevdet Paşa Belgeseli."

36. Şevket Pamuk, "Institutional Change and the Longevity of the Ottoman Empire, 1500–1800."

37. On the sociolegal approach, see Kitty Calavita, *Invitation to Law and Society: An Introduction to the Study of Real Law*; Roger Cotterrell, *Law, Culture and Society: Legal Ideas in the Mirror of Social Theory.*

1. OTTOMAN LEGALISM

1. This exchange is reported in *Annales judiciaires*, July 9, 1881. It is also cited in Uzunçarşılı, *Midhat Paşa ve Yıldız Mahkemesi*, 299–302.

2. See, for instance, David M. Trubek, "Where the Action Is: Critical Legal Studies and Empiricism"; and Mark Kelman, *A Guide to Critical Legal Studies.*

3. Judith N. Shklar, *Legalism: An Essay on Law, Morals, and Politics*, 1.

4. Ibid., 5.

5. Ibid., 9.

6. Ibid., 10.

7. Ibid., 10.

8. Ibid., 17.

9. Brian Z. Tamanaha, *On the Rule of Law: History, Politics, Theory*; Joseph Raz, *The Authority of Law: Essays on Law and Morality*; Michael Neumann, *The Rule of Law: Politicizing Ethics.*

10. Shklar, *Legalism*, 34.

11. Alan Watson, *Legal Transplants: An Approach to Comparative Law*; Avi Rubin, "Legal Borrowing and Its Impact on Ottoman Legal Culture in the Late Nineteenth Century."

12. Classical Islamic law does not recognize criminal law as a single branch of the law. Rudolph Peters, *Crime and Punishment in Islamic Law*, 7.

13. Ruth A. Miller, *Legislating Authority: Sin and Crime in the Ottoman Empire and Turkey*; Avi Rubin, *Ottoman Nizamiye Courts: Law and Modernity.*

14. Agmon, *Family and Court*, 74.

15. Rubin, *Ottoman Nizamiye Courts*; Avi Rubin, "From Legal Representation to Advocacy: Attorneys and Clients in the Ottoman Nizamiye Courts."

16. Miller, *Legislating Authority*; Hıfzı Veldet Velideoğlu, *Kanunlaştırma Hareketleri ve Tanzimat*; Zafer Toprak, "From Plurality to Unity: Codification and Jurisprudence in the Late Ottoman Empire." The present discussion is based on Avi Rubin, "Modernity as a Code: The Ottoman Empire and the Global Movement of Codification."

17. Zachary Lockman, *Contending Visions of the Middle East: The History and Politics of Orientalism.*

18. Jeremy Bentham, *Papers Relative to Codification and Public Instruction.*

19. Csaba Varga, *Codification as a Socio-Historical Phenomenon.*

20. Damiano Canale, "The Many Faces of the Codification of Law in Modern Continental Europe."

21. Werner Menski, *Comparative Law in a Global Context: The Legal Systems of Asia and Africa*, 493–593; John W. Head and Yanping Wang, *Law Codes in Dynastic China: A Synopsis of Chinese Legal History in the Thirty Centuries from Zhou to Qing.*

22. Marion W. Gray, *Prussia in Transition: Society and Politics under the Stein Reform Ministry of 1808*, 37.

23. Alan Watson, *The Evolution of Western Private Law*, 256; Varga, *Codification as a Socio-Historical Phenomenon*, 75–79.

24. Varga, *Codification as a Socio-Historical Phenomenon*, 103.

25. Ibid.

26. Lindsay Farmer, "Reconstructing the English Codification Debate: The Criminal Law Commissioners, 1833–45."

27. Tatiana Borisova, "The Digest of Laws of the Russian Empire: The Phenomenon of Autocratic Legality."

28. Andrew P. Morriss, "Codification and Right Answers."

29. Maria Luisa Murillo, "The Evolution of Codification in the Civil Law Legal Systems: Towards Decodification and Recodification."

30. Ishii Ryosuke, *Japanese Legislation in the Meiji Era.*

31. Jianfu Chen, *Chinese Law: Towards an Understanding of Chinese Law, Its Nature, and Development*, 17–22.

32. Ruud Peters, "'For His Correction and as a Deterrent Example for Others': Mehmed Ali's First Criminal Legislation (1829–1330)."

33. Kenneth M. Cuno, *Modernizing Marriage: Family, Ideology, and Law in Nineteenth- and Early Twentieth-Century Egypt.*

34. Duncan Kennedy, "Two Globalizations of Law and Legal Thought: 1850–1968."

35. Ibid., 637.

36. Ibid., 640.

37. Cengiz Kırlı, *Yolsuzluğun İcadı: 1840 Ceza Kanunu, İktidar ve Bürokrasi.*

38. Colin Imber, *The Ottoman Empire, 1300–1650: The Structure of Power.* As Baki Tezcan notes, "The basis of the legality of the *kanun* was custom." See Tezcan, *The Second Ottoman Empire: Political and Social Transformation in the Early Modern World*, 49.

39. Uriel Heyd, *Studies in Old Ottoman Criminal Law*, 173, 178.

40. James E. Baldwin, "The Deposition of Defterdar Ahmed Pasha and the Rule of Law in Seventeenth-Century Egypt," 154.

41. On Ottoman legislation, see Ehud R. Toledano, "The Legislative Process in the Ottoman Empire in the Early Tanzimat Period."

42. Tobias Heinzelmann, "The Ruler's Monologue: The Rhetoric of the Ottoman Penal Code of 1858."

43. Ibid., 308–9.

44. Rubin, *Ottoman Nizamiye Courts*. For a discussion of the difference between Ottoman modern codification and the *fiqh*, see Rudolph Peters, "From Jurists' Law to Statute Law; or, What Happens When the Sharia Is Codified."

45. According to Robin West, in addition to its commitment to rules, legalism is equally based on the conviction that the alternative to the sovereignty of the state as an expression of the people's interest is the violence emanating from "individual vainglory." See West, "Reconsidering Legalism."

46. Avi Rubin, "British Perceptions of Ottoman Judicial Reform in the Nineteenth Century: Some Preliminary Insights."

47. Timur Kuran, *The Long Divergence: How Islamic Law Held Back the Middle East*, 295.

48. Amy Singer, *Constructing Ottoman Beneficence: An Imperial Soup Kitchen in Jerusalem*; Kırlı, *Yolsuzluğun İcadı*.

49. Metin M. Çoşgel et al., "Crime and Punishment in Ottoman Times: Corruption and Fines."

50. Raz, *Authority of Law*; Tamanaha, *On the Rule of Law*. For a founding text of the substantive approach, see John Rawls, *A Theory of Justice*.

51. Pietro Costa, "The Rule of Law: A Historical Introduction."

52. See, for instance, Shklar's criticism on the theories of Friedrich Hayek, Ronald Dworkin, and others in Judith N. Shklar, "Political Theory and the Rule of Law," 7–9.

53. Lauren Benton, "Not Just a Concept: Institutions and the 'Rule of Law,'" 120.

54. Paul W. Kahn, *The Cultural Study of Law: Reconstructing Legal Scholarship*, 98.

55. Ibid., 76.

56. Rubin, *Ottoman Nizamiye Courts*, 83–111.

57. James E. Baldwin, *Islamic Law and Empire in Ottoman Cairo*.

58. Uzunçarşılı, *Vesikalar*, 87–88.

59. European observers who wrote on everyday life in the Ottoman domains during the middle decades of the nineteenth century reported that capital punishment had been rarely applied since the beginning of the Tanzimat. For a discussion on the application of the death penalty in this period and an innovative explanation about the impact of Shar'i considerations on the imposition of the death penalty, see Ebru Aykut, "Judicial Reforms, Sharia Law, and the Death Penalty in the Late Ottoman Empire."

60. *Annales judiciaires*, July 9, 1881.

61. Ibid.

62. The fairness of the trial was discussed in British Parliament on July 29, 1881, following concerns raised by MPs Lord Stratheden and Campbell, who argued, "The fate

of Midhat Pasha was a question in which the people of this country took great interest. There was no doubt that he had not had a fair trial, and obstacles were put in the way of his defending himself. There was little doubt that Abdul Aziz had put an end to his own life." *Hansard*, July 29, 1881, vol. 264, 113–15.

63. Rubin, "From Legal Representation to Advocacy."

64. Uzunçarşılı, *Midhat Paşa ve Yıldız Mahkemesi*, 310.

65. Sait Paşa, *Sait Paşa'nın Hatıratı.*

66. Uzunçarşılı, *Midhat Paşa ve Yıldız Mahkemesi*, 322.

67. Hirisantos, *Midhat Paşa ve Rüfekasının Muhakemesi.*

68. Ibid., 4.

69. Ibid., 17.

70. Ibid., 20–21.

71. Ibid., 22.

72. Ibid., 27.

73. Ibid., 33.

74. Ibid., 18.

75. Ibid., 33.

2. POLITICAL TRIAL

1. On Selanikli Tevfik, see Mehmet Tahir, *Osmanlı Müellifleri*, 250; and Ayşe Banu Karadağ, "Türk Çeviri Tarihimizde 'Mütercim' Selanikli Tevfik."

2. *Tanin*, June 25, 1909.

3. On the eve of the Revolution, Arabs, for instance, did not constitute a coherent faction with distinct political priorities. See Hasan Kayalı, *Arabs and Young Turks: Ottomanism, Arabism, and Islamism in the Ottoman Empire, 1908–1918*, 17–51. For inclinations of other ethnic groups, see M. Şükrü Hanioğlu, *The Young Turks in Opposition.*

4. In 2012 Turkish journalist Murat Bardakçı released a three-minute voice recording of Mahmut Şevket Paşa, the commander of the Third Army. In this remarkable original recording, Şevket Paşa is heard instigating his troops with much pathos before marching on to Istanbul, calling them to save the nation and constitutionalism. See "Mahmud Şevket Paşa'nın 31 Mart Olayı Sırasındaki Ses Kaydı."

5. William Hale, *Turkish Politics and the Military*, 35–41; Feroz Ahmad, *The Making of Modern Turkey*, 31–37.

6. Ron Christenson, *Political Trials: Gordian Knots in the Law*, 2.

7. Interest in the political aspects of the law started with the American movement of legal realism in the 1920s. Members of this school were the first to demonstrate the fictitious nature of claims about the law as a sphere of human activity that is detached from political and social considerations through its alleged rationality. Scholars have demonstrated the political aspects of the law in the fields of adjudication and jurisprudence. For

a discussion of the impact of legal realism and its later scholarly offshoots, see Mathieu Deflem, *Sociology of Law: Visions of a Scholarly Tradition.*

8. Michael R. Belknap, "Introduction: Political Trials in the American Past," 3; Theodore L. Becker, ed., *Political Trials*, i. An example of the court as a guardian of hegemonic political perceptions is evident by the approach of the Israeli Supreme Court to the occupation of the Palestinian territories. In a definitive study covering the years 1967–2000, Kretzmer shows that as far as the occupation was concerned, the main function of the Supreme Court has been to legitimize government actions in the occupied territories. See David Kretzmer, *The Occupation of Justice: The Supreme Court of Israel and the Occupied Territories.*

9. See, for instance, Otto Kirchheimer, *Political Justice: The Use of Political Procedure for Political Ends*, 46; and Christenson, *Political Trials*, 8–11.

10. Christenson, *Political Trials*, 8–11.

11. Ken Kyle and Pat Lauderdale, "The Rule of Law or Unruly Law? Reflections on the Study of Political Trials."

12. Shklar, *Legalism*, 147–48.

13. Ibid., 149.

14. Ibid., 152–56.

15. Hannah Arendt, *Eichmann in Jerusalem: A Report on the Banality of Evil*, 253. For an analysis of Arendt's report and its interpretation as a legal critique, and the discourse that it provoked, see Shoshana Felman, *The Juridical Consciousness: Trials and Traumas in the Twentieth Century*, 106–30.

16. İbnülemin Mahmut Kemal İnal, *Son Sadrazamlar*, 101.

17. See, for instance, Niyazi Berkes, *The Development of Secularism in Turkey*; Bernard Lewis, *The Emergence of Modern Turkey.*

18. Edhem Eldem, "Istanbul: From Imperial to Peripheralized Capital"; Beshara Doumani, *Rediscovering Palestine: Merchants and Peasants in Jabal Nablus, 1700–1900.* For an overview of these historiographical trends, see Dror Ze'evi, "Back to Napoleon? Thoughts on the Beginning of the Modern Era in the Middle East."

19. İnal, *Son Sadrazamlar*, 102.

20. For an overview on the Ottoman patronage system, see Ehud R. Toledano, *As If Silent and Absent: Bonds of Enslavement in the Islamic Middle East*, 24–34.

21. Roderic H. Davison, *Reform in the Ottoman Empire, 1856–1876*, 327.

22. Ahmet Cevdet Paşa, *Tarih-i Cevdet*; Ahmet Cevdet Paşa, *Tezakir.*

23. Christoph K. Neumann, "Whom Did Ahmed Cevdet Represent?"

24. İnal, *Son Sadrazamlar*, 315.

25. Stanford J. Shaw and Ezel Kural Shaw, *History of the Ottoman Empire and Modern Turkey*, 67.

26. Carter V. Findley, "The Evolution of the System of Provincial Administration as Viewed from the Center."

27. Midhat's innovations went beyond the administrative field. For instance, the state orphanages (ıslahhane), which he developed in the Tuna Province, became a standard provincial institution across the empire. As noted by Nazan Maksudyan, Abdülhamit changed the title of this institution "since the organic link of the institution with Midhat Pasha was problematic." See Nazan Maksudyan, *Orphans and Destitute Children in the Late Ottoman Empire*, 80.

28. Ebubekir Ceylan, *The Ottoman Origins of Modern Iraq: Political Reform, Modernization, and Development in the Nineteenth-Century Middle East*; Gökhan Çetinkaya, *Ottoman Administration of Iraq, 1890–1908*.

29. The independence of the grand vizier vis-à-vis the sultan and other senior posts had been the subject of constant political negotiation since the sixteenth century. See Hüseyin Yılmaz, "Containing Sultanic Authority: Constitutionalism in the Ottoman Empire before Modernity," 235–39.

30. Davison, *Reform in the Ottoman Empire*, 289.

31. Edhem Eldem, "Stability against All Odds: The Imperial Ottoman Bank, 1875–1914."

32. For Ottoman accounts of the coup, in addition to Süleyman Paşa's report that is discussed below, see Nureddin Tevfik, *Sultan Aziz'in Hal'ı ve İntiharı*; and Mahmut Celaleddin Paşa, *Mirat-ı Hakikat: Tarih-i Mahmut Cellaleddin Paşa*.

33. Uzunçarşılı, *Vesikalar*, 52.

34. Ibid., 52.

35. Ibid., 55.

36. In 1878 Sülyman Paşa stood a military trial for his responsibility for the defeat in the Russo-Ottoman War of 1877–78. See Süleyman Paşa, *Süleyman Paşa Muhakemesi*, 46–47.

37. Süleyman Paşa, *Hiss-i İnkilap yahut Sultan Abdülaziz Hal'i ile Sultan Murat-ı Hamisin Cülusu*.

38. Robert Devereux, "Süleyman Pasha's 'The Feeling of the Revolution,'" 4.

39. Davison, *Reform in the Ottoman Empire*, 336; Haluk Y. Şehsuvaroğlu, *Sultan Aziz: Hususi, Siyası Hayatı, Devri ve Ölümü*, 95–96.

40. Süleyman Paşa, *Hıss-ı İnkilap*, 13.

41. Ibid., 60.

42. Dipesh Chakrabarty, *Provincializing Europe: Postcolonial Thought and Historical Difference*.

43. Baki Tezcan, who identifies "constitutionalist groups" in the seventeenth century, offers a different view. Tezcan describes the janissaries, for instance, as constitutionalists who sought to limit sultanic authority through legal means. He admits his anachronistic use of the term: "The two political groups—the absolutists and the constitutionalists—did not exist as such in the seventeenth-century Ottoman Empire and

are my invention." Nevertheless, he argues, the absence of these terms does not imply an absence of inclinations that conform with constitutionalism the same way that "gender" was not part of Ottoman vocabulary, but it played a major role in Ottoman society and politics. See Tezcan, *Second Ottoman Empire*, 48. To my mind, this rationalization of Tezcan's anachronistic use of terms is problematic for two reasons. For one, it falls into the trap of employing categories of social practice as categories of analysis while reproducing reifications. If constitutionalism is defined in such broad terms and can be found in every action intended to limit the sovereign's power, it becomes an obscure and timeless category. Such categories may be effective as categories of practice, but much less so as categories of analysis. Second, reading categories backward in history carries the risk of historicism. For the problem of confusing categories of social practice with categories of analysis, see Rogers Brubaker and Frederick Cooper, "Beyond 'Identity.'"

44. Aylin Koçunyan, "The Transcultural Dimension of the Ottoman Constitution."

45. Nader Sohrabi, *Revolution and Constitutionalism in the Ottoman Empire and Iran*, 39–45.

46. Şerif Mardin, *The Genesis of Young Ottoman Thought: A Study in the Modernization of Turkish Political Ideas*, 280–21.

47. Ibid., 308–13.

48. Joseph G. Rahme, "Namık Kemal's Constitutional Ottomanism and Non-Muslims."

49. Madeline C. Zilfi, *The Politics of Piety: The Ottoman Ulema in the Postclassical Age, 1600–1800*; Ariel Salzmann, *Tocqueville in the Ottoman Empire: Rival Paths to Modern State.*

50. For the full text, see Kemal Beydilli, "Kabakcı İsyanı Akabinde Hazırlanan Hüccet-i Şer'iyye."

51. Ali Yaycioğlu, *Partners of the Empire: The Crisis of the Ottoman Order in the Age of Revolutions*, 226. The study includes an excellent translation of the Deed of Alliance.

52. For the full annotated text of the pact, see Ali Akyıldız, "Sened-i İttifak'ın İlk Tam Metni."

53. Hakan T. Karateke, "Who Is the Next Ottoman Sultan? Attempts to Change the Rule of Succession during the Nineteenth Century."

54. Uzunçarşılı, *Vesikalar*, 93.

55. British National Archives (henceforth, BNA), FO 78/2462.

56. Davison, *Reform in the Ottoman Empire*, 353.

57. BNA, FO 78/2462.

58. Ibid.

59. The full text of the Basic Law is available in Kemal Gözler, *Türk Anayasaları*, 30–36.

60. İnal, *Son Sadrazamlar*, 345; Davison, *Reform in the Ottoman Empire*, 377.

61. *Tanin*, June 16, 1909.

62. Mirjan Damaska, "The Shadow Side of Command Responsibility," 455.

63. The Code pénal provides more systematic guidance as to the matter of liability, under the title "Des Personnes Punissables, Excusables ou Responsables, pour Crimes ou Pour Délits." The relevant articles to command responsibility are 59, 60, 64. See Julien-Michel Dufour, *Code criminel avec instructions: Deuxième partie, Code pénal.*

64. Chantal Meloni, "Command Responsibility: Mode of Liability for the Crimes of Subordinates or Separate Offence of the Superior?"

65. Iryna Marchuk, *The Fundamental Concept of Crime in International Law: A Comparative Law Analysis*, 38.

66. Timothy Wu and Yong-Sung (Jonathan) Kang, "Criminal Liability for the Actions of Subordinates: The Doctrine of Command Responsibility and Its Analogues in United States Law," 279.

67. *Tanin*, July 6, 1909.

68. "Ceza Kanunname-i Hümayunu," in *Düstur.*

69. *Annales judiciaires*, July 9, 1881.

70. The following exchanges are reported in *Annales judiciaires*, July 9, 1881.

71. Celaleddin Paşa, *Mırat-ı Hakikat*, 121. For the text of the report, see Ahmet Midhat, *Üss-i Inkilap*, 398–400.

72. Dr. Markel uses the term *murder* (*katil*). This is an odd word choice, considering that he had signed the statement suggesting suicide, together with the other physicians. His account about the woman's testimony provides further support to his initial stand, namely, that it was a case of suicide, so he did not seem to change his mind. Perhaps the reporter who recorded the testimony omitted the word *alleged.*

73. *Tanin*, July 1, 1909.

74. Uzunçarşılı, *Vesikalar*, 120.

75. Ibid., 128.

76. Butrus Abu-Manneh, "Arab-Ottomanists' Reactions to the Young Turk Revolution," 155.

77. Uzunçarşılı, *Vesikalar*, 120.

78. Ibid., 129–30.

79. Ibid., 136–37.

80. Ibid., 138–39.

81. Ibid., 146–47.

82. Ibid., 165.

83. Ibid., 167.

84. Uzunçarşılı, *Midhat Paşa ve Yıldız Mahkemesi*, 303.

85. *Annales judiciaires*, July 9, 1881.

86. BOA Y.EE. 16/9.

87. Uzunçarşılı, *Midhat Paşa ve Yıldız Mahkemesi*, 319–20.

88. Kirchheimer, *Political Justice*, 118.

3. PERFORMING A SHOW TRIAL

1. Ebru Boyar and Kate Fleet, *A Social History of Ottoman Istanbul.*

2. Uzunçarşılı, *Midhat Paşa ve Yıldız Mahkemesi*, 228.

3. For the linguistic meanings of performance, see J. L. Austin, *How to Do Things with Words: The William James Lectures Delivered at Harvard University in 1955.*

4. Henning Grunwald, *Courtroom to Revolutionary Stage: Performance and Ideology in Weimar Political Trials*, 174–78.

5. Julie Stone Peters, "Legal Performance Good and Bad," 185.

6. For an analysis of a political trial applying theories of the theater, see Pnina Lahav, "Theater in the Courtroom."

7. Peirce, *Morality Tales*, 9.

8. Agmon, *Family and Court*, 100.

9. For a revisionist view of Müteferrika's printing venture, see Orlin Sabev, "The First Ottoman Turkish Printing Enterprise: Success or Failure?"

10. Nile Green, "Journeymen, Middlemen: Travel, Transculture, and Technology in the Origins of Muslim Printing," 218.

11. Jale Baysal, *Müteferrika'dan Birinci Meşrutiyete Kadar Osmanlı Türklerinin Bastıkları Kitaplar.* On the emergence of private printing in Cairo, see Kathryn A. Schwartz, "The Political Economy of Private Printing in Cairo as Told from a Commissioning Deal Turned Sour, 1871."

12. *Cosmopolitanism* appears here in quotation marks following Edhem Eldem's argument concerning the nature of Istanbul's so-called cosmopolitanism. According to Eldem, and based on the assumption that diversity should not be treated as a synonym of cosmopolitanism, a sort of rather limited cosmopolitanism developed no earlier than the second half of the nineteenth century. Its limited nature was evident, among other things, in the exclusion of the majority of the population while transforming the upper middle class. Edhem Eldem, "Istanbul as a Cosmopolitan City: Myths and Realities."

13. Orhan Koloğlu, "Newspapers"; Johann Strauss, "'Kütüp ve Resail-i Mevkufe': Printing and Publishing in a Multi-ethnic Society." On Hamidian censorship, see Fatmagül Demirel, *II Abdülhamid Döneminde Sansür.*

14. For instance, see Osman Recep Bahadır and H. H. Günhan Danışman, "Late Ottoman and Early Republican Science Periodicals: Center and Periphery Relationship in Dissemination of Knowledge."

15. Matar, who served as the tutor of Cevdet's son, studied law and medicine in Istanbul and worked as a medical doctor, lawyer, professor, and civil servant. On the life of Matar and his role as the founder of Syrian historiography, see Youssef M. Choueiri, *Modern Arab Historiography: Historical Discourse and the Nation-State*, 48–53.

16. For studies that use the *Ceride-i Mehakim* as a source for institutional and sociolegal histories of the late Ottoman empire, see Fatmagül Demirel, *Adliye Nezareti:*

Kuruluşu ve Faaliyetleri, 1876–1914; Noémi Lévy-Aksu, *Ordre et désordres dans l'Istanbul ottomane, 1879–1909: De l'état au quartier*; and Rubin, *Ottoman Nizamiye Courts.*

17. Metin M. Çoşgel et al., "Crime and Punishment in Ottoman Times." According to Haim Gerber, early-modern Anatolian Sharia courts exhibited a high degree of consistency and predictability in their practice. Gerber, *State, Society and Law in Islam: Ottoman Law in Comparative Perspective.*

18. On the new publicity of violence in the press, see Noémi Lévy-Aksu, "A Capital Challenge: Managing Violence and Disorders in Late Ottoman Istanbul."

19. *Vakit*, June 28, 1881.

20. *Tercüman-ı Hakikat*, June 28, 1881.

21. *Tercüman-ı Hakikat*, May 18, 1881.

22. *Tercüman-ı Hakikat*, June 29, 1881.

23. *Tercüman-ı Hakikat*, July 9, 18, 1881.

24. Selim Deringil, *The Well-Protected Domains: Ideology and the Legitimation of Power in the Ottoman Empire, 1876–1909*, 135–49.

25. Ahmet Midhat, *Üss-i İnkilap.*

26. Bernard Lewis, "Ahmed Midhat"; Shaw and Shaw, *History of the Ottoman Empire*, 252. For a nuanced analysis of Ahmet Midhat's work, see Abdulhamit Kırmızı, "Authoritarianism and Constitutionalism Combined: Ahmed Midhat Efendi between the Sultan and the Kanun-i Esasi."

27. Uzunçarşılı, *Vesikalar*, 57.

28. *Vakit*, July 4, 1881.

29. *Vakit*, June 28, 1881; *Tercüman-ı Hakikat*, June 28, 1881.

30. Dwayne R. Winseck and Robert M. Pike, *Communication and Empire: Media, Markets, and Globalization, 1860–1930.*

31. *Reuters*, May 17, 1881.

32. *New York Times*, June 5, 1876.

33. *Sydney Morning Herald*, July 26, 1876.

34. *Tablet*, July 2, 1881.

35. *New York Times*, August 22, 1881.

36. *New York Times*, May 12, 1884.

37. *Tablet*, July 5, 1884.

38. See, for instance, *Launceston Examiner*, May 13, 1884.

39. Ali Haydar, *Life of Midhat Paşa*, 208.

40. Ibid., 209.

41. Ibid., 210.

42. Ibid., 213.

43. Ibid., 215.

44. Ibid., 217.

45. Ibid., 218.

46. *Annales judiciaires*, July 9, 1881.

47. *Annales judiciaires*, June 27, 1881; Ali Haydar Midhat, *Life of Midhat Paşa*, 208–9.

48. Petra de Bruijn, "Turkish Theatre: Autonomous Entity to Multicultural Compound," 186–92.

49. Martin Heidegger, *The Question Concerning Technology, and Other Essays*, 129–30.

50. Uzunçarşılı, *Midhat Paşa ve Yıldız Mahkemesi*, 256.

51. Anthony G. Amsterdam and Jerome Bruner, *Minding the Law: How Courts Rely on Storytelling, and How Their Stories Change the Ways We Understand the Law—and Ourselves*, 184.

52. *Tanin*, June 25, 1909.

53. *Annales judiciaires*, July 9, 1881.

54. Ibid.

55. For show trials as a medium for addressing the general public, see Eyal Ginio, "Debating the Nation in Court: The Torlakian Trial (Istanbul, 1921)"; and Yoram Meital, *Revolutionary Justice: Special Courts and the Formation of Republican Egypt*.

56. Awol K. Allo, "The 'Show' in the 'Show Trial': Contextualizing the Politicization of the Courtroom," 51.

57. Uzunçarşılı, *Midhat Paşa ve Yıldız Mahkemesi*, 291.

58. On the position of the Public Prosecution, see Rubin, *Ottoman Nizamiye Courts*, 133–52.

59. *Annales judiciaires*, July 9, 1881.

60. Ibid.

61. Rubin, "From Legal Representation to Advocacy."

62. Hirisantos, *Midhat Paşa ve Rüfekasının Muhakemesi*, 29.

63. *Tanin*, July 10, 1909.

64. *Tanin*, July 12, 1909.

65. Ibid.

66. Shaw and Shaw, *History of the Ottoman Empire*, 164.

67. *Tanin*, July 12, 1909.

68. *Annales judiciaires*, July 9, 1881.

69. *Tanin*, July 3, 1909.

70. On the use of narratives in court, see Amsterdam and Bruner, *Minding the Law*, 11–164; and Peter Brooks and Paul Gewirtz, eds., *Law's Stories: Narrative and Rhetoric in the Law*, 8.

71. John Phillip Dawson, *The Oracles of the Law*, 376.

72. Mitchell de S.-O.-l'E. Lasser, "Judicial (Self-)Portraits: Judicial Discourse in the French Legal System."

73. Ibid., 1341–42.

74. Rubin, *Ottoman Nizamiye Courts*, 13, 87–89.

75. Dawson, *Oracles of the Law*, 400–431.

76. This claim, made by François Gény, is quoted in Lasser, "Judicial (Self-)Portraits," 1345.

77. Perhaps there is no room for expecting such a critique in the first place, considering that Ottoman academic doctrine on the codified normative law was quite limited in scope and sophistication.

78. BOA Y.EE, 16/9.

79. Sociolinguists have debated the meaning of *register*. Broadly defined, it signifies the type of rhetorical and linguistic style of choice, conditioned by particular context, occupation, or level of formality. See Peter Trudgill, *Sociolinguistics: An Introduction to Language and Society*; and James A. Coleman and Robert Crawshaw, eds., *Discourse Variety in Contemporary French: Descriptive and Pedagogical Approaches*, 8.

80. Celia Kerslake, "Ottoman Turkish."

81. Davison, *Reform in the Ottoman Empire*, 176.

82. BOA Y.EE, 16/9.

83. BOA Y.EE, 16/9.

84. BOA Y.EE. 18/96.

85. Yoram Meital demonstrates this function of the show trial in his recent study on the trials held at the special tribunals that the Egyptian Free Officers established in the aftermath of the 1952 revolution. He brings out the drama of these trials, which formed a battleground of competing narratives, the revolutionary regime on the one hand, and its major opponent—the Muslim Brothers—on the other. See Meital, *Revolutionary Justice*.

4. LEGAL BURDENS AND POLITICAL LEGACIES

1. BOA Y.PRK.MK. 13/66.

2. BOA İ.DH. 1295/4/162168.

3. Heda Reindle-Kiel, "The Tragedy of Power: The Fate of Grand Vezirs according to the 'Menakibname-i Mahmud Paşa-i Veli.'"

4. Deringil, *Well-Protected Domains*, 165.

5. *Ceride-i Mehakim*, 1138, 6431.

6. Uzunçarşılı, *Midhat Paşa ve Taif Mahkumları*, 12.

7. Ibid., 16.

8. William Ochsenwald, *Religion, Society, and the State in Arabia: The Hijaz under Ottoman Control, 1840–1908*, 18.

9. Ibid., 64–72.

10. Ibid., 28–29.

11. Uzunçarşılı, *Midhat Paşa ve Taif Mahkumları*, 17.

12. Davison, *Reform in the Ottoman Empire*, 322–26.

13. On Abdülhamit's achievements and style of rule, see Kemal H. Karpat, *The Politicization of Islam: Reconstructing Identity, State, Faith, and Community in the Late Ottoman State*, 155–82.

14. Ochsenwald, *Religion, Society, and the State in Arabia*, 7–9.

15. M. Talha Çiçek, "Negotiating Power and Authority in the Desert: The Arab Bedouin and the Limits of the Ottoman State in the Hijaz, 1840–1908."

16. Ş. Tufan Buzpinar, "Vying for Power and Influence in the Hijaz: Ottoman Rule, the Last Emirate of Abdulmuttalib and the British (1880–1882)," 1–3.

17. Ochsenwald, *Religion, Society, and the State in Arabia*, 180–82.

18. Uzunçarşılı, *Midhat Paşa ve Taif Mahkumları*, 32–33.

19. Ochsenwald, *Religion, Society, and the State in Arabia*, 182; Mostafa Minawi, *The Ottoman Scramble for Africa: Empire and Diplomacy in the Sahara and the Hijaz*, 136.

20. Uzunçarşılı, *Midhat Paşa ve Taif Mahkumları*, 35–36.

21. On the Ottoman-Sanusi alliance, see Minawi, *Ottoman Scramble for Africa*, 94–95.

22. In 1878, Ali Suavi, a journalist and former Young Ottoman, led an attempted coup, aimed at reinstating Murat V. In 1905, Abdülhamit was saved from an assassination attempted by Armenian revolutionaries during a Friday prayer ceremony.

23. Patricia O'Brien, *The Promise of Punishment: Prisons in Nineteenth-Century France*.

24. Kent F. Schull, *Prisons in the Late Ottoman Empire: Microcosms of Modernity*, 42–46.

25. Ibid., 45.

26. BOA Y.EE. 88/74.

27. The telegraph logs of the Hijaz contain daily reports following interception of British telegraph correspondence and observation of movement of British forces on the Egyptian coast of the Red Sea, as well as frequent requests for reinforcements. See BOA Y.EE.D. 1090.

28. Uzunçarşılı, *Midhat Paşa ve Taif Mahkumları*, 47–50.

29. Bilal N. Şimşir, *Fransız Belgelerine Göre Midhat Paşa'nın Sonu*, 152–59.

30. Kahn, *Cultural Study of Law*.

31. Ibid., 67.

32. BOA Y.PRK.ASK 22/40.

33. According to Sam White, historians often confused anthrax with the bubonic plague, which caused the Black Death pandemic in medieval Europe. See Sam White, "Rethinking Disease in Ottoman History."

34. Uzunçarşılı, *Midhat Paşa ve Taif Mahkumları*, 59.

35. Ibid., 64.

36. Ibid., 63.

37. BOA Y.EE. 16/36/3.

38. BOA Y.EE. 16/36/4.

39. BOA Y.EE 16/33.

40. Uzunçarşılı, *Midhat Paşa ve Taif Mahkumları*, 68.

41. Ibid., 68–70.

42. BOA Y.EE. 16/35.

43. Fanny Davis, *The Ottoman Lady: A Social History from 1718–1918*, 180.

44. BOA İ.DH. 917/72743. In 1909 Şehriban Hanım petitioned for a raise in her pension following the death of the first wife, Naime. This petition indicates that the financial support of the family continued for many years. BOA BEO 3498/262303.

45. Sibel Zandi-Sayek, *Ottoman Izmir: The Rise of a Cosmopolitan City, 1840–1880.*

46. Ali Haydar Midhat, *Osmanlı'dan Cumhuriyet'e Hatıralarım, 1872–1946*, 143.

47. Ibid.

48. BOA BEO. 274/20523.

49. Ali Haydar Midhat, *Osmanlı'dan Cumhuriyet'e Hatıralarım*, 149–56.

50. Ibid., 163.

51. BOA Y.EE. 14/80.

52. BOA Y.EE. 150/21; HR.SYS. 1706/96.

53. Hanioğlu, *Young Turks in Opposition*, 151.

54. For the bundles sent to the palace, see BOA Y.EE. 56/7/1–6. For the other bundles, see BOA Y.EE. 56/7/7–47.

55. BOA Y.EE. 56/7/43.

56. BOA Y.EE. 56/7/9 Y.EE. 56/7/4.

57. Ali Haydar Midhat, *Life of Midhat Paşa*, 237–38.

58. Davis, *Ottoman Lady*, 107–8.

59. BOA Y.EE. 56/7/9–10.

60. BOA Y.EE. 56/7/9–10; BOA Y.EE. 56/7/5. For the English translation of the letter, see Ali Haydar Midhat, *Life of Midhat Paşa*, 241–42.

61. A French version of the book came out in 1908. Ali Haydar Mithat, *Midhat-Pacha: Sa vie, son oeuvre.*

62. Ali Haydar Midhat, *Life of Midhat Pasha*, viii.

63. Ibid., 256.

64. For Hayrullah's account in the Turkish version of Ali Haydar Midhat's biography of his father, see *Midhat Paşa'nın Hatıraları* 2:361–82.

65. Ali Haydar Midhat, *Life of Midhat Pasha*, 242.

66. Ibid., 245.

67. In fact, Cevdet Paşa retired in 1882 in order to work on his magnum opus, *Tarih-i Cevdet*, and other works. In 1886 he returned to public service.

68. Ali Haydar Midhat, *Life of Midhat Pasha*, 246.

69. Ibid., 255.

70. Ibid., 254.

71. For the short version, see BOA Y.EE. 18/103; for the longer version, see BOA Y.EE. 16/26.

72. Uzunçarşılı, *Midhat Paşa ve Taif Mahkumları*, 74–77.

73. Ibid., 78–105.

74. Ibid., 79–80; BOA Y.EE. 16/26.

75. BOA DH.MKT. 2663/79.

76. BOA DH.MKT. 2885/64.

77. Ali Haydar Midhat, *Osmanlı'dan Cumhuriyet'e Hatıralarım*, 204.

78. Ibid., 204–6.

79. BOA DH.D. 23/4.

80. Kayalı, *Arabs and Young Turks*, 184.

CONCLUSION

1. Hasan Cemal, "Hukuk Devleti de Yok, Kanun Devleti de Yok, Erdoğan Devleti Var!"

2. Brubaker and Cooper, "Beyond 'Identity,'" 4.

3. Charles de Secondat Montesquieu, *The Spirit of Laws*.

4. Brubaker and Cooper, "Beyond 'Identity,'" 6.

5. Shklar, "Political Theory and the Rule of Law," 1.

6. Ibid., 16.

7. Tamanaha, *On the Rule of Law*.

8. For a critical discussion on the parochial perspective of "Westernization" in the context of Japanese legal change, see Daniel Hedinger, "Globalization of Legal Cultures in the 19th Century: Criminal Trials, Gender, and the Public in Meiji Japan."

9. On the law as a constitutive force in the early-modern Ottoman Empire, evident in legal institutions, practices, and regulations, see for instance, Engin Deniz Akarlı, "The Ruler and Law Making in the Ottoman Empire"; Tezcan, *Second Ottoman Empire*; Baldwin, *Islamic Law and Empire in Ottoman Cairo*; Peirce, *Morality Tales*; and Metin Coşgel and Boğaç Ergene, *The Economics of Ottoman Justice Settlement and Trial in the Sharia Courts*.

10. See, for instance, Gerber, *State, Society and Law*; and Eyal Ginio, "Coping with the State's Agents 'From Below': Petitions, Legal Appeal, and the Sultan's Justice in Ottoman Legal Practice."

11. Boğaç E. Ergene, *Local Court, Provincial Society, and Justice in the Ottoman Empire: Legal Practice and Dispute Revolution in Çankırı and Kastamonu (1652–1744)*; Agmon, *Family and Court*. On the practice of amicable agreements, see Işık Tamdoğan, "Sulh and the 18th Century Ottoman Courts of Üsküdar and Adana."

12. Ekrem Buğra Ekinci, *Osmanlı Mahkemeleri: Tanzimat ve Sonrası*.

13. Rubin, *Ottoman Nizamiye Courts.*

14. George H. Hodos, *Show Trials: Stalinist Purges in Eastern Europe, 1948–1954,* 77.

15. Meital, *Revolutionary Justice.*

16. Allo, "'Show' in the 'Show Trial,'" 50.

17. Yaşar Şahin Anıl, *Osmanlı'da Hukuk Skandalları.*

18. İsmail Safa Üstün, "Heresy and Legitimacy in the Ottoman Empire in the Sixteenth Century."

19. According to Carlo Ginzburg, it is the meaning of *context* that signifies the huge gap between judges and historians. While judges treat contexts as arrays of mitigating factors, assessed in terms of their possible impact on verdicts, historians are concerned with contexts as collections of possibilities and conjectures that allow them to fill in what is not revealed by documents. I wish to stress this point. The sorts of contexts conceived by historians are not assortments of determined facts but of assumptions. Any pretension to "recovering" contextual facts must be a denial of the "haphazard and unpredictable dimension that forms such an important part (if not all) of an individual life." Carlo Ginzburg, *The Judge and the Historian: Marginal Notes on a Late-Twentieth-Century Miscarriage of Justice,* 117.

Bibliography

ARCHIVAL SOURCES AND PUBLISHED OFFICIAL RECORDS

Başbakanlık Osmanlı Arşivi (BOA, Turkish Prime Minister's Ottoman Archives), Istanbul

Askeri Maruzat (Y.PRK.ASK)
Bab-ı Ali Evrak Odası (BEO)
Dahiliye Nezareti Defterleri (DH.d)
Dahiliye Nezareti Mektubı Kalemi (DH.MKT)
Düstur, 1st ed. (Istanbul: Matbaa-yı Amire)
İrade Dahiliye (İ.DH)
Siyası Kısmı Belgeleri (HR.SYS)
Yıldız Esas Evrakı Defterleri (Y.EE.d)
Yıldız Evrakı Defterleri (Y.EE)
Yıldız Perakende Müfettişlikler ve Komiserlikler Tahriratı (Y.PRK.MK)

British National Archives (BNA, London)

Foreign Office (FO)
Hansard

NEWSPAPERS

Annales judiciaires de l'Empire Ottoman: Revue hebdomadaire de la jurisprudence, de la legislation et des débats judiciaires
Ceride-i Mehakim
Launceston Examiner
New York Times

Reuters
Sydney Morning Herald
Tablet
Tanin
Tercüman-ı Hakikat
Vakit

OTHER SOURCES

"131 Yılık Yalan Sultan Abdülaziz İntihar Etmedi Öldürüldü." YouTube. https://www.youtube.com/watch?v=7G_2EC9EvEI.

Abu-Manneh, Butrus. "Arab-Ottomanists' Reactions to the Young Turk Revolution." In *Late Ottoman Palestine: The Period of Young Turk Rule*, edited by Yuval Ben-Bassat and Eyal Ginio, 145–64. London: I. B. Tauris, 2011.

Adamiak, Patrick, Jeffery Dyer, and Michael Christopher Low. "The End of an Era: The Less than Grand Opening of the New Ottoman Archives." Jadaliyya. http://www.jadaliyya.com/Details/28498/The-End-of-an-Era-The-Less-than-Grand-Opening-of-the-New-Ottoman-Archives.

Agmon, Iris. *Family and Court: Legal Culture and Modernity in Late Ottoman Palestine*. Syracuse, NY: Syracuse Univ. Press, 2006.

———. "Recording Procedures and Legal Culture in the Late Ottoman Shari'a Court of Jaffa, 1865–1890." *Islamic Law and Society* 11 (2004): 333–77.

Agmon, Iris, and Ido Shahar. "Theme Issue—Shifting Perspectives in the Study of Shari'a Courts: Methodologies and Paradigms." *Islamic Law and Society* 15 (2008): 1–19.

Ahmad, Feroz. *The Making of Modern Turkey*. London: Routledge, 1993.

Ahmet Cevdet Paşa. *Tarih-i Cevdet*. Istanbul: Matbaa-yı Osmaniye, 1309 [1893].

———. *Tezakir*. Ankara: Türk Tarih Kurumu, 1933.

"Ahmet Cevdet Paşa Belgeseli." YouTube. https://www.youtube.com/watch?v=STMoy5fyymE.

Ahmet Midhat. *Üss-i İnkilap*. Vol. 1. Istanbul, 1294–95 [1877–78].

Akarlı, Engin Deniz. "The Ruler and Law Making in the Ottoman Empire." In *Law and Empire: Ideas, Practices, Actors*, edited by Jeroen Duindam, Jill Harries, Caroline Humfress, and Nimrod Hurvitz, 87–109. Leiden: Brill, 2013.

Akyıldız, Ali. "Sened-i İttifak'ın İlk Tam Metni." *İslam Araştırmaları Dergisi* 2 (1998): 209–22.

Ali Haydar Midhat. *The Life of Midhat Pasha: A Record of His Services, Political Reforms, Banishment, and Judicial Murder, Derived from Private Documents and Reminiscences.* London: J. Murray, 1903.

———. *Midhat-Pacha: Sa vie, son oeuvre.* Paris: Stock, 1908.

———. *Midhat Paşa'nın Hayatı Siyasiyesi, Hidematı, Menfa Hayatı.* Istanbul: Hilal Matbaası, 1325 [1909].

———. *Osmanlı'dan Cumhuriyet'e Hatıralarım, 1872–1946.* Istanbul: Bengi Yayınları, 2008.

Allo, Awol K. "The 'Show' in the 'Show Trial': Contextualizing the Politicization of the Courtroom." *Barry Law Review* 15, no. 1 (2010): 41–72.

Amsterdam, Anthony G., and Jerome Bruner. *Minding the Law: How Courts Rely on Storytelling, and How Their Stories Change the Ways We Understand the Law—and Ourselves.* Cambridge, MA: Harvard Univ. Press, 2002.

Anıl, Yaşar Şahin. *Osmanlı'da Hukuk Skandalları.* Ankara: Panama Yayıncılık, 2014.

Arendt, Hannah. *Eichmann in Jerusalem: A Report on the Banality of Evil.* New York: Viking Press, 1964.

Austin, J. L. *How to Do Things with Words: The William James Lectures Delivered at Harvard University in 1955.* Oxford: Oxford Univ. Press, 1962.

Aykut, Ebru. "Judicial Reforms, Sharia Law, and the Death Penalty in the Late Ottoman Empire." *Journal of the Ottoman and Turkish Studies Association* 4, no. 1 (2017): 7–29.

Bahadır, Osman Recep, and H. H. Günhan Danışman. "Late Ottoman and Early Republican Science Periodicals: Center and Periphery Relationship in Dissemination of Knowledge." In *Turkish Studies in the History and Philosophy of Sciences*, edited by Gürol Irzik and Güven Güzeldere, 285–308. Dordrecht: Springer, 2005.

Baldwin, James E. "The Deposition of Defterdar Ahmed Pasha and the Rule of Law in Seventeenth-Century Egypt." *Osmanlı Araştırmaları/Journal of Ottoman Studies* 46 (2015): 131–61.

———. *Islamic Law and Empire in Ottoman Cairo.* Edinburgh: Edinburgh Univ. Press, 2017.

Banu Karadağ, Ayşe. "Türk Çeviri Tarihimizde 'Mütercim' Selanikli Tevfik." *Turkish Studies* 8, no. 10 (2013): 355–63.

Başbuğ, İlker. *20. Yüzyilin En Büyük Lideri Atatürk.* Istanbul: Remzi Kitabevi, 2012.

———. *Ermeni Suçlamaları ve Gerçekler.* Istanbul: Remzi Kitabevi, 2015.

Baysal, Jale. *Müteferrika'dan Birinci Meşrutiyete Kadar Osmanlı Türklerinin Bastıkları Kitaplar.* Istanbul: Edebiyet Fakültesi, 1968.

Becker, Theodore L., ed. *Political Trials.* Indianapolis: Bobbs-Merril, 1971.

Belknap, Michael R. "Introduction: Political Trials in the American Past." In *American Political Trials*, edited by Michael R. Belknap. Westport, CT: Greenwood Press, 1981.

Bentham, Jeremy. *Papers Relative to Codification and Public Instruction.* London: J. M'Creery, 1817.

Benton, Lauren. "Not Just a Concept: Institutions and the 'Rule of Law.'" *Journal of Asian Studies* 68, no. 1 (2009): 117–22.

Berkes, Niyazi. *The Development of Secularism in Turkey.* Montreal: McGill Univ. Press, 1964.

Berktay, Halil. "The Search for the Peasant in Western and Turkish History/Historiography." In *New Approaches to State and Peasant in Ottoman History*, edited by Halil Berktay and Suraiya Faroqhi, 109–84. London: Frank Cass, 1992.

Beydilli, Kemal. "Kabakcı İsyanı Akabinde Hazırlanan Hüccet-i Şer'iyye." *Türk Kültürü İncelemeleri Dergisi* 4 (2001): 33–48.

Borisova, Tatiana. "The Digest of Laws of the Russian Empire: The Phenomenon of Autocratic Legality." *Law and History Review* 30, no. 5 (2012): 901–25.

Boyar, Ebru, and Kate Fleet. *A Social History of Ottoman Istanbul.* Cambridge: Cambridge Univ. Press, 2010.

Brooks, Peter, and Paul Gewirtz, eds. *Law's Stories: Narrative and Rhetoric in the Law.* New Haven, CT: Yale Univ. Press, 1996.

Brubaker, Rogers, and Frederick Cooper. "Beyond 'Identity.'" *Theory and Society* 29, no. 1 (2000): 1–47.

Bruijn, Petra de. "Turkish Theatre: Autonomous Entity to Multicultural Compound." In *Theatre Intercontinental: Forms, Functions, Correspondences*, edited by C. C. Barfoot and Cobi Bordewijk, 175–92. Amsterdam and Atlanta: Rodopi, 1993.

Buzpinar, Ş. Tufan. "Vying for Power and Influence in the Hijaz: Ottoman Rule, the Last Emirate of Abdulmuttalib and the British (1880–1882)." *Muslim World* 95, no. 1 (2005): 1–22.

Calavita, Kitty. *Invitation to Law and Society: An Introduction to the Study of Real Law.* Chicago: Univ. of Chicago Press, 2010.

Canale, Damiano. "The Many Faces of the Codification of Law in Modern Continental Europe." In *A History of the Philosophy of Law in the Civil Law World, 1600–1900*, edited by Damiano Canale, Paolo Grossi, and Hasso Hofman, 135–83. Dordrecht and New York: Springer, 2005.

Carr, E. H. *What Is History?* New York: Vintage Books, 1961.

Chakrabarty, Dipesh. *Provincializing Europe: Postcolonial Thought and Historical Difference.* Princeton, NJ: Princeton Univ. Press, 2008.

Celaleddin Paşa, Mahmut. *Mirat-ı Hakikat: Tarih-i Mahmut Cellaleddin Paşa.* Istanbul: Matbaa-yı Osmaniye, 1326–27 [1908].

Cemal, Hasan. "Hukuk Devleti de Yok, Kanun Devleti de Yok, Erdoğan Devleti Var!" *T24*: Bağımsız İnternet Gazetesi. http://t24.com.tr/yazarlar/hasan-cemal/hukuk-devleti-de-yok-kanun-devleti-de-yok-erdogan-devleti-var,11592.

Çetinkaya, Gökhan. *Ottoman Administration of Iraq, 1890–1908.* London and New York: Routledge, 2006.

Ceylan, Ebubekir. *The Ottoman Origins of Modern Iraq: Political Reform, Modernization, and Development in the Nineteenth-Century Middle East.* London: I. B. Tauris, 2011.

Chen, Jianfu. *Chinese Law: Towards an Understanding of Chinese Law, Its Nature, and Development.* The Hague and Boston: Kluwer Law International, 1999.

Choueiri, Youssef M. *Modern Arab Historiography: Historical Discourse and the Nation-State.* London and New York: RoutledgeCurzon, 2003.

Christenson, Ron. *Political Trials: Gordian Knots in the Law.* New Brunswick, NJ: Transaction, 1999.

Çiçek, M. Talha. "Negotiating Power and Authority in the Desert: The Arab Bedouin and the Limits of the Ottoman State in the Hijaz, 1840–1908." *Middle Eastern Studies* 52, no. 2 (2016): 260–79.

Coleman, James A., and Robert Crawshaw, eds. *Discourse Variety in Contemporary French: Descriptive and Pedagogical Approaches.* London: Association for French Language Studies in association with the Centre for Information on Language Teaching and Research, 1994.

Çoşgel, Metin, and Boğaç Ergene. *The Economics of Ottoman Justice: Settlement and Trial in the Sharia Courts.* Cambridge: Cambridge Univ. Press, 2016.

Çoşgel, Metin M., Boğaç Ergene, Haggay Etkes, and Thomas J. Miceli. "Crime and Punishment in Ottoman Times: Corruption and Fines." *Journal of Interdisciplinary History* 43, no. 3 (2013): 353–76.

Costa, Pietro. "The Rule of Law: A Historical Introduction." In *The Rule of Law: History, Theory and Criticism*, edited by Pietro Costa and Danilo Zolo, 73–149. Dordrecht: Springer, 2010.

Cotterrell, Roger. *Law, Culture and Society: Legal Ideas in the Mirror of Social Theory*. Aldershot, UK: Ashgate, 2006.

Cuno, Kenneth M. *Modernizing Marriage: Family, Ideology, and Law in Nineteenth- and Early Twentieth-Century Egypt*. Syracuse, NY: Syracuse Univ. Press, 2015.

Damaska, Mirjan. "The Shadow Side of Command Responsibility." *American Journal of Comparative Law* 49 (2001): 455–96.

Davis, Fanny. *The Ottoman Lady: A Social History from 1718–1918*. New York: Greenwood Press, 1986.

Davison, Roderic H. *Reform in the Ottoman Empire, 1856–1876*. Princeton, NJ: Princeton Univ. Press, 1963.

Dawson, John Phillip. *The Oracles of the Law*. Ann Arbor: Univ. of Michigan Law School, 1968.

Deflem, Mathieu. *Sociology of Law: Visions of a Scholarly Tradition*. Cambridge: Cambridge Univ. Press, 2008.

Demirel, Fatmagül. *II Abdülhamid Döneminde Sansür*. Istanbul: Bağlam, 2007.

———. *Adliye Nezareti: Kuruluşu ve Faaliyetleri, 1876–1914*. Istanbul: Boğaziçi Üniversitesi, 2008.

Deringil, Selim. *The Well-Protected Domains: Ideology and the Legitimation of Power in the Ottoman Empire, 1876–1909*. London: I. B. Tauris, 1998.

Devereux, Robert. "Süleyman Pasha's 'The Feeling of the Revolution.'" *Middle Eastern Studies* 15, no. 1 (1979): 3–35.

Doumani, Beshara. *Rediscovering Palestine: Merchants and Peasants in Jabal Nablus, 1700–1900*. Berkeley: Univ. of California Press, 1995.

Dufour, Julien-Michel. *Code criminel avec instructions: Deuxième partie, code penal*. Vol. 1. Paris: Chez Arthus-Bertrand, 1811.

Durukan, Kaan. "Ideology and Historiography: State, Society and Intellectuals in Modern Turkey." PhD thesis, Univ. of Wisconsin–Madison, 2007.

Ecevit, Bülent. *Mithat Paşa ve Türk Ekonomisinin Tarihsel Süreci*. Ankara: Demokratik Sol Parti Yayını, 1990.

Ekinci, Ekrem Buğra. *Osmanlı Mahkemeleri: Tanzimat ve Sonrası*. Istanbul: Arı Sanat, 2004.

Eldem, Edhem. "Istanbul: From Imperial to Peripheralized Capital." In *The Ottoman City between East and West: Aleppo, Izmir and Istanbul*, edited by

Edhem Eldem, Daniel Goffman, and Bruce Masters, 135–206. Cambridge: Cambridge Univ. Press, 1999.

———. "Istanbul as a Cosmopolitan City: Myths and Realities." In *A Companion to Diaspora and Transnationalism*, edited by Ato Quayson and Girish Daswani, 212–30. Malden, MA: Wiley-Blackwell, 2013.

———. "Stability against All Odds: The Imperial Ottoman Bank, 1875–1914." In *Banking and Finance in the Mediterranean: A Historical Perspective*, edited by John A. Consiglo, Juan Carlos Martinez Oliva, and Gabriel Tortella, 95–118. Farnham, UK, and Burlington, VT: Ashgate, 2012.

Ergene, Boğaç E. "Evidence in Ottoman Courts: Oral and Written Documentation in Early-Modern Courts of Islamic Law." *Journal of the American Oriental Society* 124, no. 3 (2004): 471–91.

———. *Local Court, Provincial Society, and Justice in the Ottoman Empire: Legal Practice and Dispute Revolution in Çankırı and Kastamonu (1652–1744).* Leiden: Boston: Brill, 2003.

"Ergenekon Iddianamesi." Vikikaynak. http://tr.wikisource.org/wiki/Ergenekon_iddianamesi.

Ersanlı, Buşra. "The Empire in the Historiography of the Kemalist Era." In *The Ottomans and the Balkans: A Discussion of Historiography*, edited by Fikret Adanir and Suraiya Faroqhi, 115–54. Leiden: Brill, 2002.

Ertür, Başak. "The Conspiracy Archive: Turkey's 'Deep State' on Trial." In *Law, Memory, Violence: Uncovering the Counter-Archive*, edited by Stewart Motha and Honni van Rijswijk, 177–94. New York: Routledge, 2016.

———. "Spectacles and Spectres: Political Trials, Performativity and Scenes of Sovereignty." PhD thesis, Univ. of London, 2015.

Fahri Bey. *Ibretnuma: Mabeynci Fahri Bey'in Hatıraları ve İlgili Bazı Belgeler.* Edited by Bekir Sitki Baykal. Ankara: Türk Kurumu Basimevi, 1968.

Farmer, Lindsay. "Reconstructing the English Codification Debate: The Criminal Law Commissioners, 1833–45." *Law and History Review* 18, no. 2 (2000): 397–425.

Felman, Shoshana. *The Juridical Consciousness: Trials and Traumas in the Twentieth Century.* Cambridge, MA: Harvard Univ. Press, 2002.

Findley, Carter V. "The Evolution of the System of Provincial Administration as Viewed from the Center." In *Palestine in the Late Ottoman Period*, edited by David Kushner, 3–29. Jerusalem: Yad Izhak Ben-Zvi, 1986.

Gerber, Haim. *State, Society and Law in Islam: Ottoman Law in Comparative Perspective.* Albany: State Univ. of New York Press, 1994.

Ginio, Eyal. "Coping with the State's Agents 'from Below': Petitions, Legal Appeal, and the Sultan's Justice in Ottoman Legal Practice." In *Popular Protest and Political Participation in the Ottoman Empire: Studies in Honor of Suraiya Faroqhi*, edited by Eleni Gara, M. Erdem Kabadayı and Christoph K. Neumann, 41–55. Istanbul: Istanbul Bilgi Univ. Press, 2011.

———. "Debating the Nation in Court: The Torlakian Trial (Istanbul, 1921)." *Armenian Review* 55, nos. 1–2 (2015): 1–16.

Ginzburg, Carlo. *The Judge and the Historian: Marginal Notes on a Late-Twentieth-Century Miscarriage of Justice*. London and New York: Verso, 2002.

Gözler, Kemal. *Türk Anayasaları*. Bursa: Ekin Kitabevi, 1999.

Gray, Marion W. *Prussia in Transition: Society and Politics under the Stein Reform Ministry of 1808*. Philadelphia: American Philosophical Society, 1986.

Green, Nile. "Journeymen, Middlemen: Travel, Transculture, and Technology in the Origins of Muslim Printing." *International Journal of Middle East Studies* 41, no. 2 (2009): 203–24.

Grunwald, Henning. *Courtroom to Revolutionary Stage: Performance and Ideology in Weimar Political Trials*. Oxford: Oxford Univ. Press, 2012.

Gürsoy, Yaprak. "Turkish Public Opinion on the Coup Allegations: Implications for Democratization." *Political Science Quarterly* 130, no. 1 (2015): 103–32.

Hale, William. *Turkish Politics and the Military*. London and New York: Routledge, 1994.

Hanioğlu, Şükrü. *The Young Turks in Opposition*. New York: Oxford Univ. Press, 1995.

Head, John W., and Yanping Wang. *Law Codes in Dynastic China: A Synopsis of Chinese Legal History in the Thirty Centuries from Zhou to Qing*. Durham, NC: Carolina Academic Press, 2005.

Hedinger, Daniel. "Globalization of Legal Cultures in the 19th Century: Criminal Trials, Gender, and the Public in Meiji Japan." *InterDisciplines* 2 (2012): 135–65.

Heidegger, Martin. *The Question Concerning Technology, and Other Essays*. Translated by William Lovitt. New York: Harper and Row, 1977.

Heinzelmann, Tobias. "The Ruler's Monologue: The Rhetoric of the Ottoman Penal Code of 1858." *Die Welt des Islams* 54, nos. 3–4 (2014): 292–321.

Heyd, Uriel. *Studies in Old Ottoman Criminal Law*. Oxford: Clarendon Press, 1973.

Hirisantos, Tomaidis. *Midhat Paşa ve Rüfekasının Muhakemesi Hakkında Esbab-ı Mücibeyi Havi İade-yi Muhakeme Layihası*. Dersaadet: Hilal Matbaası, 1326 [1910].

Hodos, George H. *Show Trials: Stalinist Purges in Eastern Europe, 1948–1954.* New York and London: Praeger, 1987.

"İbretlik Midhat Paşa Davası ve Bugün." İlker Başbuğ Resmi Web Sitesi. http://www.ilkerbasbug.com.tr/?p=1887.

Imber, Colin. *The Ottoman Empire, 1300–1650: The Structure of Power.* New York: Palgrave Macmillan, 2002.

İnal, İbnülemin Mahmut Kemal. *Son Sadrazamlar.* Vol. 1. Istanbul: Dergah Yayınları, 1982.

Ismail Kemal Bey. *The Memoirs of Ismail Kemal Bey.* Edited by S. Story. London: Constable, 1920.

Kahn, Paul W. *The Cultural Study of Law: Reconstructing Legal Scholarship.* Chicago: Univ. of Chicago Press, 1999.

Kalkan, İbrahim Halil. "Between Medicine and Honor: The Legal Ban on Torture in the Ottoman Empire, 1840–1858." *Journal of the Ottoman and Turkish Studies Association* 4, no. 1 (2017): 31–53.

Karateke, Hakan T. "Who Is the Next Ottoman Sultan? Attempts to Change the Rule of Succession during the Nineteenth Century." In *Ottoman Reform and Muslim Regeneration: Studies in Honour of Butrus Abu-Manneh*, edited by Itzchak Weismann and Fruma Zachs, 37–53. London: I. B. Tauris, 2005.

Karpat, Kemal H. *The Politicization of Islam: Reconstructing Identity, State, Faith, and Community in the Late Ottoman State.* Oxford: Oxford Univ. Press, 2001.

Kayalı, Hasan. *Arabs and Young Turks: Ottomanism, Arabism, and Islamism in the Ottoman Empire, 1908–1918.* Berkeley: Univ. of California Press, 1997.

Kayaoğlu, Barın. "Has AKP Sacrificed Turkey's Ottoman Heritage?" Almonitor. http://www.al-monitor.com/pulse/originals/2015/02/turkey-ottoman-archives-undermine-akp.html.

Kelman, Mark. *A Guide to Critical Legal Studies.* Cambridge, MA: Harvard Univ. Press, 1988.

Kennedy, Duncan. "Two Globalizations of Law and Legal Thought, 1850–1968." *Suffolk University Law Review* 36, no. 3 (2003): 631–79.

Kerslake, Celia. "Ottoman Turkish." In *The Turkic Languages*, edited by Lars Johanson and Eva A. Csato, 179–82. London and New York: Routledge, 1998.

Kirchheimer, Otto. *Political Justice: The Use of Political Procedure for Political Ends.* Princeton, NJ: Princeton Univ. Press, 1961.

Kırlı, Cengiz. *Yolsuzluğun İcadı: 1840 Ceza Kanunu, İktidar ve Bürokrasi.* Istanbul: Verita, 2015.

Kırmızı, Abdulhamit. "Authoritarianism and Constitutionalism Combined: Ahmed Midhat Efendi between the Sultan and the Kanun-i Esasi." In *The First Ottoman Experiment in Democracy*, edited by Christoph Herzog and Malek Sharif, 53–65. Würzburg: Ergon in Kommission, 2010.

Kocahanoğlu, Osman Selim. *Midhat Paşa'nın Hatıraları: Yıldız Mahkemesi ve Taif Zindanı*. Istanbul: Temel Yayınları, 1997.

Koçunyan, Aylin. "The Transcultural Dimension of the Ottoman Constitution." In *Well-Connected Domains: Towards an Entangled Ottoman History*, edited by Pascal W. Firges, Tobias P. Graf, Christian Roth, and Gülay Tulasoğlu, 235–58. Leiden and Boston: Brill, 2014.

Koloğlu, Orhan. "Newspapers." In *Encyclopedia of the Ottoman Empire*, edited by Gabor Agoston and Bruce Masters, 431–35. New York: Facts of File, 2009.

Kretzmer, David. *The Occupation of Justice: The Supreme Court of Israel and the Occupied Territories*. New York: State Univ. of New York Press, 2002.

Kuran, Timur. *The Long Divergence: How Islamic Law Held Back the Middle East*. Princeton, NJ: Princeton Univ. Press, 2011.

Kyle, Ken, and Pat Lauderdale. "The Rule of Law or Unruly Law? Reflections on the Study of Political Trials." *Humanity and Society* 24, no. 1 (2000): 52–73.

Lahav, Pnina. "Theater in the Courtroom." *Law and Literature* 16, no. 3 (2004): 381–474.

Lasser, Mitchell de S.-O.-l'E. "Judicial (Self-)Portraits: Judicial Discourse in the French Legal System." *Yale Law Journal* 104 (1995): 1325–1410.

Lévy-Aksu, Noémi. "A Capital Challenge: Managing Violence and Disorders in Late Ottoman Istanbul." In *Urban Violence in the Middle East: Changing City Spaces in the Transition from Empire to Nation State*, edited by Ulrike Freitag, Claudia Ghrawi, and Nora Lafi, 52–69. New York and Oxford: Berghahn, 2015.

———. *Ordre et désordres dans l'Istanbul ottomane, 1879–1909: De l'état au quartier*. Paris: Karthala, 2013.

Lewis, Bernard. "Ahmed Midhat." In *Encyclopaedia of Islam*, edited by P. Bearman, Th. Bianquis, C. E. Bosworth, E. van Donzel, and W. P. Heinrichs. 2nd ed. http://dx.doi.org/10.1163/1573-3912_islam_SIM_0412.

———. *The Emergence of Modern Turkey*. London: Oxford Univ. Press, 1961).

Lockman, Zachary. *Contending Visions of the Middle East: The History and Politics of Orientalism*. Cambridge: Cambridge Univ. Press, 2004.

"Mahmud Şevket Paşa'nın 31 Mart Olayı Sırasındaki Ses Kaydı." YouTube. https://www.youtube.com/watch?v=xIRUC8p0t7M.

Maksudyan, Nazan. *Orphans and Destitute Children in the Late Ottoman Empire*. Syracuse, NY: Syracuse Univ. Press, 2014.

Marchuk, Iryna. *The Fundamental Concept of Crime in International Law: A Comparative Law Analysis*. Heidelberg: Springer, 2014.

Mardin, Şerif. *The Genesis of Young Ottoman Thought: A Study in the Modernization of Turkish Political Ideas*. Syracuse, NY: Syracuse Univ. Press, 2000.

Mehmet Tahir. *Osmanlı Müellifleri*. Istanbul: Matbaa-yı Amire, 1333 [1914].

Meital, Yoram. *Revolutionary Justice: Special Courts and the Formation of Republican Egypt*. Oxford: Oxford Univ. Press, 2017.

Meloni, Chantal. "Command Responsibility: Mode of Liability for the Crimes of Subordinates or Separate Offence of the Superior?" *Journal of International Criminal Justice* 5 (2007): 619–37.

Menski, Werner. *Comparative Law in a Global Context: The Legal Systems of Asia and Africa*. Cambridge: Cambridge Univ. Press, 2006.

Midhat Paşa. *Mir'at-ı Hayret*. Istanbul, 1325 [1909].

Miller, Ruth A. *Legislating Authority: Sin and Crime in the Ottoman Empire and Turkey*. New York and London: Routledge, 2005.

Minawi, Mostafa. *The Ottoman Scramble for Africa: Empire and Diplomacy in the Sahara and the Hijaz*. Stanford, CA: Stanford Univ. Press, 2016.

Montesquieu, Charles de Secondat. *The Spirit of Laws*. Translated by Thomas Nuget. Chicago: Encyclopaedia Britannica, 1952.

Morriss, Andrew P. "Codification and Right Answers." *Chicago-Kent Law Review* 74 (1999): 355–92.

Murillo, Maria Luisa. "The Evolution of Codification in the Civil Law Legal Systems: Towards Decodification and Recodification." *Journal of Transnational Law and Policy* 11 (2001): 1–20.

Neumann, Christoph K. "Whom Did Ahmed Cevdet Represent?" In *Late Ottoman Society: The Intellectual Legacy*, edited by Elizabeth Özdalga, 117–33. London and New York: Routledge, 2005.

Neumann, Michael. *The Rule of Law: Politicizing Ethics*. Aldershot, Hants, UK, and Burlington, VT: Ashgate, 2002.

Nora, Pierre. "Between Memory and History: *Les lieux de mémoire*." *Representations* 26 (1989): 7–24.

O'Brien, Patricia. *The Promise of Punishment: Prisons in Nineteenth-Century France*. Princeton, NJ: Princeton Univ. Press, 1982.

Ochsenwald, William. *Religion, Society, and the State in Arabia: The Hijaz under Ottoman Control, 1840–1908*. Columbus: Ohio State Univ. Press, 1984.

Osman Nuri, *Abdülhamid-i Sani ve Devri Saltanatı Hayatı ve Hususiyesi*. Istanbul: Kitabhane-yi İslam ve Askery—İbrahim Hami, 1327 [1910].

Pamuk, Şevket. "Institutional Change and the Longevity of the Ottoman Empire, 1500–1800." *Journal of Interdisciplinary History* 35, no. 2 (2004): 225–47.

Paz, Omri. "Documenting Justice: New Recording Practices and the Establishment of an Activist Criminal Court System in the Ottoman Provinces (1840–Late 1860s)." *Islamic Law and Society* 21 (2014): 81–113.

———. "The Usual Suspect: Worker Migration and Law Enforcement in Mid-Nineteenth-Century Anatolia." *Continuity and Change* 30, no. 2 (2015): 223–49.

Peirce, Leslie. *Morality Tales: Law and Gender in the Ottoman Court of Aintab*. Berkeley: Univ. of California Press, 2003.

Peters, Rudolph. *Crime and Punishment in Islamic Law*. Cambridge: Cambridge Univ. Press, 2005.

———. "From Jurists' Law to Statute Law; or, What Happens When the Sharia Is Codified." *Mediterranean Politics* 7, no. 3 (2002): 82–95.

Peters, Ruud. "'For His Correction and as a Deterrent Example for Others': Mehmed Ali's First Criminal Legislation (1829–1330)." *Islamic Law and Society* 6 (1999): 164–92.

Petrov, Milen V. "Everyday Forms of Compliance: Subaltern Commentaries on Ottoman Reform, 1864–1868." *Comparative Study of Society and History* 46, no. 4 (2004): 730–59.

Quataert, Donald. *The Ottoman Empire, 1700–1922*. Cambridge: Cambridge Univ. Press, 2005.

Rahme, Joseph G. "Namık Kemal's Constitutional Ottomanism and Non-Muslims." *Islam and Christian-Muslim Relations* 10, no. 1 (1999): 23–39.

Rawls, John. *A Theory of Justice*. Cambridge, MA: Belknap Press of Harvard Univ. Press, 1971.

Raz, Joseph. *The Authority of Law: Essays on Law and Morality*. Oxford: Clarendon Press, 1979.

Reindle-Kiel, Heda. "The Tragedy of Power: The Fate of Grand Vezirs according to the 'Menakibname-i Mahmud Paşa-i Veli.'" *Turcica* 35 (2003): 247–56.

Rubin, Avi. "British Perceptions of Ottoman Judicial Reform in the Nineteenth Century: Some Preliminary Insights." *Law and Social Inquiry* 37, no. 4 (2012): 991–1012.

———. "From Legal Representation to Advocacy: Attorneys and Clients in the Ottoman Nizamiye Courts." *International Journal of Middle East Studies* 44, no. 1 (2012): 111–27.

———. "Legal Borrowing and Its Impact on Ottoman Legal Culture in the Late Nineteenth Century." *Continuity and Change* 22, no. 2 (2007): 279–303.

———. "Modernity as a Code: The Ottoman Empire and the Global Movement of Codification." *Journal of the Economic and Social History of the Orient* 59, no. 5 (2016): 828–56.

———. *Ottoman Nizamiye Courts: Law and Modernity.* New York: Palgrave Macmillan, 2011.

Ryosuke, Ishii. *Japanese Legislation in the Meiji Era.* Tokyo: Pan Pacific Press, 1958.

Sabev, Orlin. "The First Ottoman Turkish Printing Enterprise: Success or Failure?" In *Ottoman Tulips, Ottoman Coffee: Leisure and Lifestyle in the Eighteenth Century*, edited by Dana Sajdi, 63–89. London: Tauris Academic Studies, 2007.

Sait Paşa. *Sait Paşa'nın Hatıratı.* Istanbul: Sabah Matbaası, 1328 [1912].

Salzmann, Ariel. *Tocqueville in the Ottoman Empire: Rival Paths to Modern State.* Leiden and Boston: Brill, 2004.

Schull, Kent F. *Prisons in the Late Ottoman Empire: Microcosms of Modernity.* Edinburgh: Edinburgh Univ. Press, 2014.

Schwartz, Kathryn A. "The Political Economy of Private Printing in Cairo as Told from a Commissioning Deal Turned Sour, 1871" *International Journal of Middle East Studies* 49, no. 1 (2017): 25–45.

Şehsuvaroğlu, Haluk Y. *Sultan Aziz: Hususi, Siyası Hayatı, Devri ve Ölümü.* Istanbul: Hilmi Kitabevi, 1949.

Shaw, Stanford J., and Ezel Kural Shaw. *History of the Ottoman Empire and Modern Turkey.* Vol. 2. Cambridge: Cambridge Univ. Press, 1977.

Shklar, Judith N. *Legalism: An Essay on Law, Morals, and Politics.* Cambridge, MA: Harvard Univ. Press, 1964.

———. "Political Theory and the Rule of Law." In *The Rule of Law: Ideal of Ideology*, edited by Alan C. Hutchinson and Patrick Monahan, 1–16. Toronto and Calgary: Carswell, 1987.

Şimşir, Bilal N. *Fransız Belgelerine Göre Midhat Paşa'nın Sonu.* Ankara: Ayyıldız Matbaası, 1970.

Singer, Amy. *Constructing Ottoman Beneficence: An Imperial Soup Kitchen in Jerusalem.* New York: State Univ. of New York Press, 2002.

Sohrabi, Nader. *Revolution and Constitutionalism in the Ottoman Empire and Iran*. Cambridge: Cambridge Univ. Press, 2011.

Stone Peters, Julie. "Legal Performance Good and Bad." *Law, Culture and the Humanities* 4 (2008): 179–200.

Strauss, Johann. "'Kütüp ve Resail-i Mevkufe': Printing and Publishing in a Multi-ethnic Society." In *Late Ottoman Society: The Intellectual Legacy*, edited by Elisabeth Özdalga, 227–54. London and New York: RoutledgeCurzon, 2005.

Süleyman Paşa. *Hiss-i İnkilap yahut Sultan Abdülaziz Hal'i ile Sultan Murat-ı Hamisin Cülusu*. Istanbul: Tanin Matbaası, 1326 [1910].

———. *Süleyman Paşa Muhakemesi*. Edited by Süleyman Paşazade Sami. Istanbul: Matbaa-yı Ebüziya, 1328 [1910].

"Sultan Abdülaziz Han'ın Katli Ağlatan Sahne." YouTube. https://www.youtube.com/watch?v=ZPB6zKDRJNU.

"Talat Paşa Mithat Paşa Yeter Artık Bıktık Bu Yalanlardan." YouTube. https://www.youtube.com/watch?v=M6Qc5JnnaM4.

Tamanaha, Brian Z. *On the Rule of Law: History, Politics, Theory*. Cambridge: Cambridge Univ. Press, 2004.

Tamdoğan, Işık. "Sulh and the 18th Century Ottoman Courts of Üsküdar and Adana." *Islamic Law and Society* 15 (2008): 55–83.

Tevfik, Nureddin. *Sultan Aziz'in Hal'ı ve İntiharı*. Istanbul: Karabet Matbaası 1324 [1908].

Tezcan, Baki. *The Second Ottoman Empire: Political and Social Transformation in the Early Modern World*. New York: Cambridge Univ. Press, 2010.

Toledano, Ehud R. *As If Silent and Absent: Bonds of Enslavement in the Islamic Middle East*. New Haven, CT: Yale Univ. Press, 2007.

———. "The Legislative Process in the Ottoman Empire in the Early Tanzimat Period." *International Journal of Turkish Studies* 11, no. 2 (1980): 99–108.

———. "Shemsigul: A Circassian Slave in Mid-Nineteenth-Century Cairo." In *Struggle and Survival in the Modern Middle East*, edited by Edmund Burke III, 59–74. London: I. B. Tauris, 1993.

———. "Social and Economic Change in 'the Long Nineteenth Century.'" In *The Cambridge History of Egypt*, edited by M. W. Daly, 2:252–83. Cambridge: Cambridge Univ. Press, 1998.

Toprak, Zafer. "From Plurality to Unity: Codification and Jurisprudence in the Late Ottoman Empire." In *Ways to Modernity in Greece and Turkey: Encounters with Europe, 1850–1950*, edited by Anna Frangoudaki and Caglar Keyder, 26–39. London: I. B. Tauris, 2007.

Trubek, David M. "Where the Action Is: Critical Legal Studies and Empiricism." *Stanford Law Review* 36 (1984): 575–622.

Trudgill, Peter. *Sociolinguistics: An Introduction to Language and Society*. Harmondsworth, UK, and New York: Penguin Books, 1983.

Üstün, İsmail Safa. "Heresy and Legitimacy in the Ottoman Empire in the Sixteenth Century." PhD thesis, Univ. of Manchester, 1991.

Uzunçarşılı, İsmail Hakki. *Bizans ve Selçukiylerle Germiyan ve Osman Oğulları zamanında Küthaya Şehri*. Istanbul: Devlet Matbaası, 1932.

———. *Midhat Paşa ve Rüştü Paşaların Tevkiflerine Dair Vesikalar*. Ankara: Türk Tarih Kurumu Basımevi, 1947.

———. *Midhat Paşa ve Taif Mahkumları*. Ankara: Türk Kurumu Basımevi, 1950.

———. *Midhat Paşa ve Yıldız Mahkemesi*. Ankara: Türk Tarih Kurumu Basimevi, 2000 [1967].

Varga, Csaba. *Codification as a Socio-Historical Phenomenon*. Budapest: Szent Istvan Tarsulat, 2010.

Velideoğlu, Hıfzı Veldet. *Kanunlaştırma Hareketleri ve Tanzimat*. Istanbul: Maarif Matbaası, 1940.

Watson, Alan. *The Evolution of Western Private Law*. Baltimore: Johns Hopkins Univ. Press, 2001.

———. *Legal Transplants: An Approach to Comparative Law*. Athens: Univ. of Georgia Press, 1993.

West, Robin. "Reconsidering Legalism." *Minnesota Law Review* 88 (2003): 119–58.

White, Sam. "Rethinking Disease in Ottoman History." *International Journal of Middle East History* 42, no. 4 (2010): 549–67.

Winseck, Dwayne R., and Robert M. Pike. *Communication and Empire: Media, Markets, and Globalization, 1860–1930*. Durham, NC: Duke Univ. Press, 2007.

Wu, Timothy, and Yong-Sung (Jonathan) Kang. "Criminal Liability for the Actions of Subordinates: The Doctrine of Command Responsibility and Its Analogues in United States Law." *Harvard International Law Journal* 38, no. 1 (1997): 272–97.

Yaycioğlu, Ali. *Partners of the Empire: The Crisis of the Ottoman Order in the Age of Revolutions*. Stanford, CA: Stanford Univ. Press, 2016.

Yılmaz, Hüseyin. "Containing Sultanic Authority: Constitutionalism in the Ottoman Empire before Modernity." *Journal of Ottoman Studies* 45 (2015): 231–64.

Zandi-Sayek, Sibel. *Ottoman Izmir: The Rise of a Cosmopolitan City, 1840–1880.* Minneapolis: Univ. of Minnesota Press, 2012.

Ze'evi, Dror. "Back to Napoleon? Thoughts on the Beginning of the Modern Era in the Middle East." *Mediterranean Historical Review* 19, no. 1 (2004): 73–94.

———. "The Use of Ottoman Shari'a Court Records as a Source for Middle Eastern Social History: A Reappraisal." *Islamic Law and Society* 5 (1998): 35–57.

Zilfi, Madeline C. *The Politics of Piety: The Ottoman Ulema in the Postclassical Age, 1600–1800.* Minneapolis: Bibliotheca Islamica, 1988.

Index

Avi Rubin is a professor in the Department of Middle East Studies at Ben-Gurion University of the Negev in Israel. His research interests lie in the area of Ottoman social and legal history, with a focus on nineteenth-century sociolegal change and modernity. Rubin is the author of *Ottoman Nizamiye Courts: Law and Modernity* (2011).